VISUAL EXPLORER GUIDE

EGYPT

VISUAL EXPLORER GUIDE

EGYPT

TREVOR NAYLOR

amber
BOOKS

First published in 2019

Published by
Amber Books Ltd
United House
North Road
London
N7 9DP
United Kingdom
www.amberbooks.co.uk
Instagram: amberbooksltd
Facebook: www.facebook.com/amberbooks
Twitter: @amberbooks

Project Editor: Sarah Uttridge
Designers: Keren Harragan
Picture Research: Terry Forshaw and Justin Willsdon

ISBN: 978-1-78274-873-1

Printed in China

Contents

Introduction	6
Ancient Egypt	8
Landmarks	52
Waterways	112
Red Sea Coast	144
Deserts	166
City Life	196
Picture Credits	224

Introduction

Egypt's allure comprises a wide mixture of historical and cultural attractions, as well as beach-side holidays and the nation's greatest asset, its friendly and fun-loving people. Its earliest sites attest to an ancient civilization stretching back more than 5000 years. The many successive eras of human endeavour over thousands of years were to create gigantic temples and pyramids, delicate mural paintings and magnificent sculptures in stone. All around the Nile, towns, temples and commerce developed hand in hand to build a successful society. Fast forward to Roman times and you will see the influence on the land they occupied for 700 years and the riches they left behind along the length of the Nile Valley. All around you in today's Egypt are the descendants of Christian settlers who arrived around 33 AD, to be followed 600 years later by the Muslim conquest of 639 AD. These great religions have given Egypt its more recent, but magnificent art and architecture. There is so much to explore in Egypt that a visitor may hardly know where to start. With this book in hand, the traveller can peruse the variety that awaits, or revive memories after a wonderful visit.

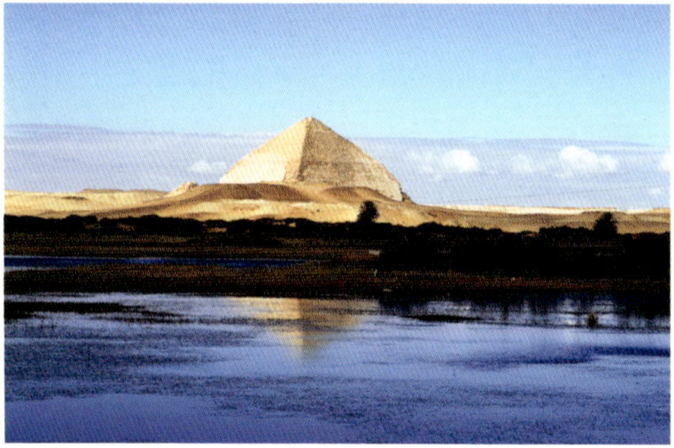

ABOVE:
Pyramids of Dahshur
OPPOSITE:
Pharaoh Ramesses II Statue, Luxor Temple

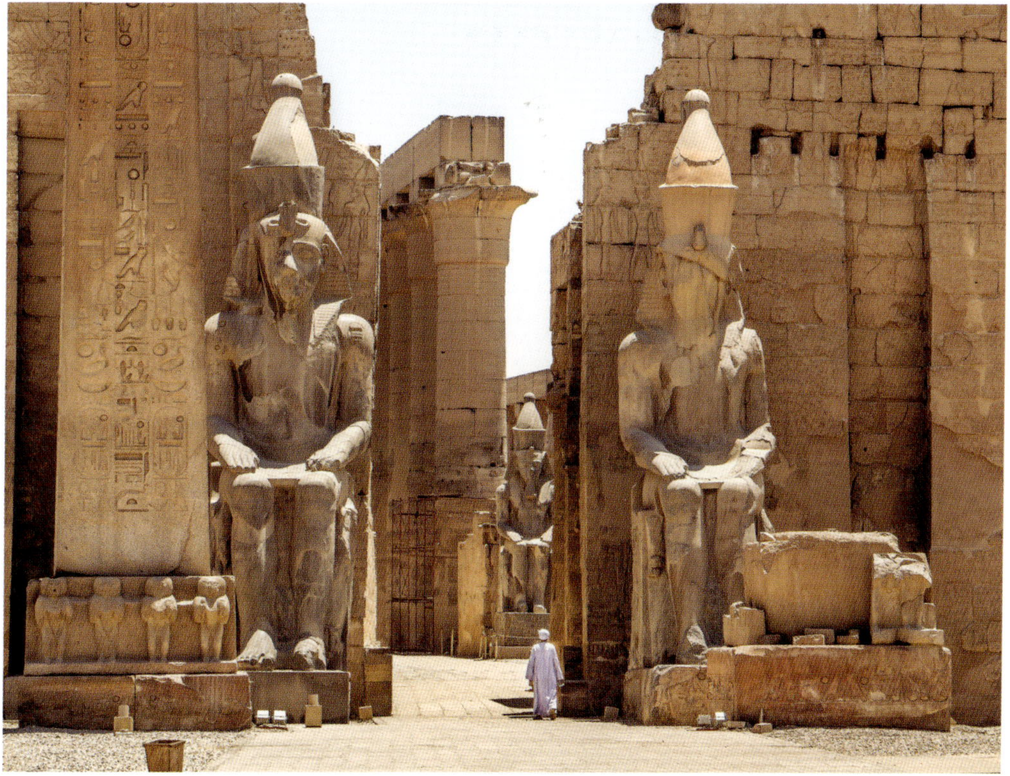

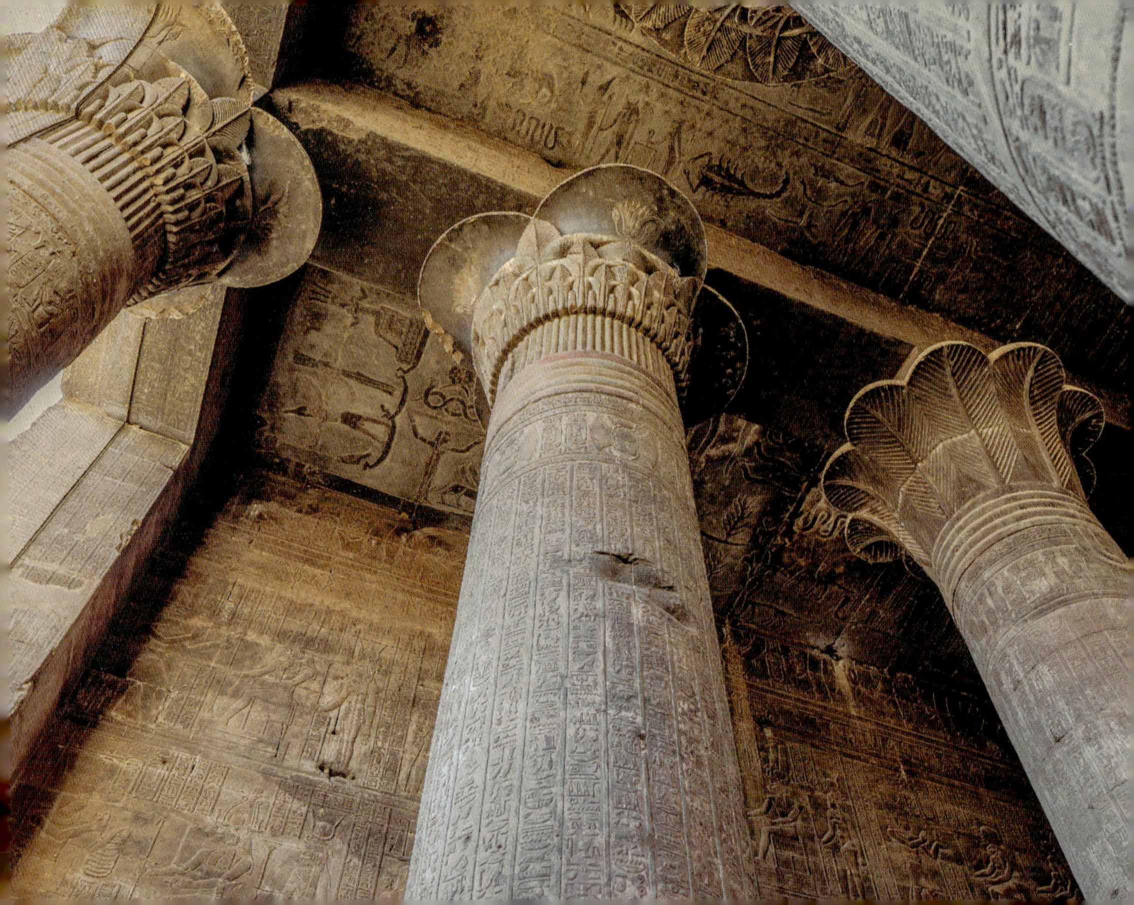

Ancient Egypt

Egypt's greatest attraction is its long, unbroken history as a country which has been home to an advanced civilization for thousands of years. The fact that today you can visit sites more than 5000 years old, see art as beautiful as when it was first created, and follow a story of ancient life and religion that was recorded in detail during its own time, is a unique mix.

From the era of the pyramids onwards, Egypt created giant monuments from the Great Pyramid and the Sphinx to Abu Simbel and Karnak Temple. Equally impressive on a more intimate scale are the painted tombs of the Valley of the Kings and the Mask of Tutankhamun. Behind these masterpieces of art and architecture lay a civilization that developed medicine and mathematics, created new and advanced methods of agriculture and irrigation, and had a writing system that allows the modern world to decipher today what happened thousands of years ago. Perhaps another facet of Ancient Egypt is that new discoveries are constantly being made and there is always something new to learn. The ongoing story will continue to excite for generations to come.

OPPOSITE:

Esna Temple, Upper Egypt

Begun by Pharaoh Tuthmose III between 1458 and 1425 BC during the 18th Dynasty, this still roofed building is of interest due to its hypostyle hall and the painted capitals of the 24 columns which support it.

Giza Pyramids
The Pyramids of Giza stand alone as the last remaining monument of the Seven Wonders of the Ancient World. Having stood for 4000 years under blazing sun, these monuments to the Old Kingdom pharaohs, Khafra (back) Khufu (centre) and Menkaure (front) are a lasting testament to the skilled labour of the thousands of workers who toiled at this site.

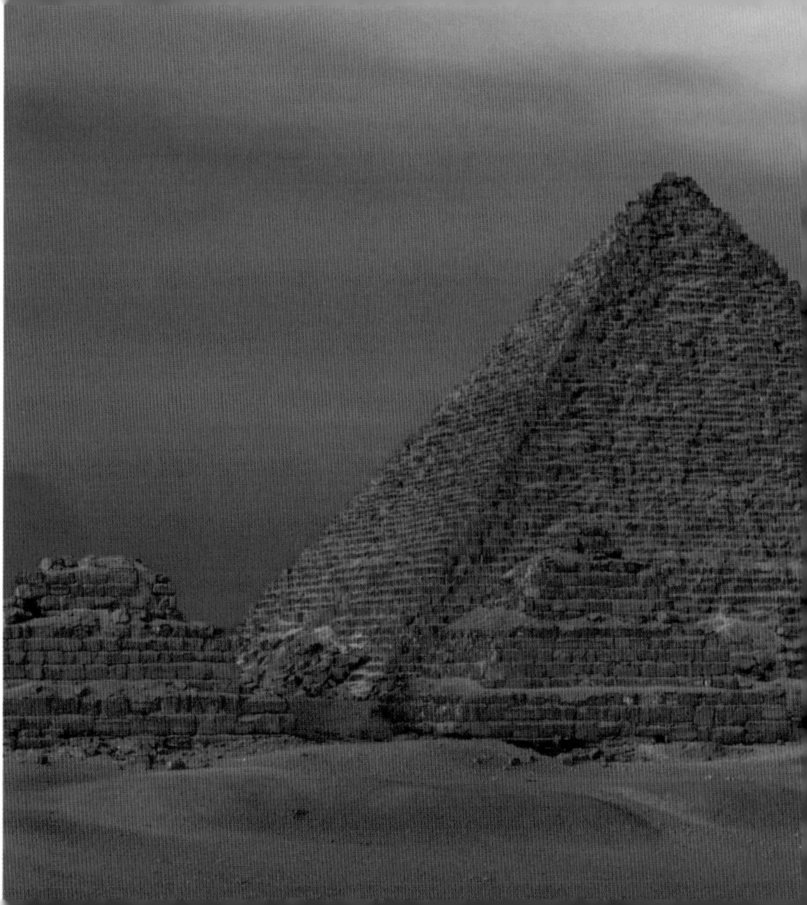

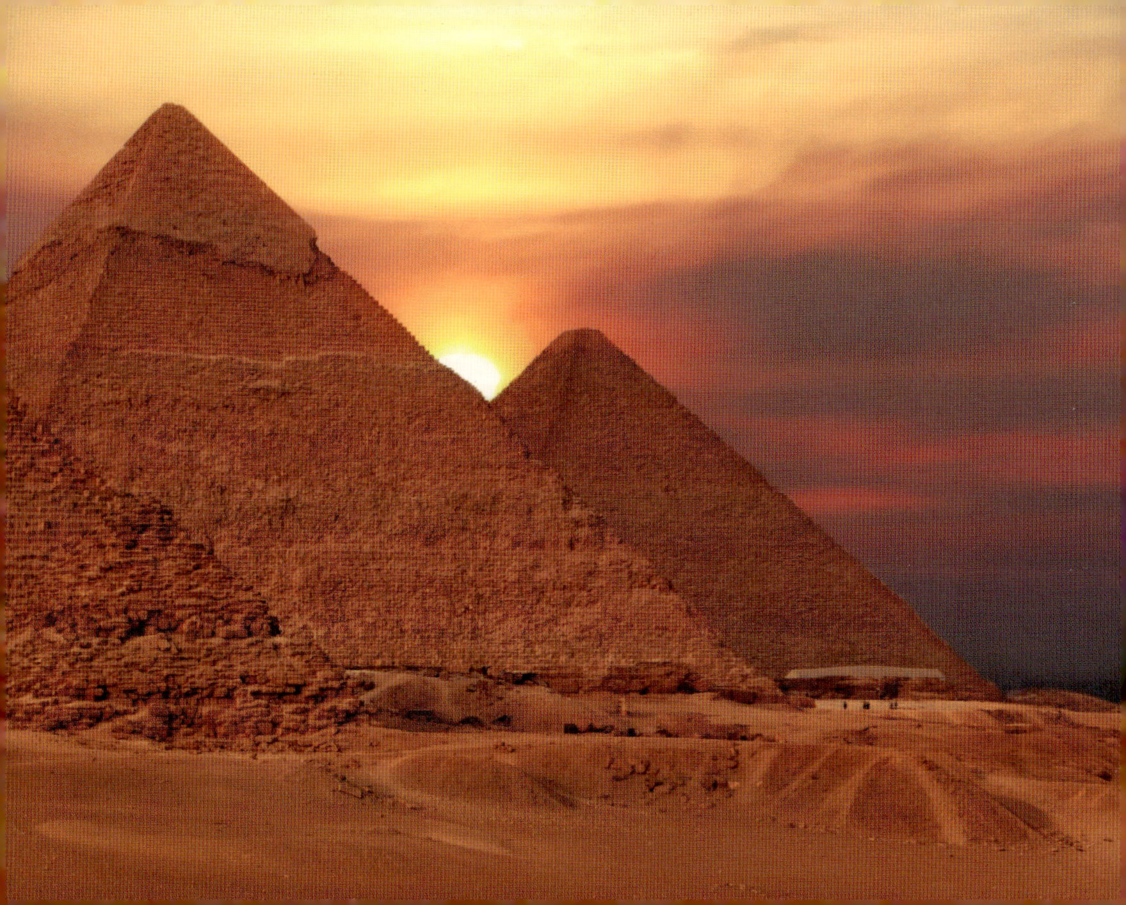

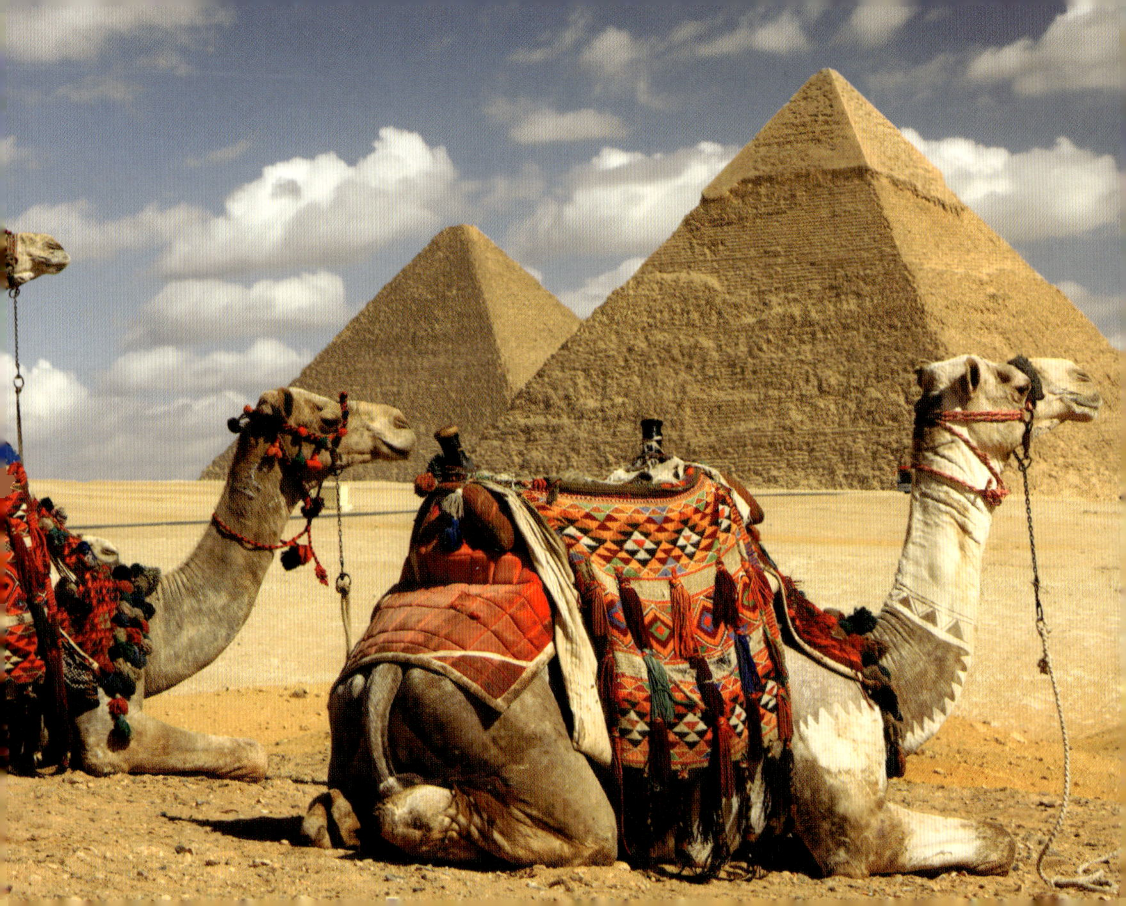

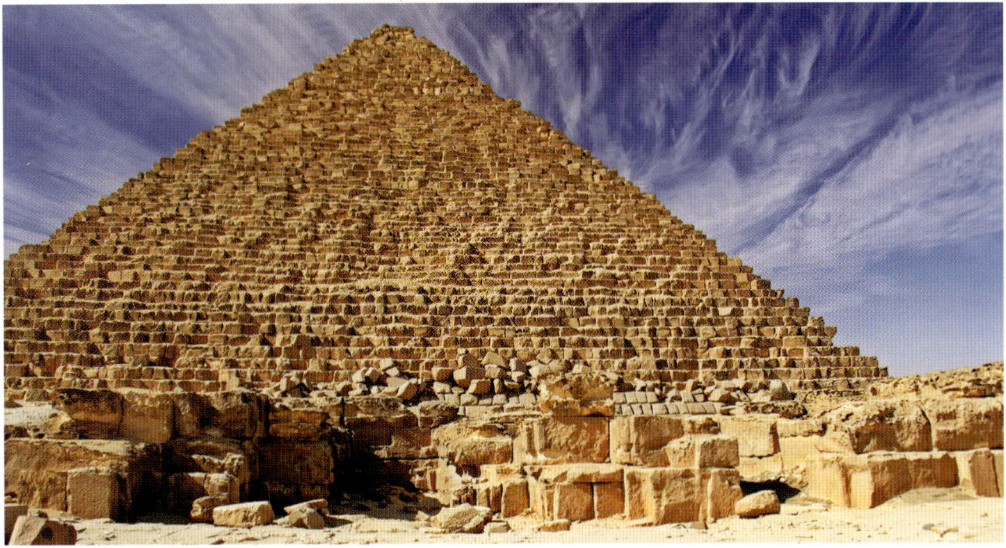

OPPOSITE:

Giza Pyramids

No visit to the Pyramids of Giza is complete without a ride on these 'Ships of the Desert'. Camels can be tricky beasts but are also comfortable, and provide a wonderful view of the Giza plateau should you take a trip to one of the excellent vantage points around the area.

ABOVE:

Menkaure Pyramid, Giza

The pyramid built for King Menkaure is the smallest in height of the main pyramids of Giza but is known for its more complex series of royal burial chambers, and for the statues of the king and his queen. Menkaure succeeded Khafra, builder of the Great Pyramid, during the Fourth Dynasty of Kings (c. 2613 to 2494 BC).

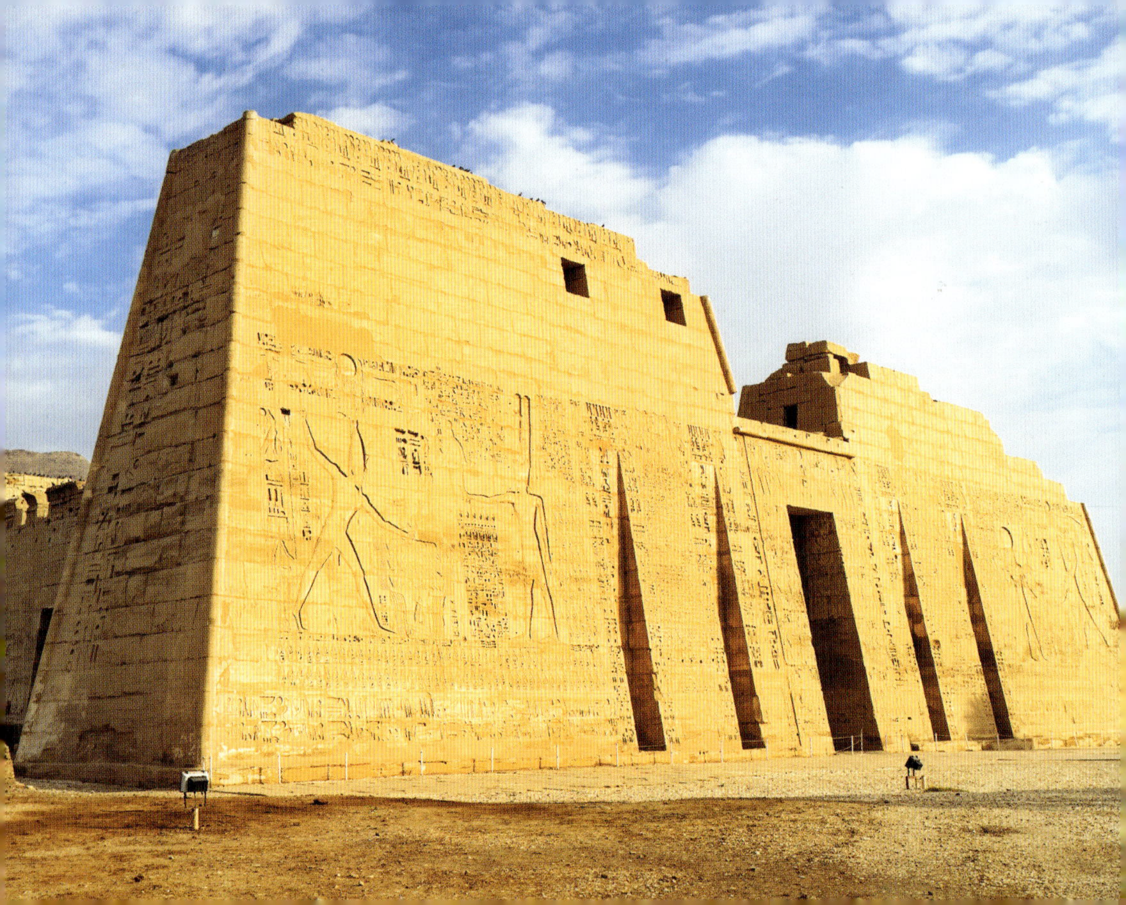

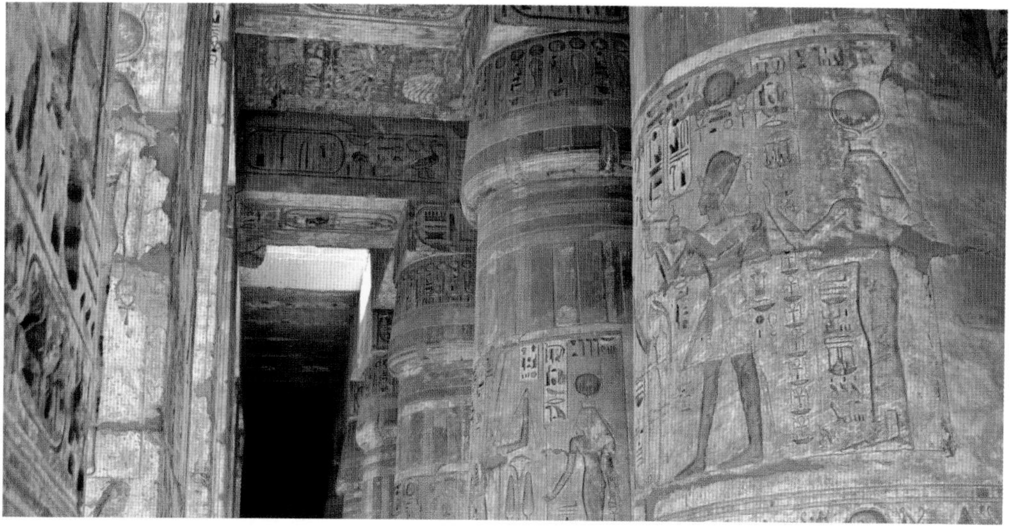

OPPOSITE:

Medinet Habu, Luxor

The first pylon of Ramesses III memorial temple at Medinet Habu is a gateway to one of Egypt's most fascinating sites. The Temple of Amun within the complex was built by Queen Hatshepsut and Thutmose III, and is one of the earliest places devoted to that local god. Medinet Habu was later greatly enlarged by the construction of the Funerary Temple of Ramesses III.

ABOVE:

Medinet Habu, Luxor

The second court of Medinet Habu features tall columns with highly coloured reliefs. These magnificent examples of Ancient Egyptian art were preserved when the temple was used as a church during the Christian era. At the time, they were fortunately painted over and thereby protected for future generations to uncover.

RIGHT:

Catacombs of Kom El Shoqafa, Alexandria

This site is the largest Roman burial place yet known in Egypt, and its complex maze of rooms and stairways present the classical look of Greco-Roman art with a twist of Pharaonic symbolism. These catacombs were one of the last places devoted to Ancient Egyptian religion despite being under Roman occupation. This necropolis was in use from the 2nd to the 4th centuries AD.

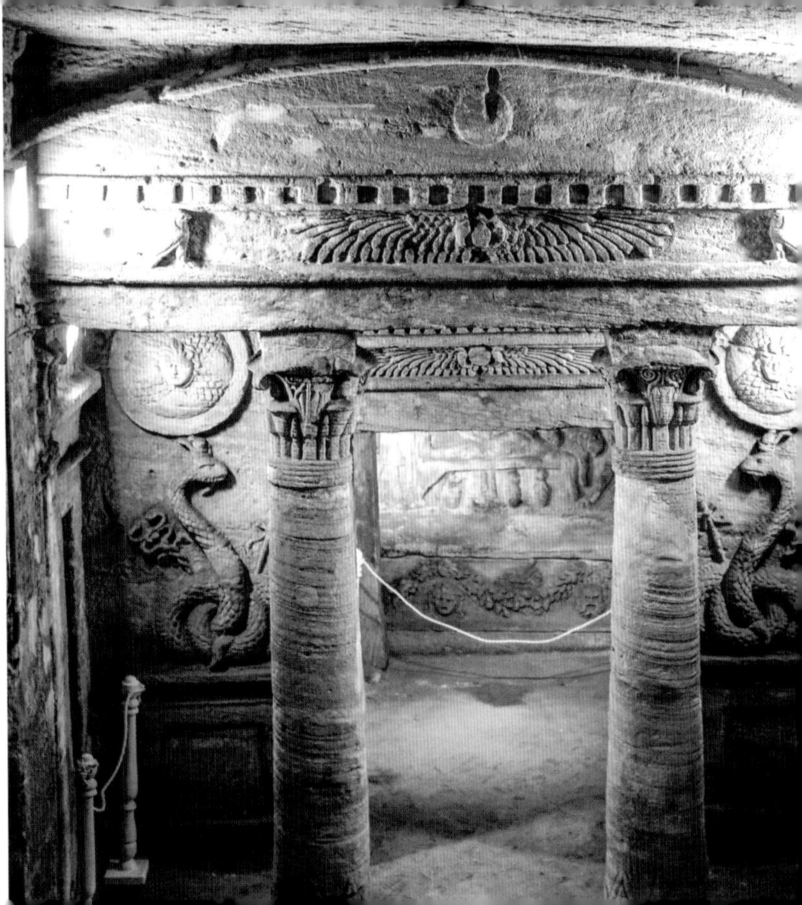

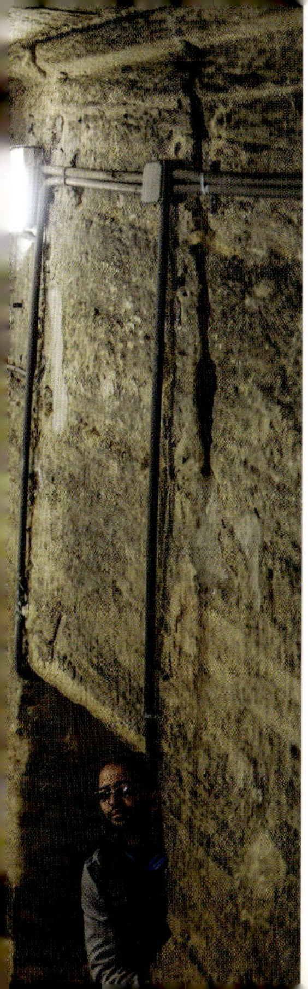

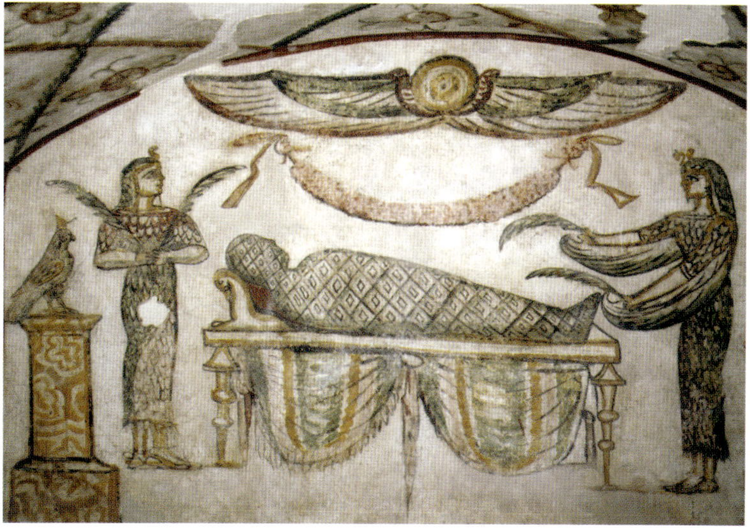

ABOVE:

Catacombs of Kom El Shoqafa, Alexandria

The catacombs were discovered at the start of the 20th century when a donkey fell through its roof. It was found to feature frescos and sarcophagi using gods from Egyptian myths. Here we see Isis assisting the embalming of a mummy in the Tomb of Tigran, whilst other walls feature a mix of Egypt's ancient history, such as the God Anubis dressed as a Roman legionary.

West Bank of Luxor

The burial place of many pharaohs and nobles of the New Kingdom era lie on the west bank of the Nile at Luxor (Thebes). These tombs are in several areas including the Valley of the Kings and the Valley of the Queens. There are 63 tombs in the Valley of the Kings, dug over a period of 500 years between the 16th and 11th centuries BC. Hiding their treasures in these desert hills did nothing to deter tomb robbers who stole much of what was buried alongside each sarcophagus.

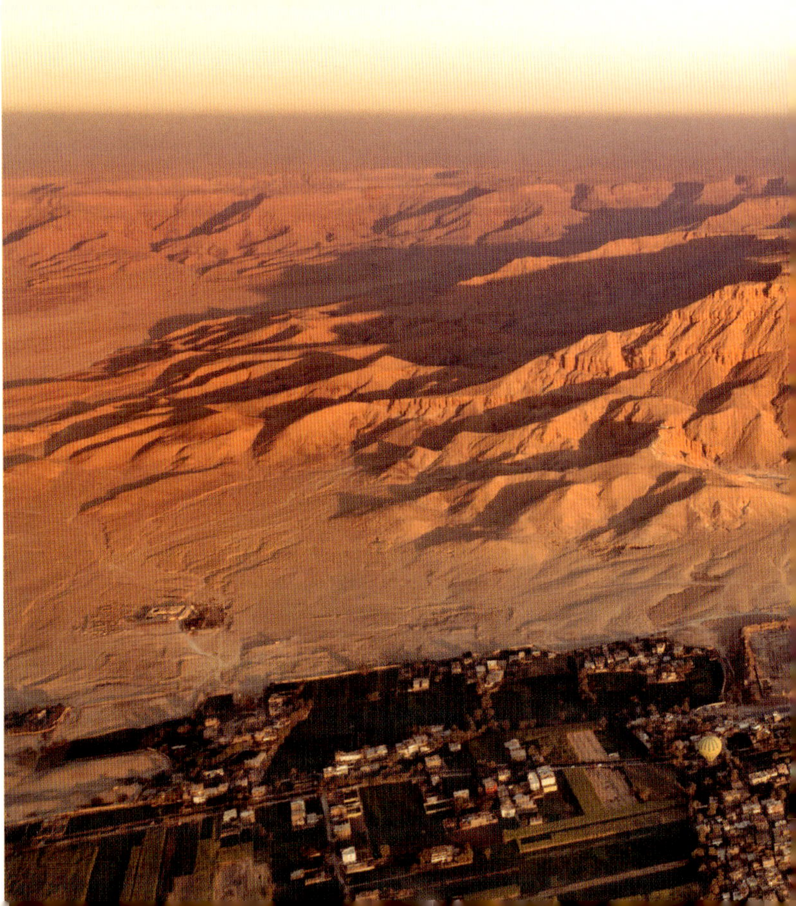

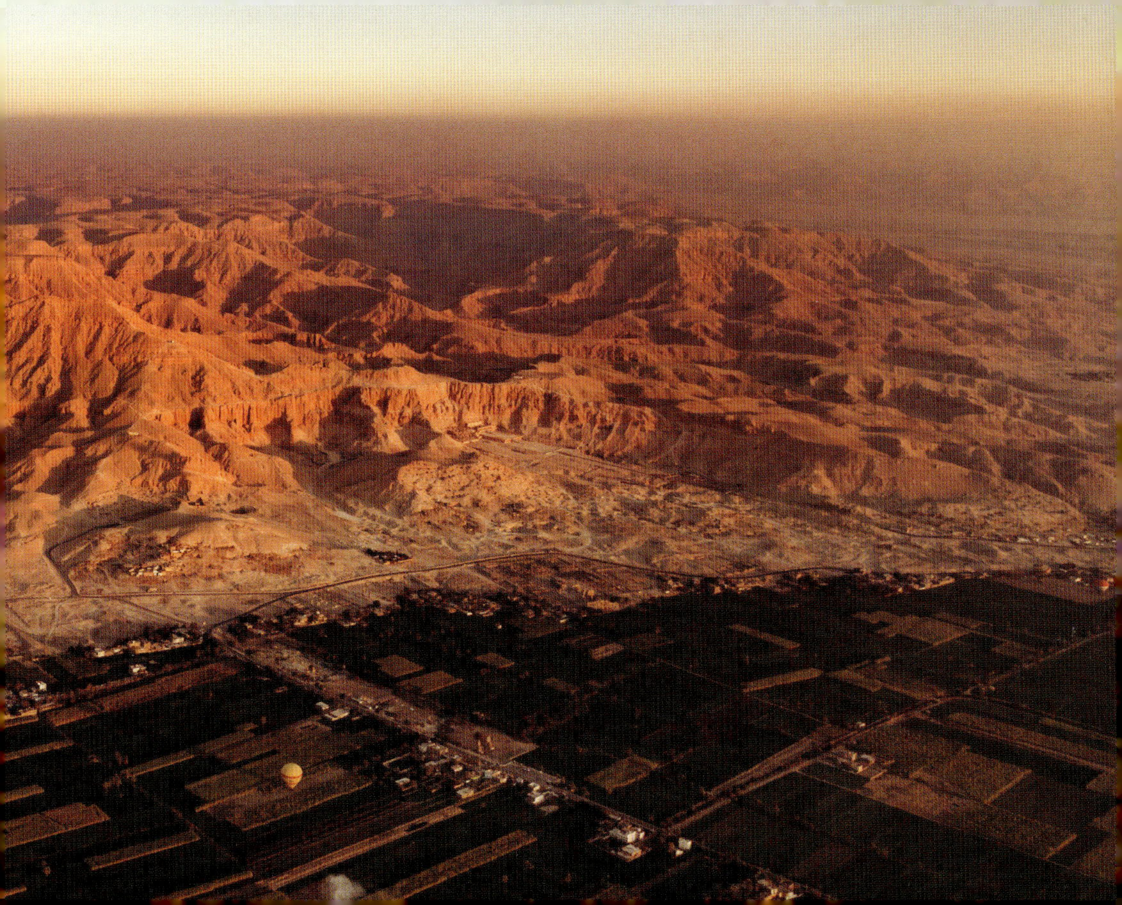

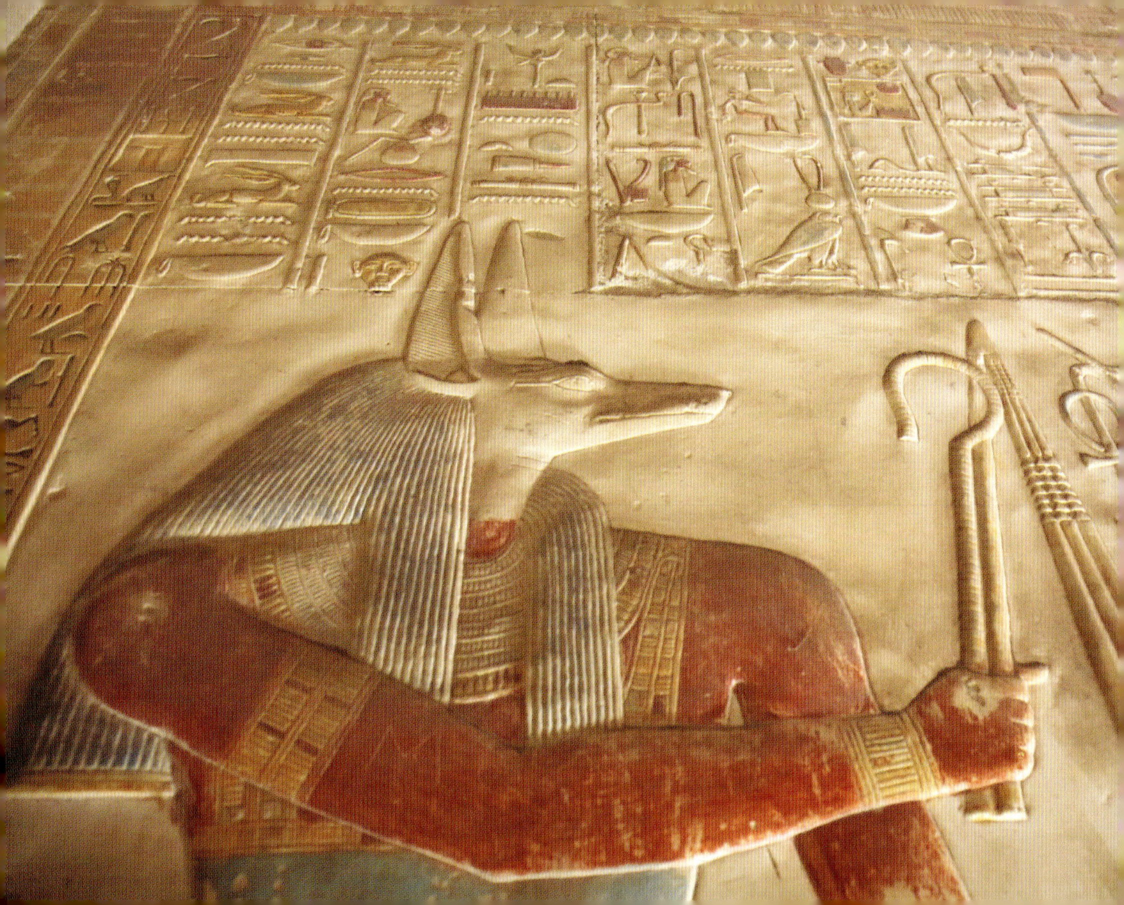

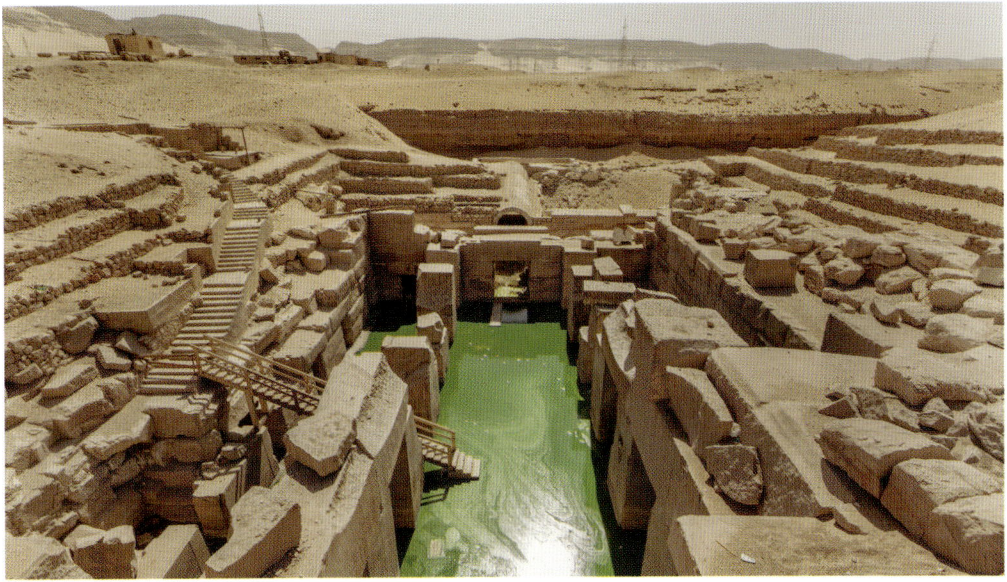

OPPOSITE:

Temple of Seti I, Abydos

Abydos was one of the holiest towns of Ancient Egypt and a major cult centre of the Goddess Osiris. Here we see a dramatic bas-relief of the God Anubis from the walls of Abydos.

ABOVE:

Abydos, The Osireion

The Osireion is also part of the Seti I funerary complex at Abydos and was built at such a level that it is now partly submerged. This temple was discovered in 1902 by archaeologists Flinders Petrie and Margaret Murray.

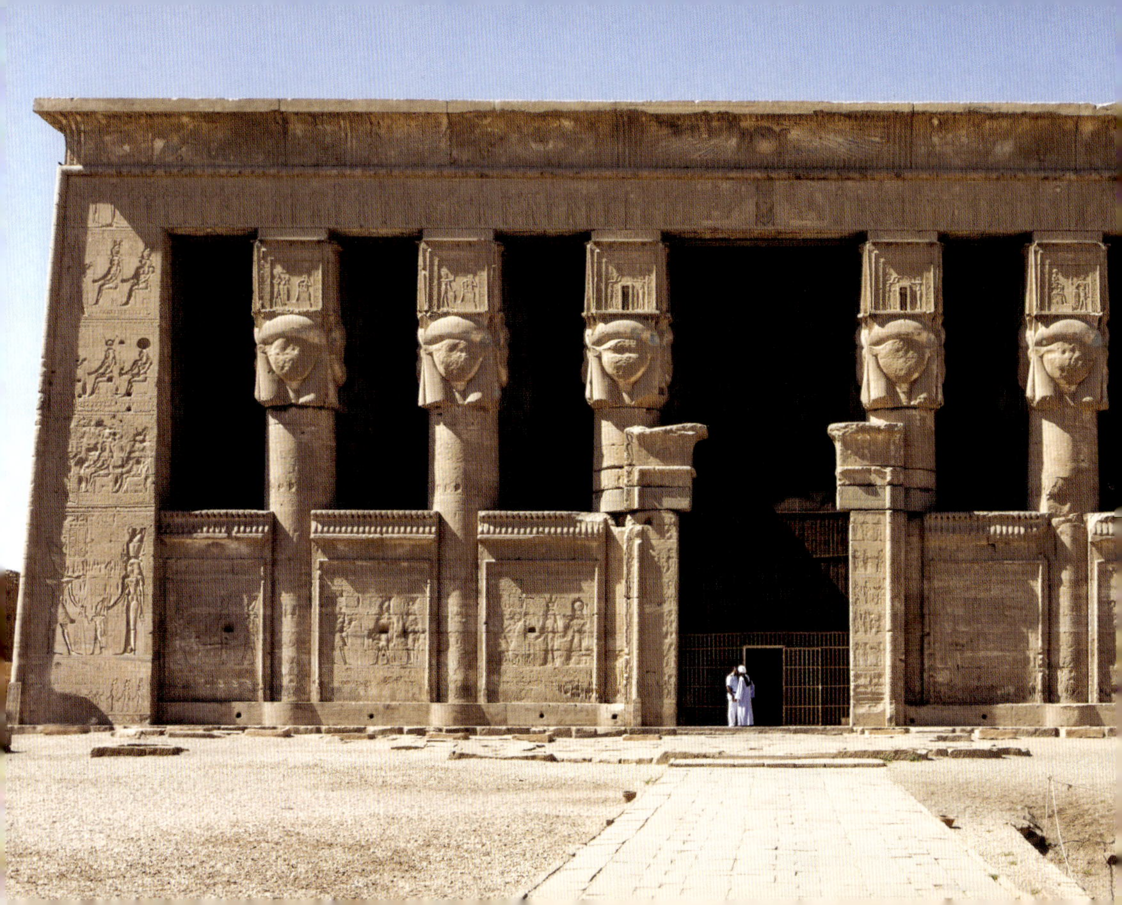

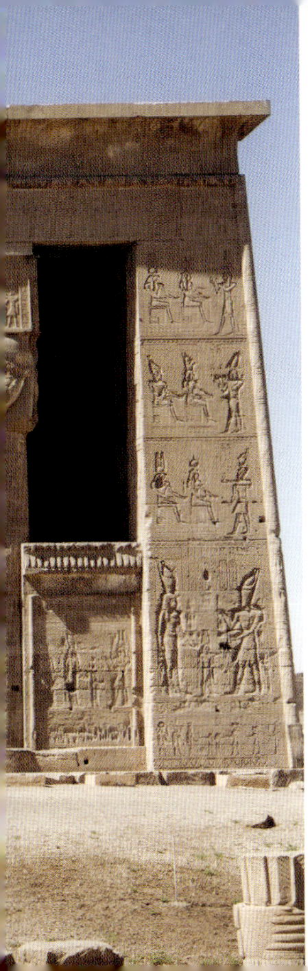

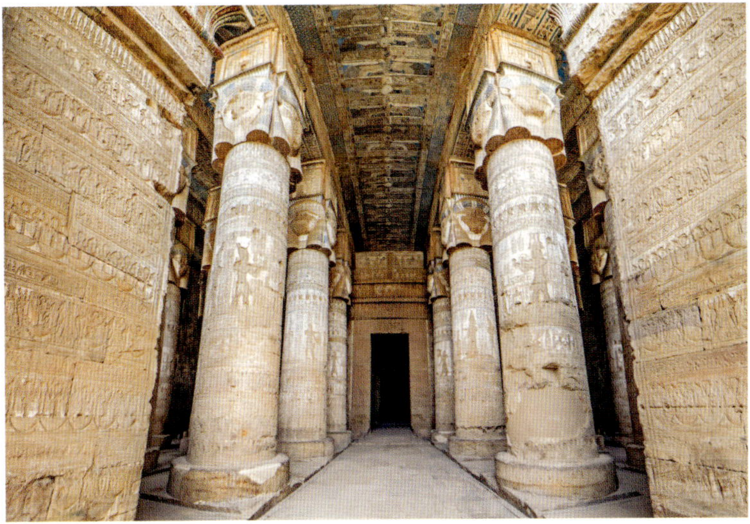

LEFT:

Temple of Hathor, Temple complex, Dendera

This site is one of the best preserved in Egypt and has a long history of active use beginning in the Old Kingdom period (2686–2181 BC).

ABOVE:

Temple of Hathor, Hypostyle Hall Dendera

The columns and ceiling are covered with art from all periods of Ancient Egypt, including gods and the famous Dendera Zodiac.

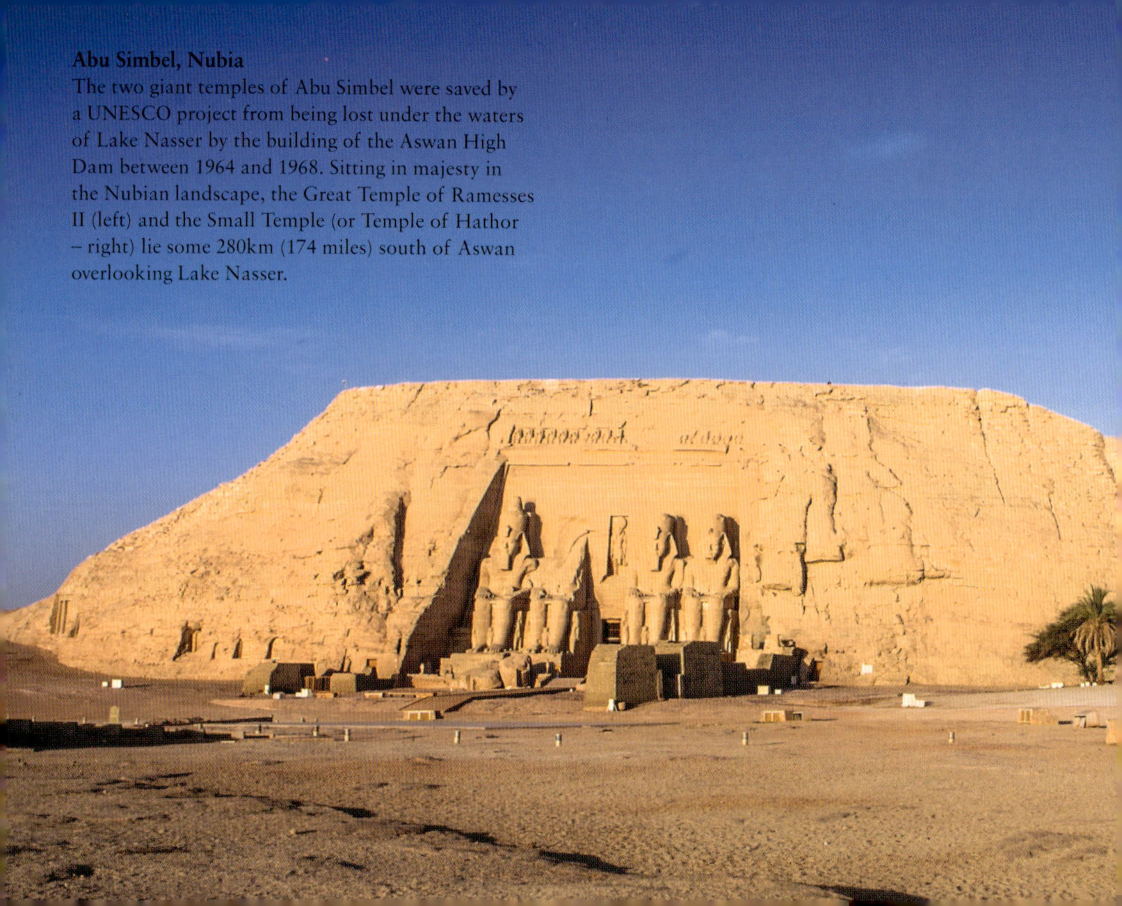

Abu Simbel, Nubia
The two giant temples of Abu Simbel were saved by a UNESCO project from being lost under the waters of Lake Nasser by the building of the Aswan High Dam between 1964 and 1968. Sitting in majesty in the Nubian landscape, the Great Temple of Ramesses II (left) and the Small Temple (or Temple of Hathor – right) lie some 280km (174 miles) south of Aswan overlooking Lake Nasser.

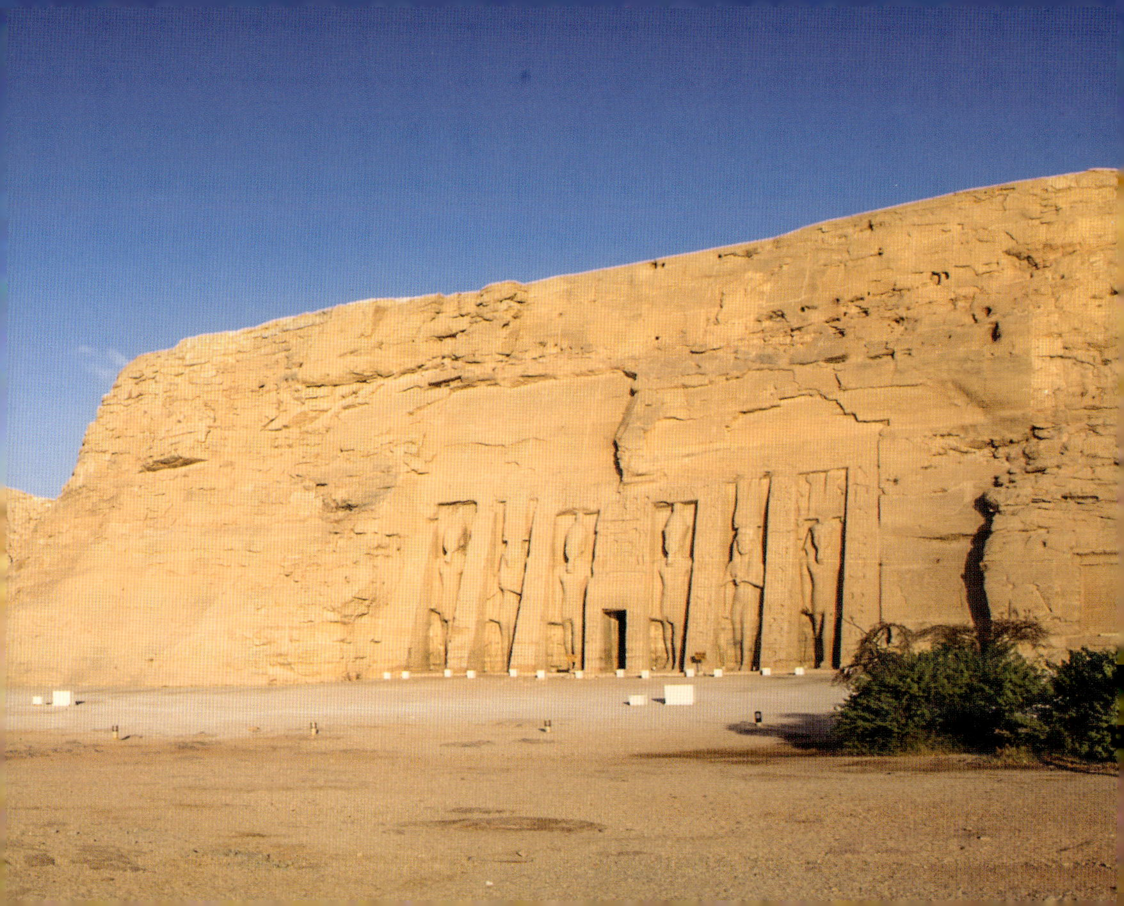

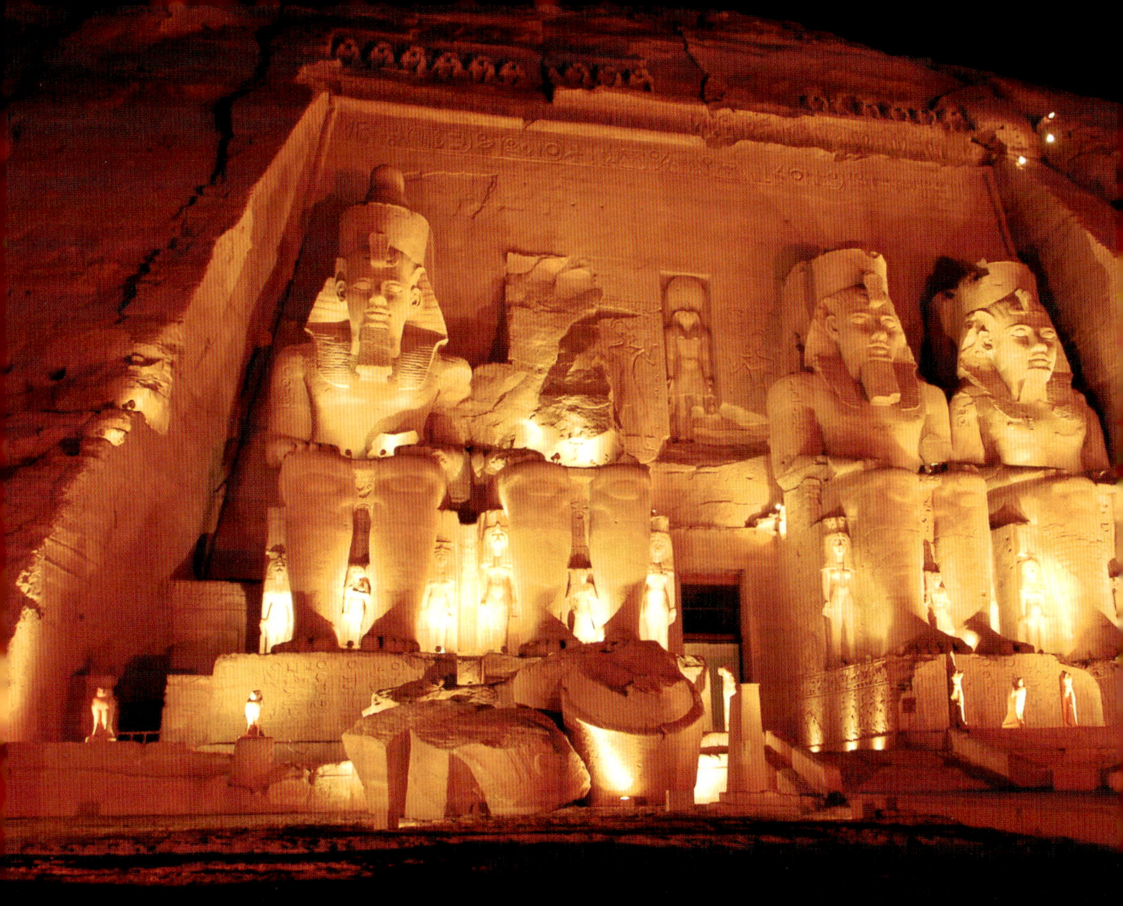

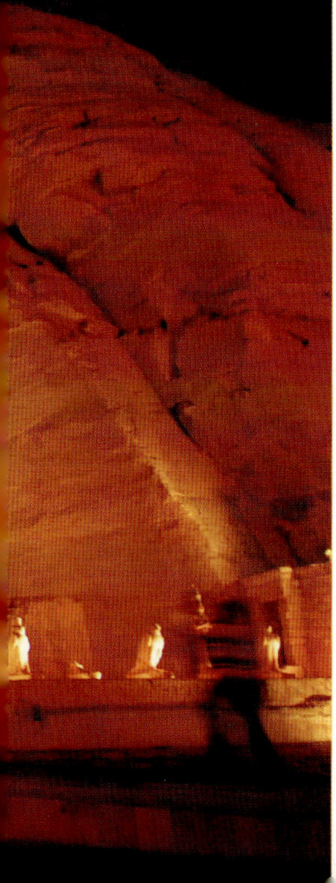

LEFT:

Abu Simbel, Nubia

The Great Temple of Ramesses II was part of this pharaoh's determination to celebrate his kingship and the campaigns and battles that he fought. He wished to achieve his own immortality across Egypt and Nubia and did so through an extensive series of building projects. In Abu Simbel, this immortal vision was made real and the giant statues are now known worldwide.

BELOW:

Abu Simbel, Nubia

Ramesses II waged war with the Nubians and the Hittites and the walls of Abu Simbel tell many stories of his successful battles. Here we see wall reliefs of captured Nubian prisoners of war.

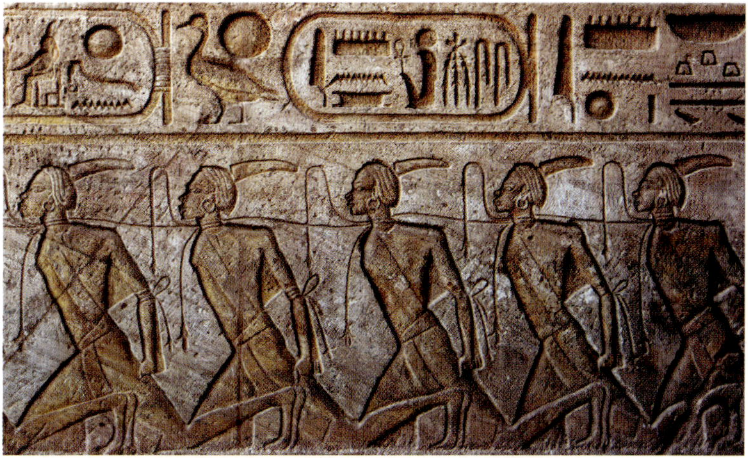

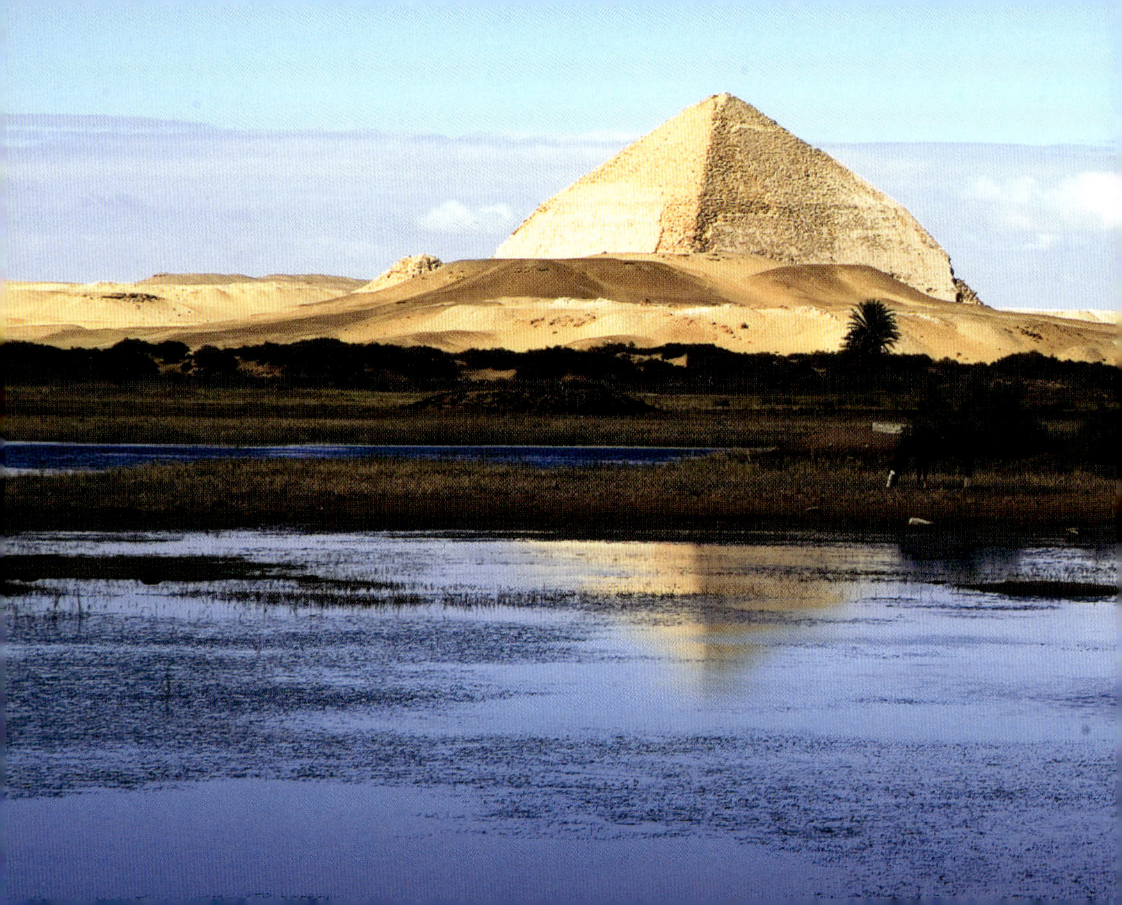

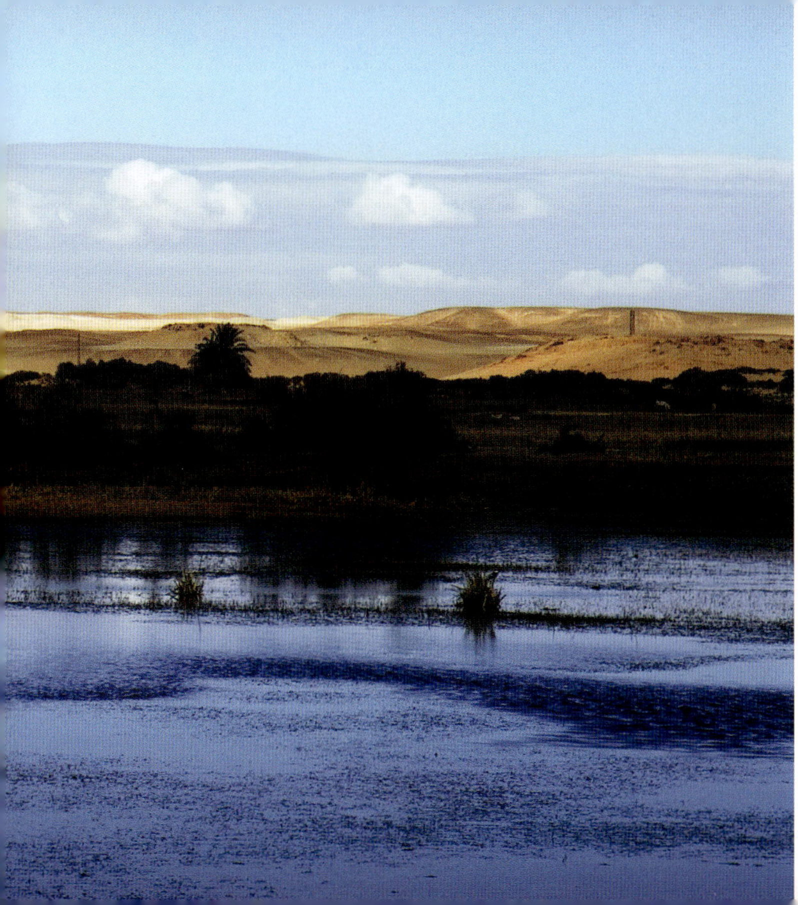

Pyramids of Dahshur
The so-called Bent Pyramid seen here is one of the two large Pyramids at Dahshur, near Cairo (the other is the Red Pyramid). Built by the pharaoh Sneferu, it is thought to be the first attempt at a smooth sided pyramid, though how this intriguing final shape came about is still not clear. One of Sneferu's several children was Khufu, the Pharaoh who is buried in the Great Pyramid.

ALL PHOTOGRAPHS:

Saqqara, near Cairo

Saqqara is a large necropolis which served as the burial ground for the Ancient Egyptian capital of Memphis.

(RIGHT) Carved cobras form a line of sculptures within the funerary complex of King Djoser, whose pyramid stands in the centre of the site.

(OPPOSITE TOP) The entrance to the main funerary complex is via this rebuilt entrance.

(OPPOSITE BOTTOM) The Step Pyramid of Djoser, constructed in the Third Dynasty, was the first monumental stone-built structure and it marked a huge change in the development of building in Egypt and beyond.

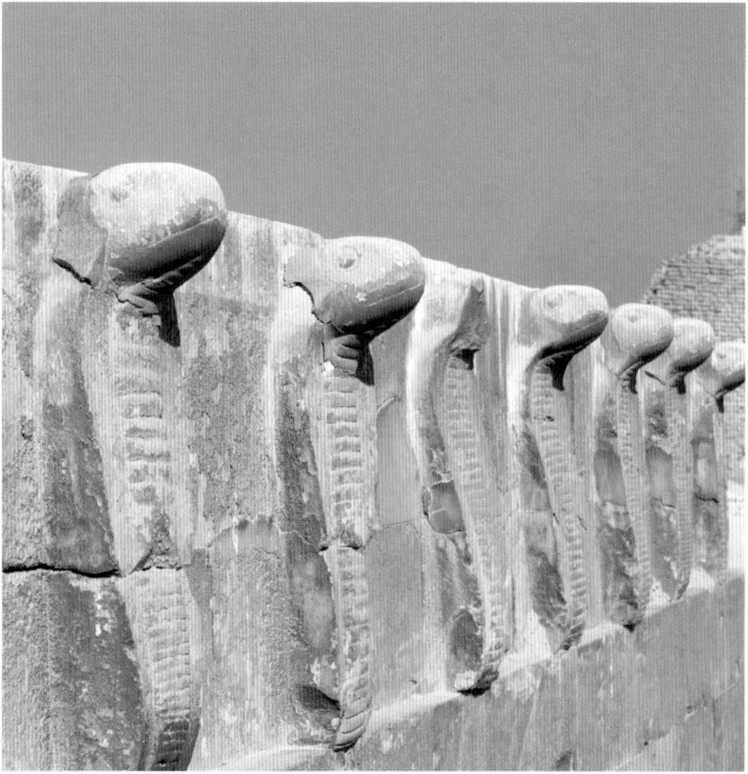

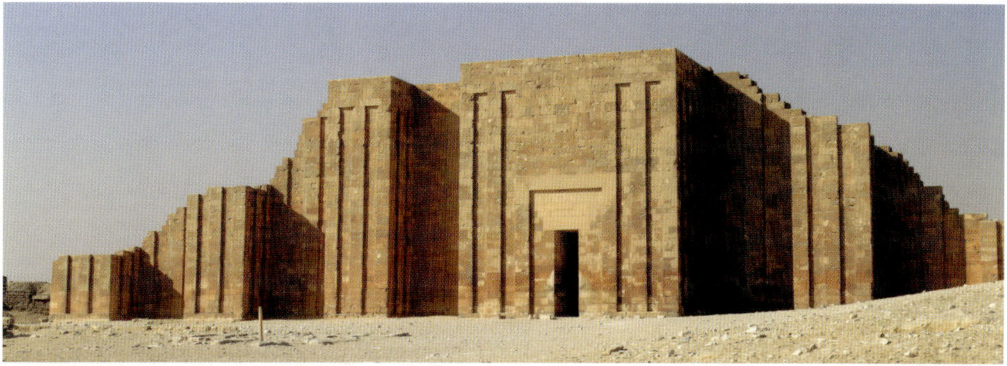

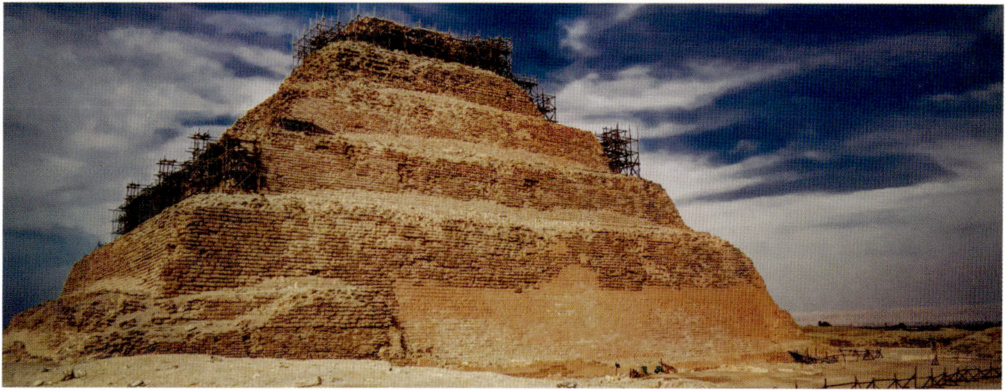

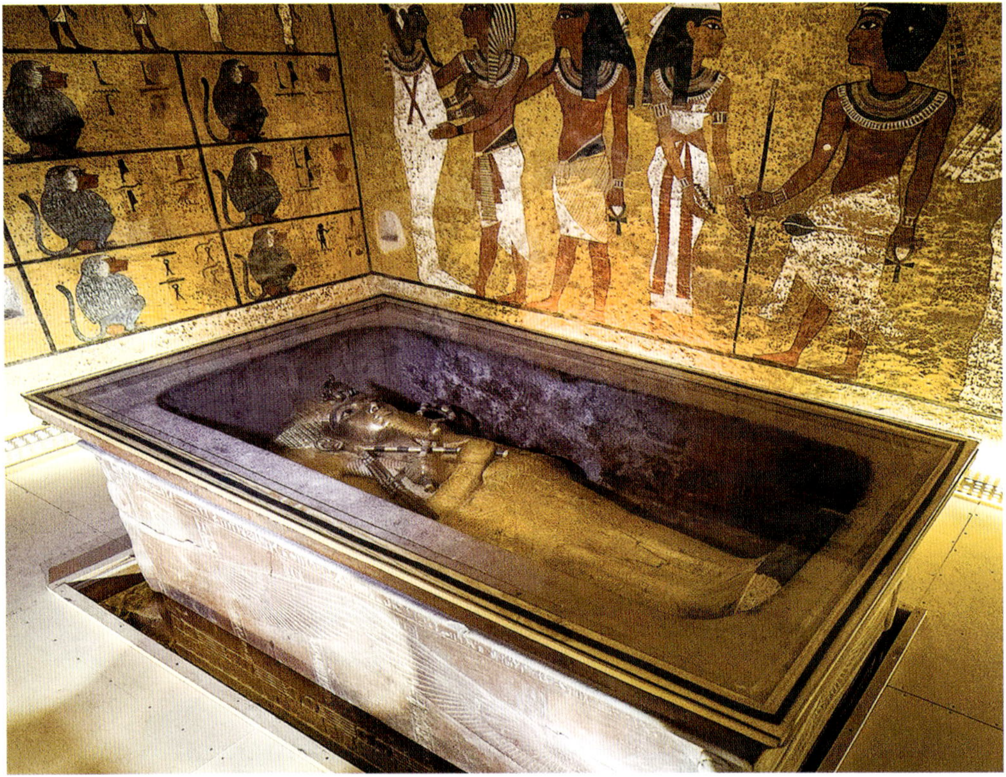

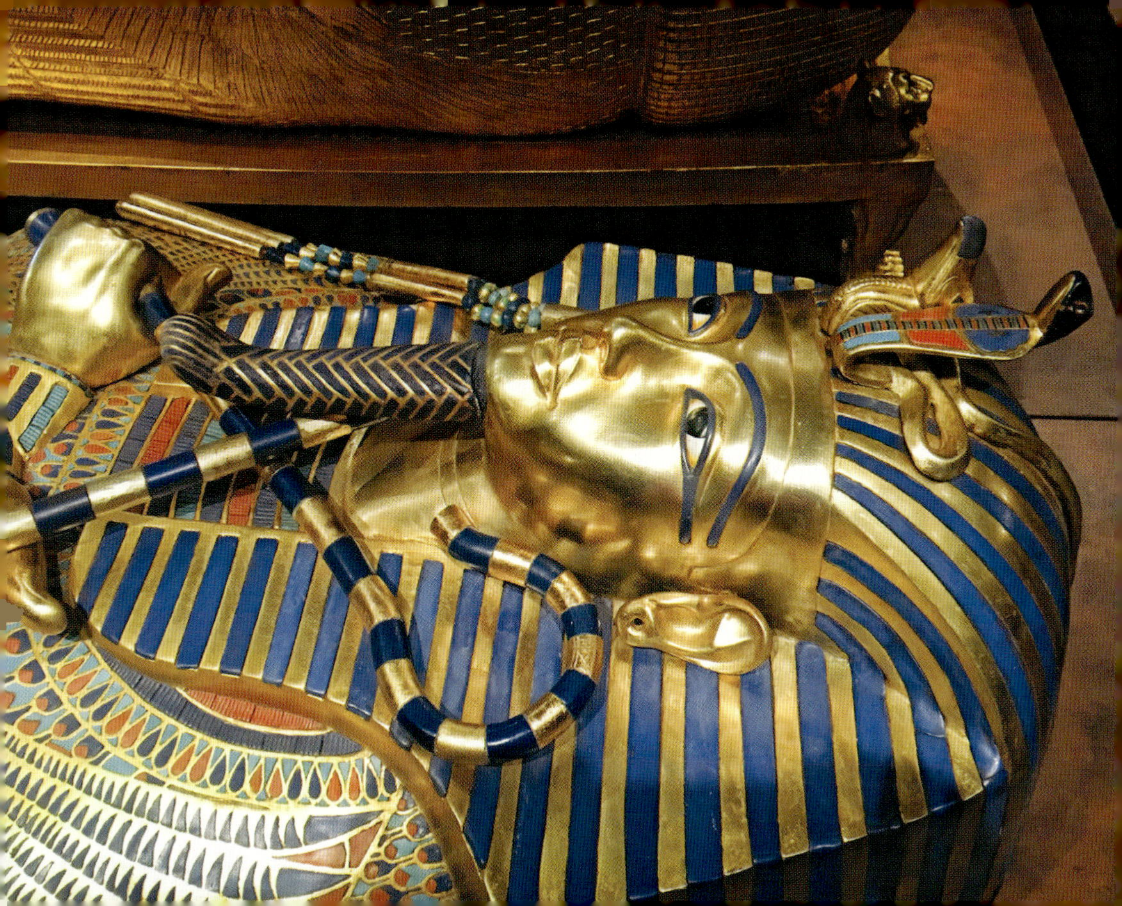

PREVIOUS PAGE, LEFT:

Tutankhamun, The Tomb, Valley of the Kings

Tutankhamun died aged 19 and was hurriedly buried. His tomb in the Valley of the Kings has recently reopened after years of restoration work.

PREVIOUS PAGE, RIGHT:

Tutankhamun's Second Coffin, Cairo

Howard Carter, on seeing this magnificent coffin for the first time, noted 'the fairness of work is superior to the first coffin, in so much that it is more delicate and purer in line and conveys almost greater feeling'. This piece of Ancient Egyptian art is a treasure made from gilded wood, glass, semiprecious stones and faience.

RIGHT:

Tutankhamun Statue, Luxor

Tutankhamun is shown here with his consort Ankhesenamun, who was also his half sister. This unusual statue can be seen in Luxor Temple, some distance from the Valley of the Kings.

OPPOSITE:

Tutankhamun Gold Coffin, Cairo

The young pharaoh's coffin was multi-layered, with the gold mask being the last of several. The outer coffin is made of cypress wood and decorated intricately with a layer of gold foil.

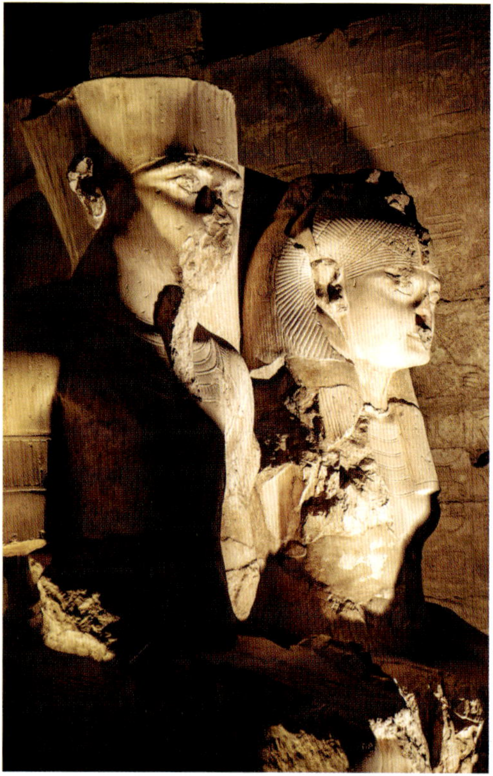

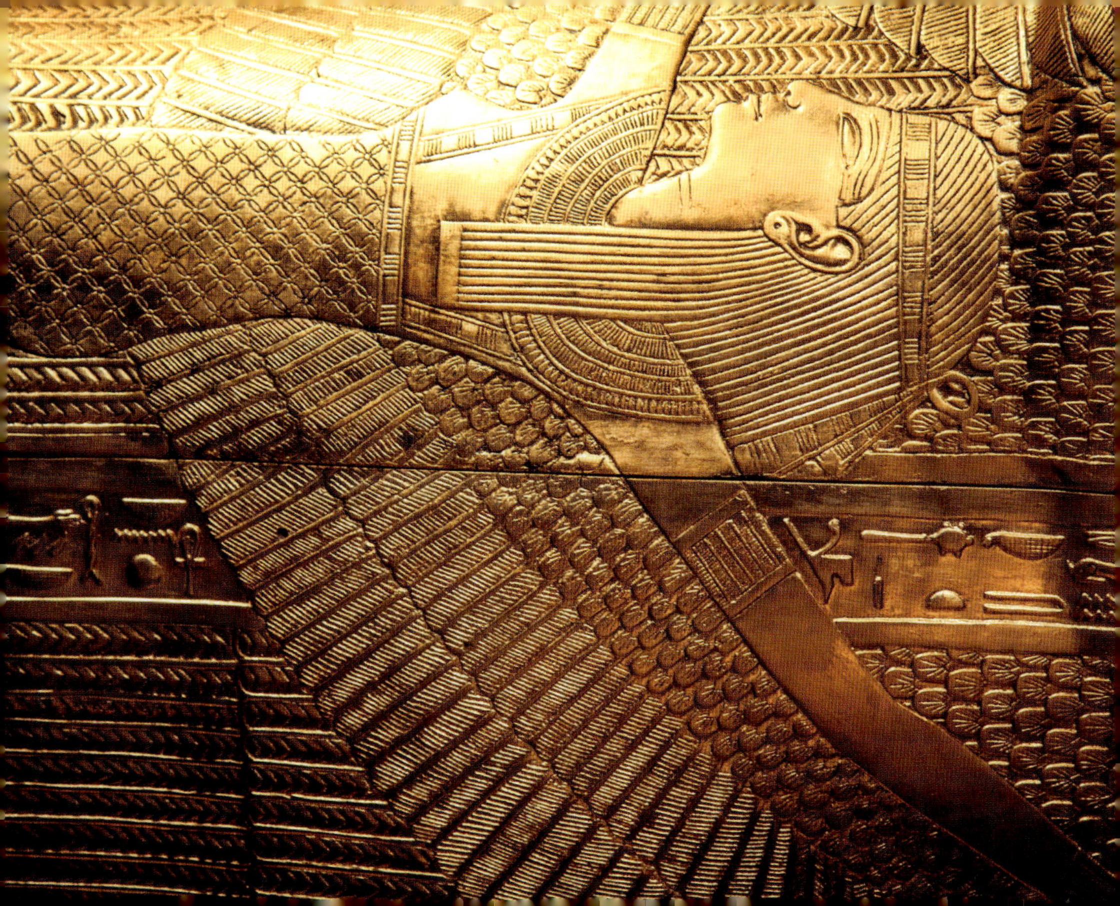

BELOW:

Roman Amphitheatre, Alexandria

Kom Al Dikka is an area of Alexandria which, in Roman times, was one of this ancient city's most affluent areas. During building work in the 1960s archaeologists found the only Roman Amphitheatre in Egypt. On the same site are some of the best preserved Roman mosaics in Egypt.

RIGHT:

Pompey's Pillar, Alexandria

Pompey's Pillar rises some 30m (98ft) from the ground and was erected in 291 AD. The area around this distinctive pillar includes the ruins of the temple dedicated to the God Serapis – a hybrid Greco-Egyptian deity introduced by Pharaoh Ptolemy I Soter as an attempt at religious unity.

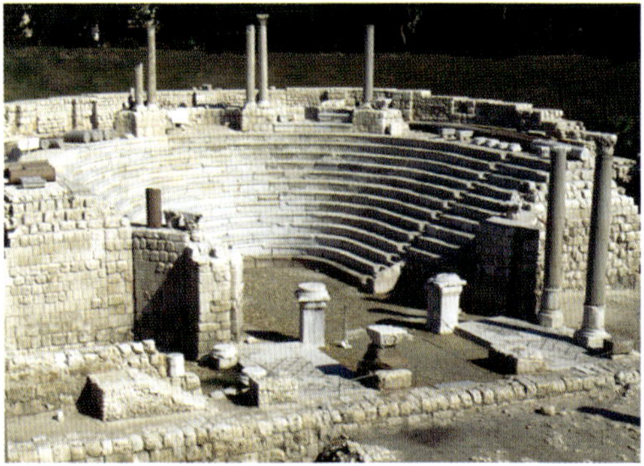

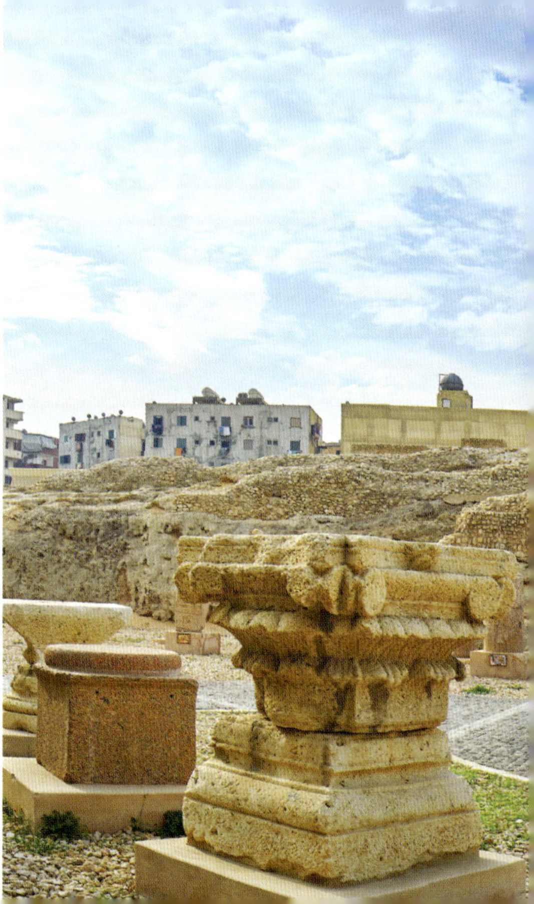

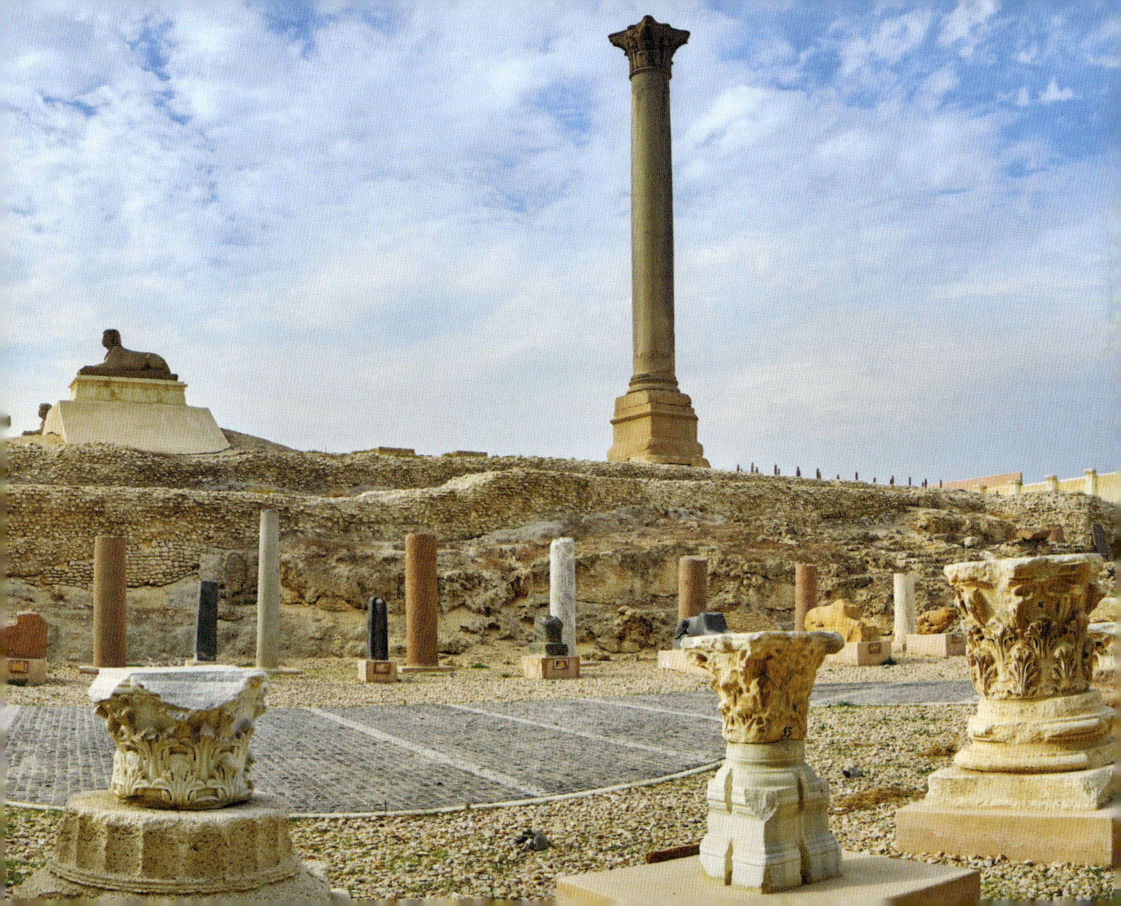

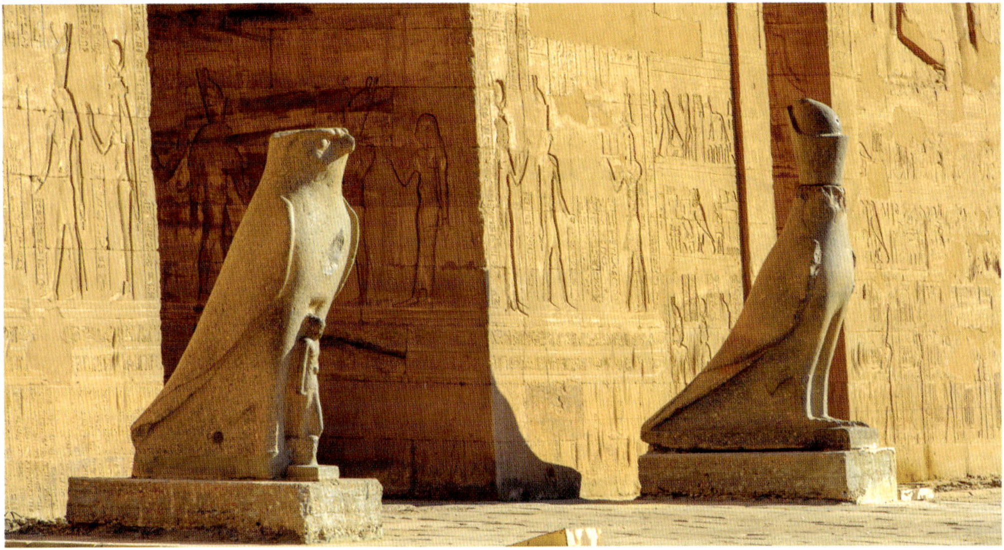

ABOVE:

Edfu Temple, Upper Egypt

One of Egypt's largest and best preserved temples, Edfu lies on the Nile between Luxor and Aswan. Originally a temple devoted to Horus, it was expanded as a Greco-Roman site during the Ptolemaic period until 57 BC. Falcon statues of Horus guard the temple and depict this sky god, whose two eyes represent the sun and the moon.

OPPOSITE:

Edfu Temple, The Façade, Upper Egypt

The main pylon at Edfu stands a massive 36m (118ft) in height and beyond the gateway lies a vast, decorated Court of Offerings. The temple was excavated from sands and rubble by the French Egyptologist Auguste Mariette in the 19th century.

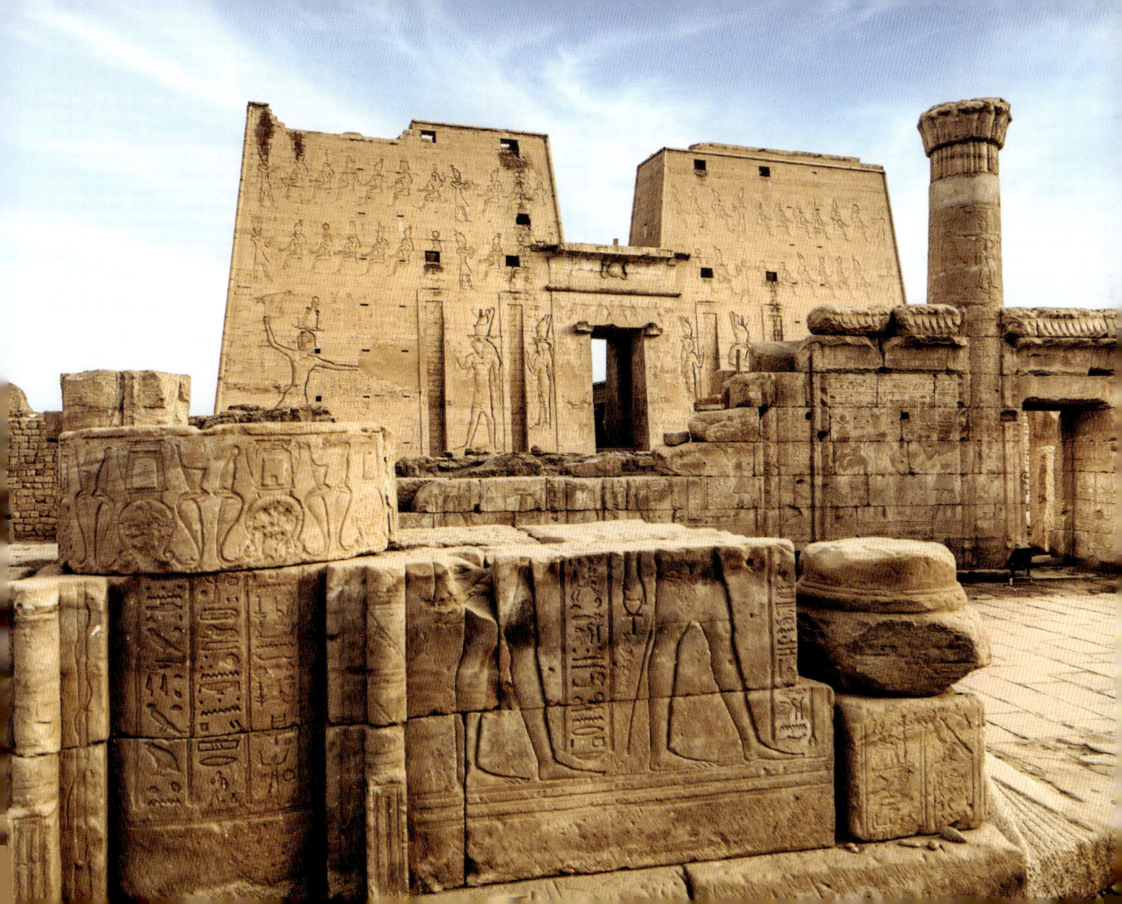

BELOW:

The Sphinx and the Great Pyramid, Giza

This iconic view of the two star attractions of the Giza plateau shows the Great Pyramid, created for the Pharaoh Khufu, standing behind the Great Sphinx of Giza. The Sphinx is believed to have been built for the Pharaoh Khafra, who constructed the second Giza Pyramid.

RIGHT:

The Great Sphinx of Giza

The Sphinx acquired its name some 2000 years after it was carved from the bedrock of the plateau. In classical antiquity, the sphinx was a mythical beast combining a lion's body, a woman's head and the wings of an eagle. This creature would kill anyone who failed to answer the riddles it set.

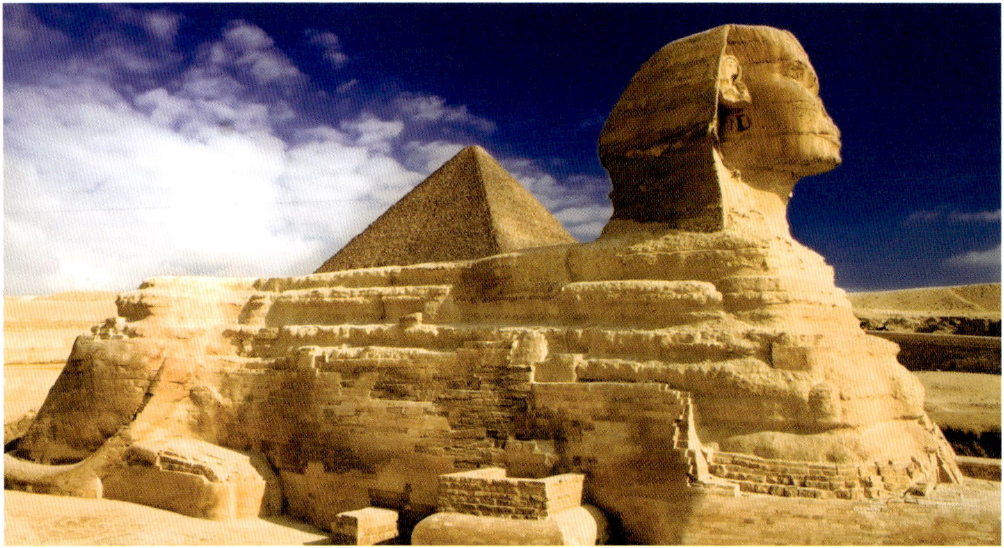

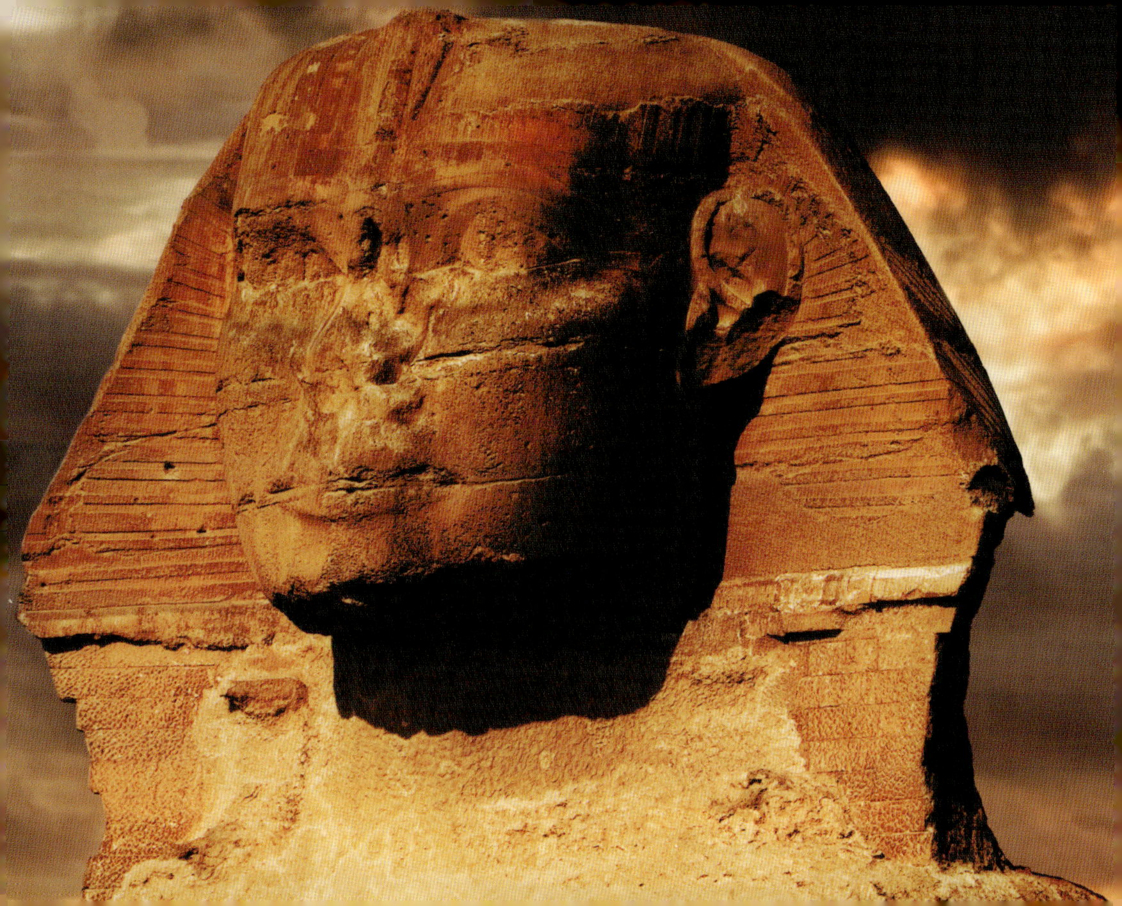

Luxor Temple

Luxor Temple comes as a sudden surprise to new visitors as it sits in the very centre of Luxor town itself. With the Nile on one side and the town square on the other, it is impressive and statuesque in its setting. Here we approach the first pylon from the Avenue of the Sphinxes and are met by the Luxor Obelisk built by Ramesses II. The twin of which is now in Paris.

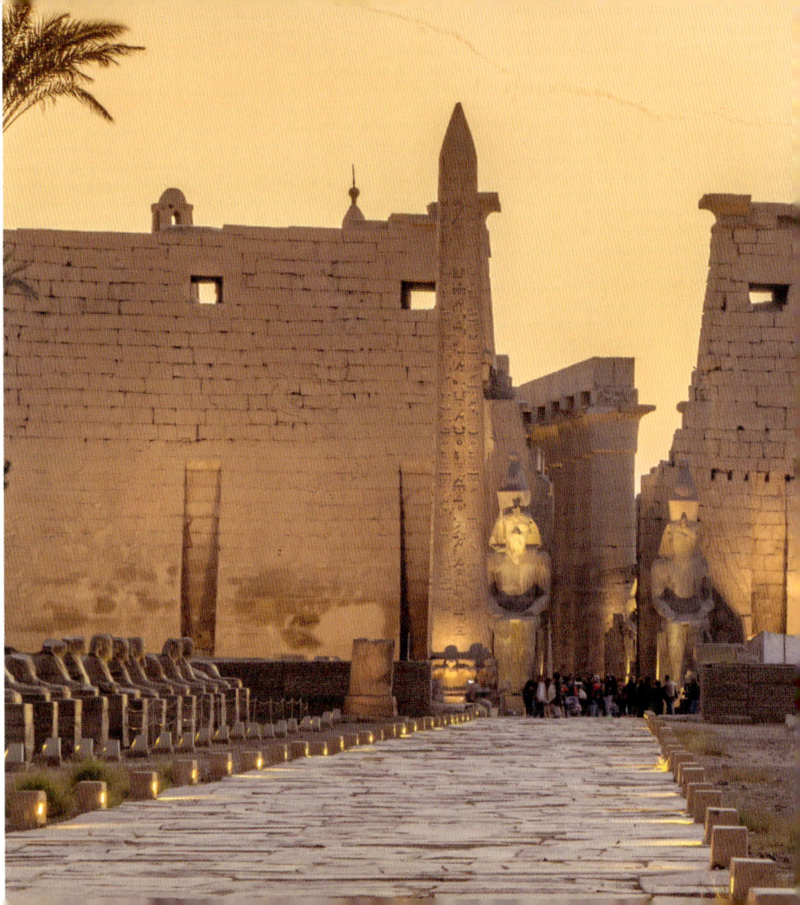

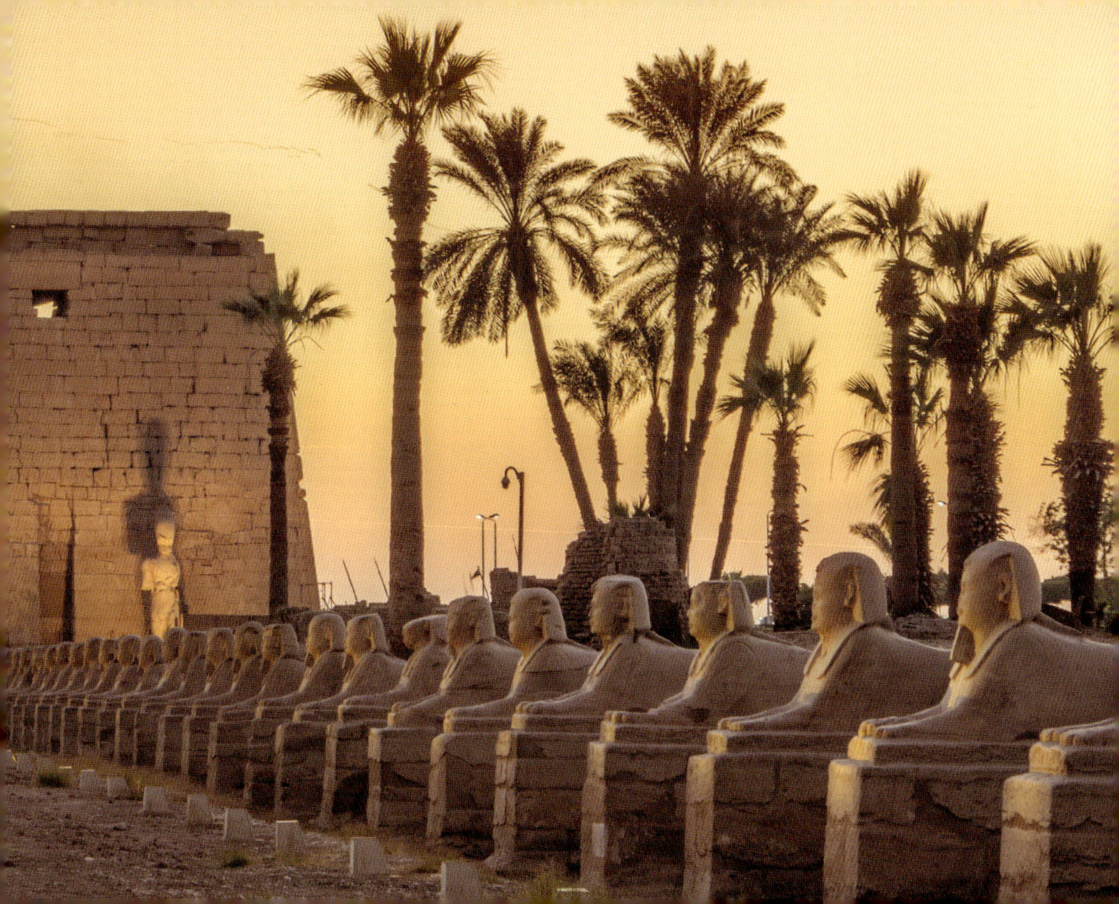

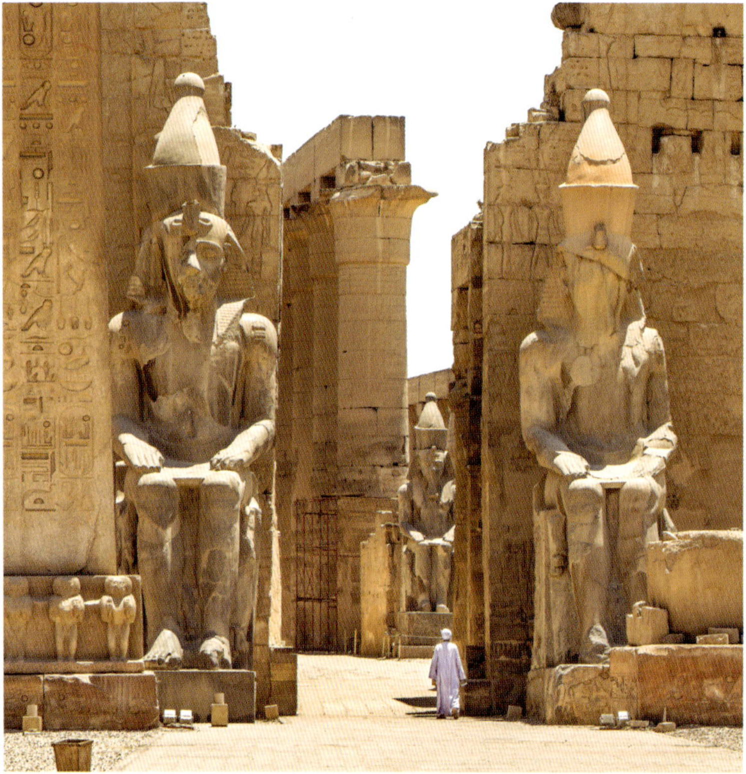

LEFT:

Luxor Temple

Two large statues of Ramesses II sit by the gateway to Luxor Temple. Appropriation of space by later pharaohs was common throughout their history. Luxor Temple was largely built by King Amenhotep III, and his collonaded Sun Court is the main highlight of this temple.

OPPOSITE:

Pyramid Of Meidum, Fayoum

This fascinating addition to Egypt's skyline was perhaps the next attempt at pyramid building after the Step Pyramid of Saqqara. It was something of a failure, thanks to a mixture of poor design, poor construction, and a bad choice of materials for its outer covering.

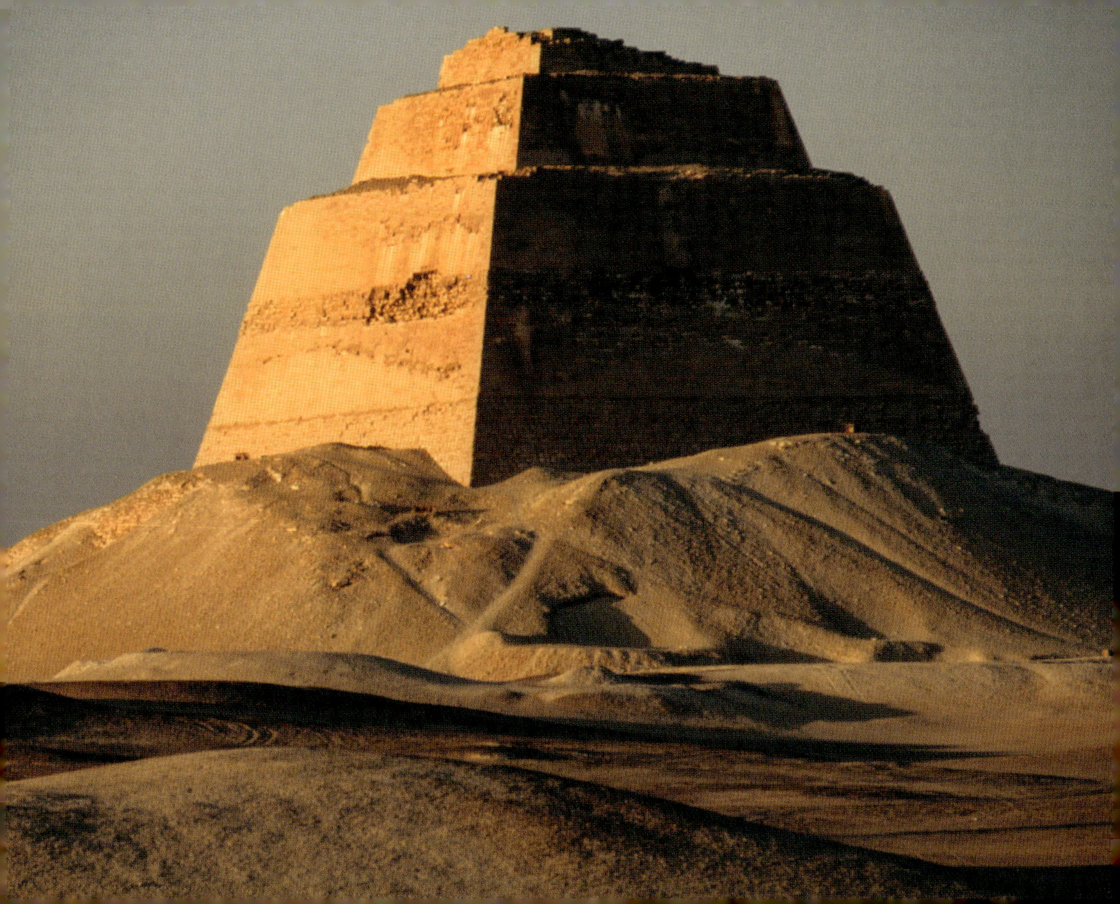

RIGHT TOP:

Fayoum Portraits

The face of a man from Hawara in the Fayoum. This district is believed to have been a burial area for the more elite members of society during Roman times.

RIGHT BOTTOM:

Roman Mummy Mask

The exterior of some mummy cases included a gold covered cartonnage mask during the Greco-Roman era.

FAR RIGHT:

Fayoum Mummy

The Fayoum district had been home to many people over the centuries up to and including the Roman era. These faces are drawn from ancestors such as Egyptians, Syrians, Libyans, Nubians, Jews and Romans.

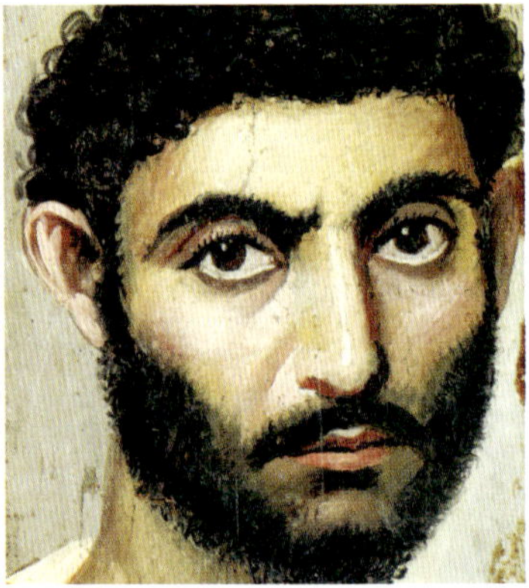

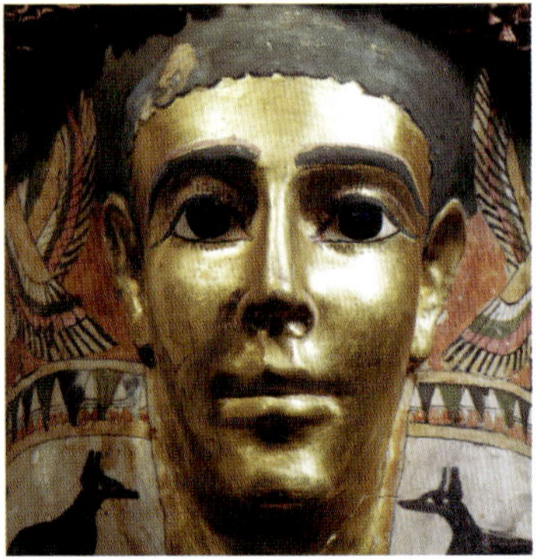

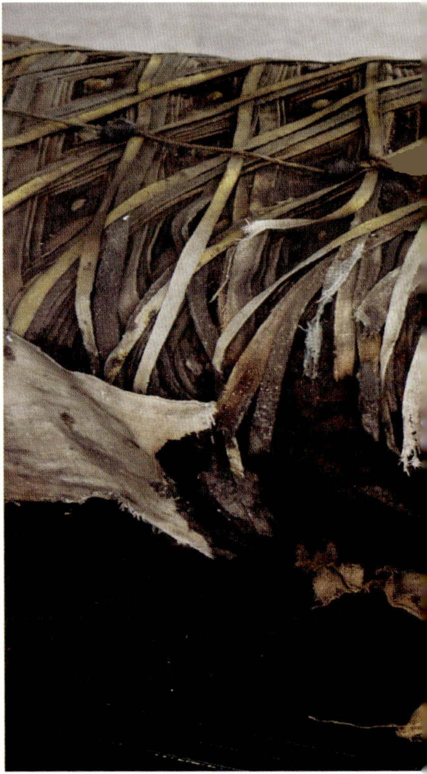

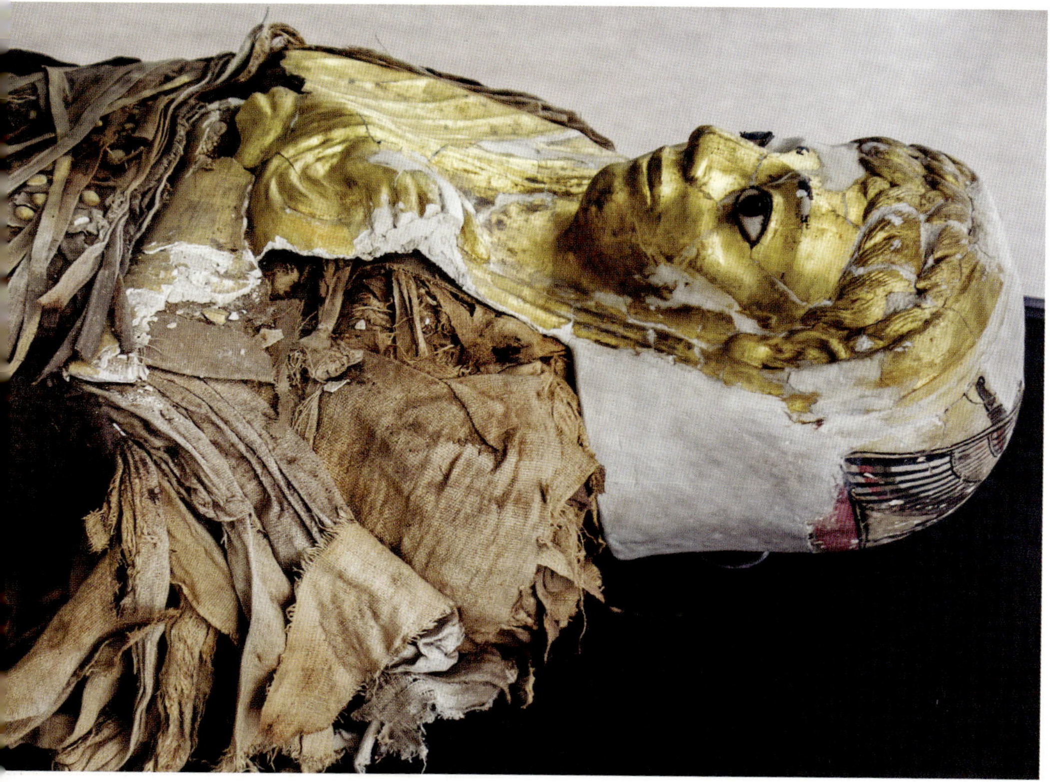

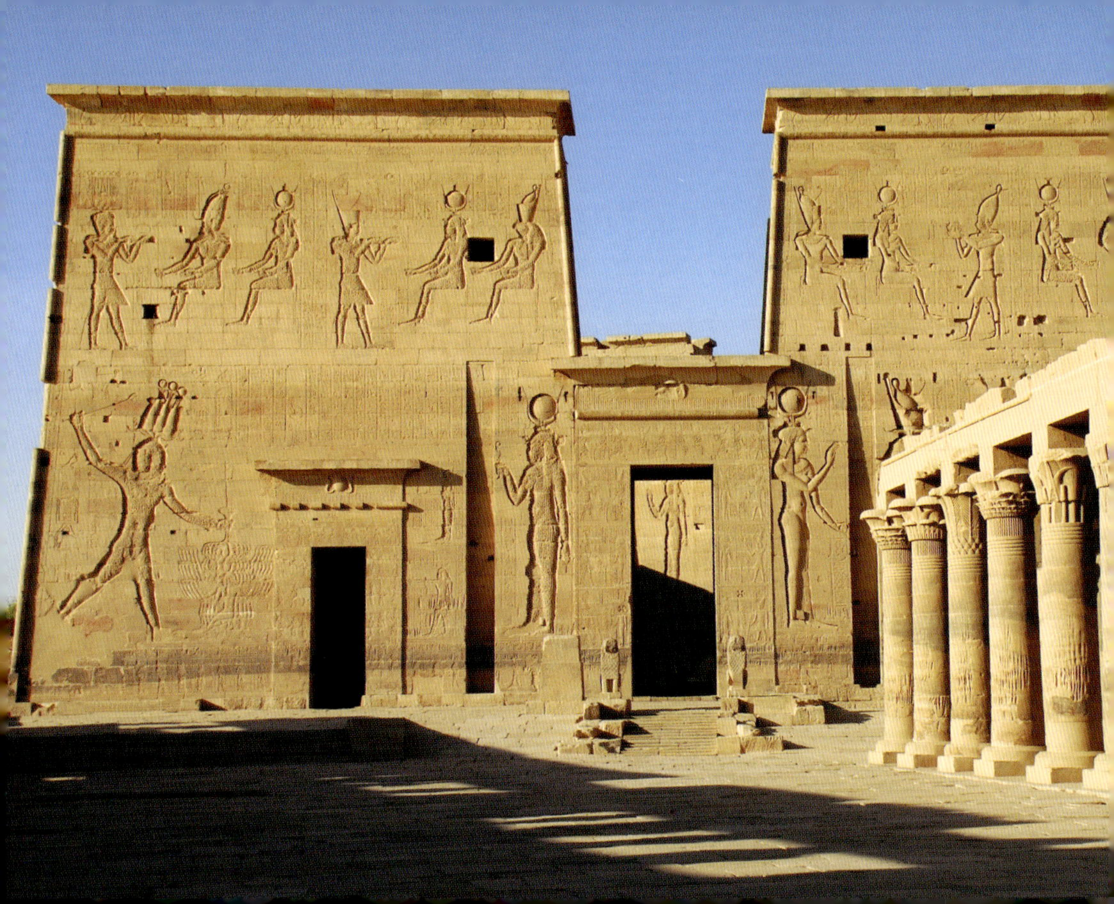

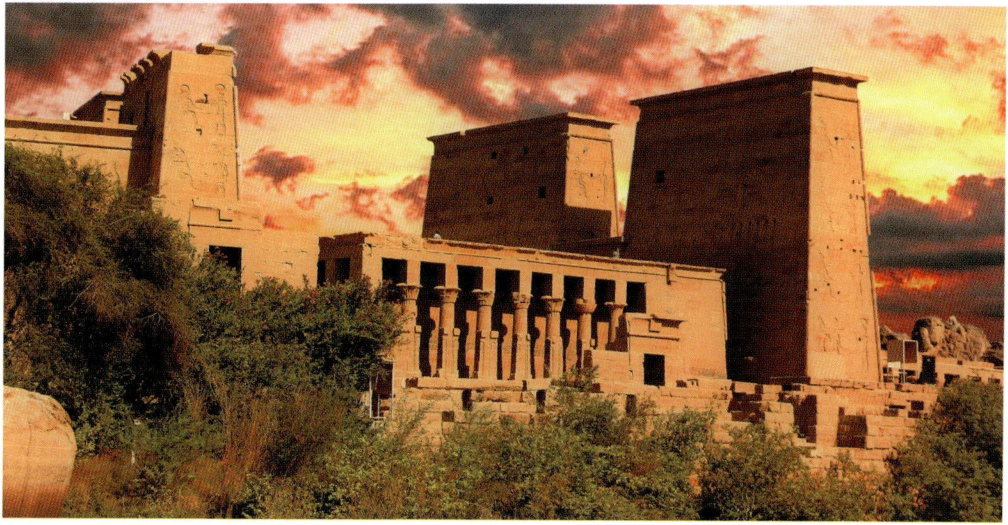

OPPOSITE:

Temple of Isis, Philae

The Temple of Isis at Philae is another treasure saved from being submerged by an international effort backed by UNESCO. The temple complex was dismantled and moved in 1970. Philae was revered by both Egyptians and Nubians because they believed that Osiris himself, god of life, death and the afterlife, was buried there.

ABOVE:

Temple of Isis, Philae

The temple itself is devoted to the Goddess Isis and carries this inscription 'Mighty one, foremost of the goddesses, Ruler in heaven, Queen on earth ... All gods are under her command.' Isis was the wife of Osiris and together they were the parents of Horus.

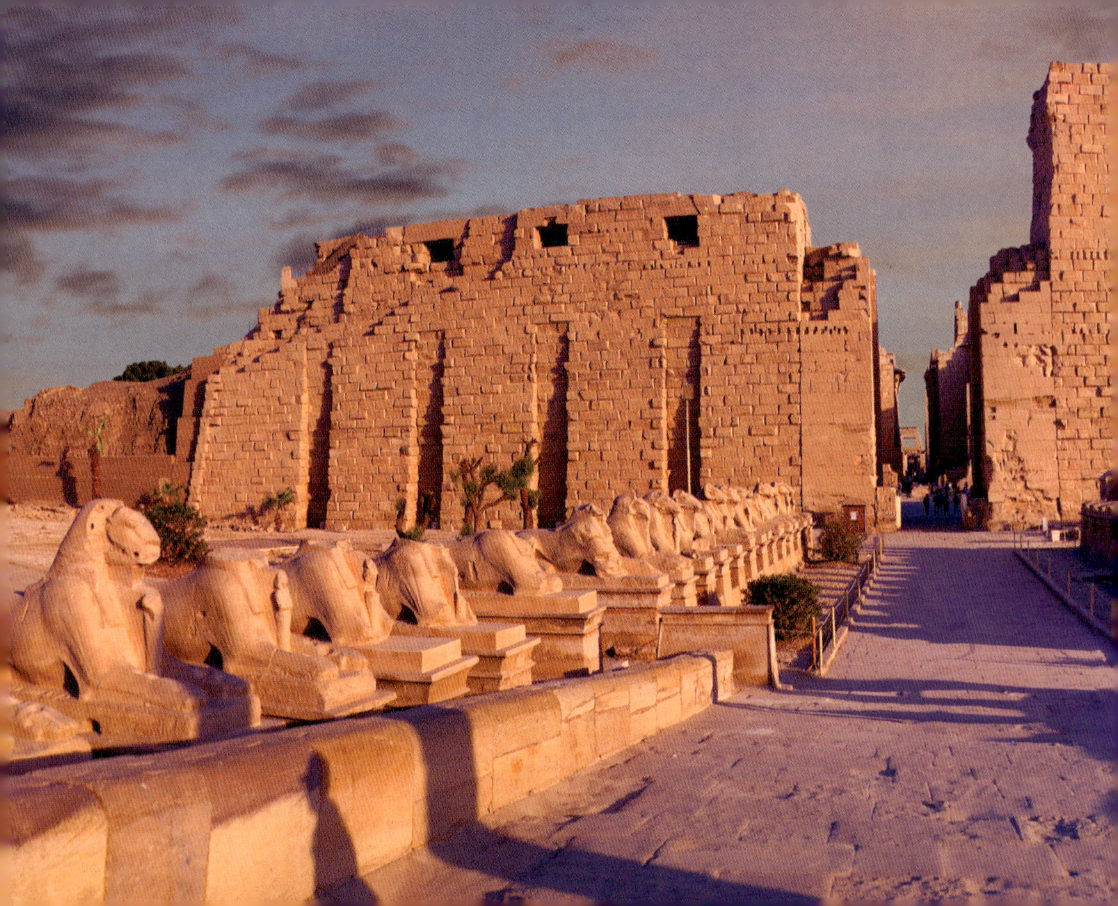

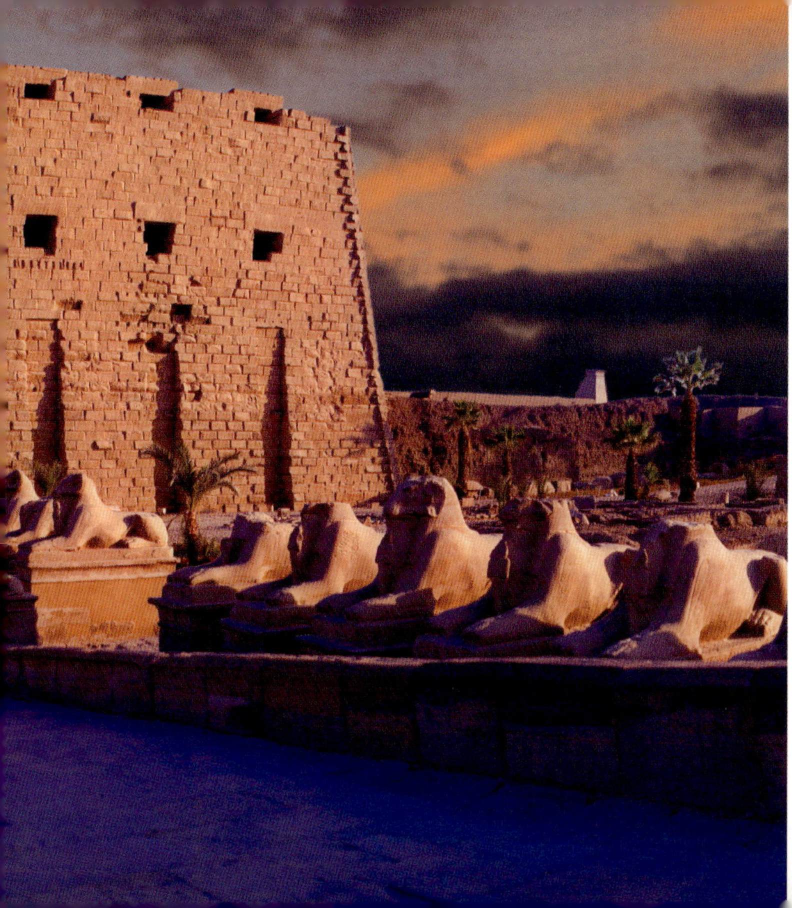

Karnak, Temple of Amun, Upper Egypt

Karnak was the centre of religious life in New Kingdom Ancient Egypt. For more than 2000 years every pharaoh added their name or face to this vast site around the Temple of Amun-Re. The people of Ancient Egypt came each day to offer devotional gifts. Its temples, statues, chapels, sanctuaries, shrines and a large sacred lake cover an area of more than 300,000 sq m (3,229,173 sq ft). Any visitor should devote more than one day to exploring this massive complex.

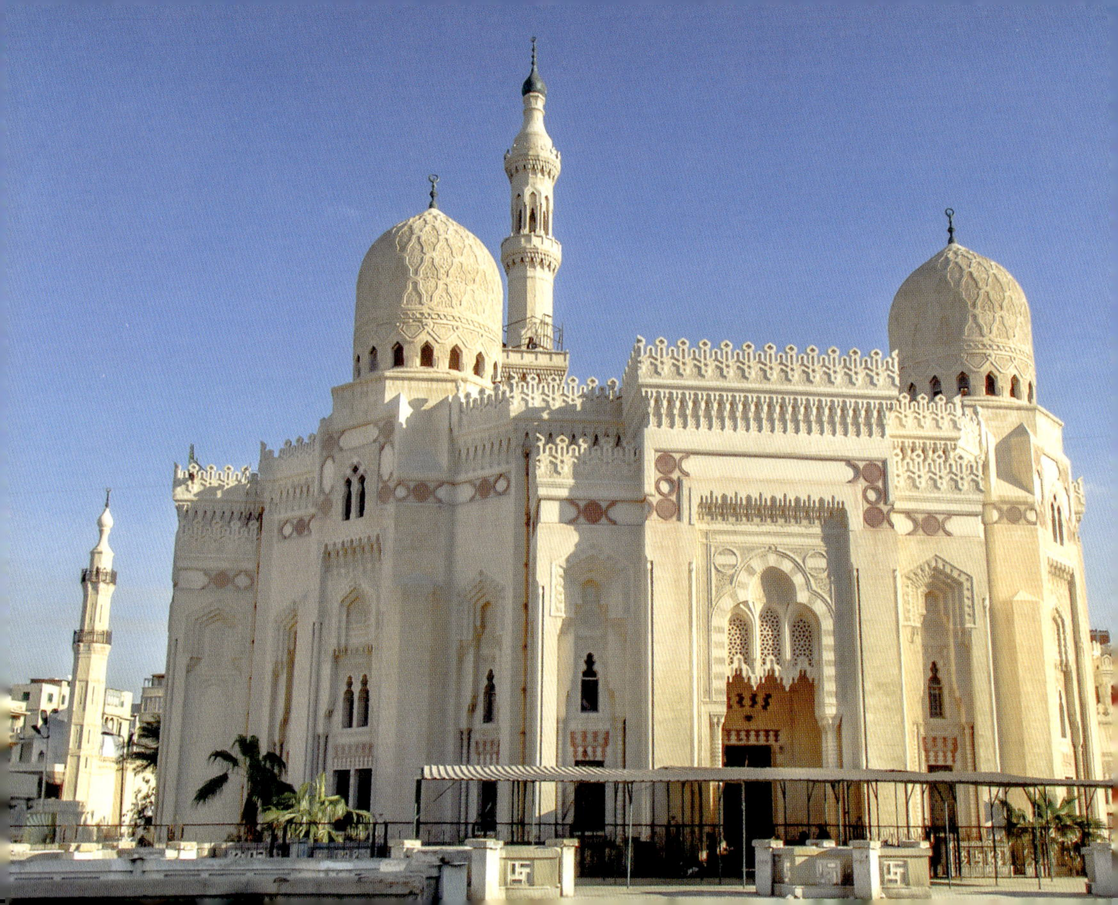

Landmarks

What makes something a landmark? In Egypt, 'almost anything' is the answer. The country's continuous history has ensured that each period, civilization, religion or ruler has left behind some symbol marking their time in Egypt. In this section, we explore examples from a country rich in buildings and monuments which are both historically important yet still very much part of daily life. These landmarks include museums, buildings from Coptic and Jewish history, mosques and architecture of the Islamic period in Cairo and Alexandria. We see the influence of Rome and the Ottomans, while in more modern times we embrace the legacy of Egypt's royal era.

Admittedly some places, such as The City of the Dead in Cairo which is home to some truly historic mosques and is surrounded by highways these days, or the more out-of-the way pyramids such as Meidum (the collapsed pyramid which is a key part of the development of these astonishing tombs), take time to track down.

So get off the beaten track and create some landmark memories for yourself.

OPPOSITE:

Abu al-Abbas al-Mursi Mosque, Alexandria

There has been a mosque dedicated to the Muslim scholar and teacher Abu Abbas al-Mursi on this site since the 13th century. The tomb of this important Sufi saint is inside.

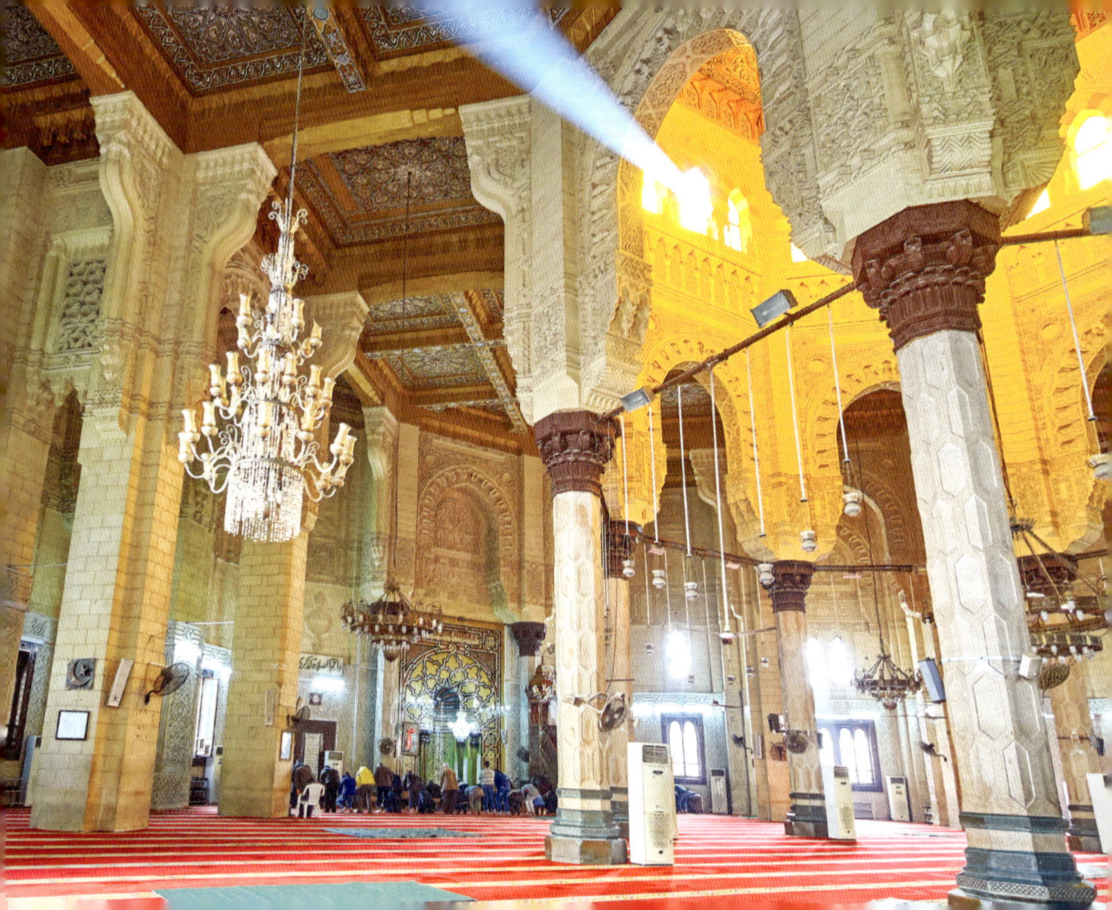

OPPOSITE:

Abu al-Abbas al-Mursi Mosque, Alexandria

Abu Abbas al-Mursi came to Egypt from Andalucia via Tunisia and lived in Alexandria for over 40 years. He devoted his life to teaching and scholarship. After his death his work became celebrated and the site of his tomb became part of the pilgrimage route to Mecca along the North African coast.

RIGHT:

Abu al-Abbas al-Mursi Mosque, Alexandria

The mosque you visit today was built in 1775, its cream coloured façade hides a huge interior of arches, elongated columns, marble flooring, coloured arabesque windows and a highly decorated roof.

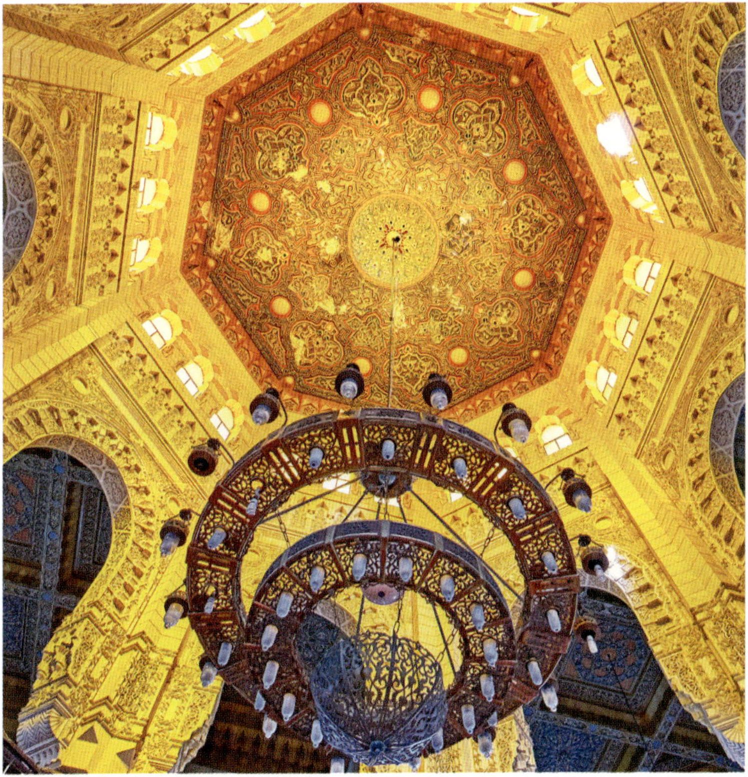

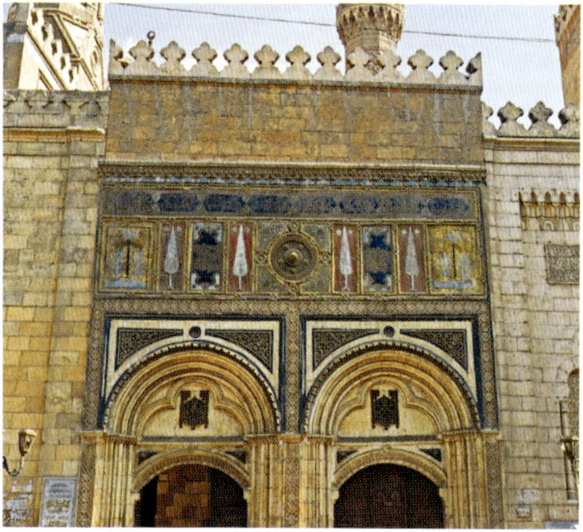

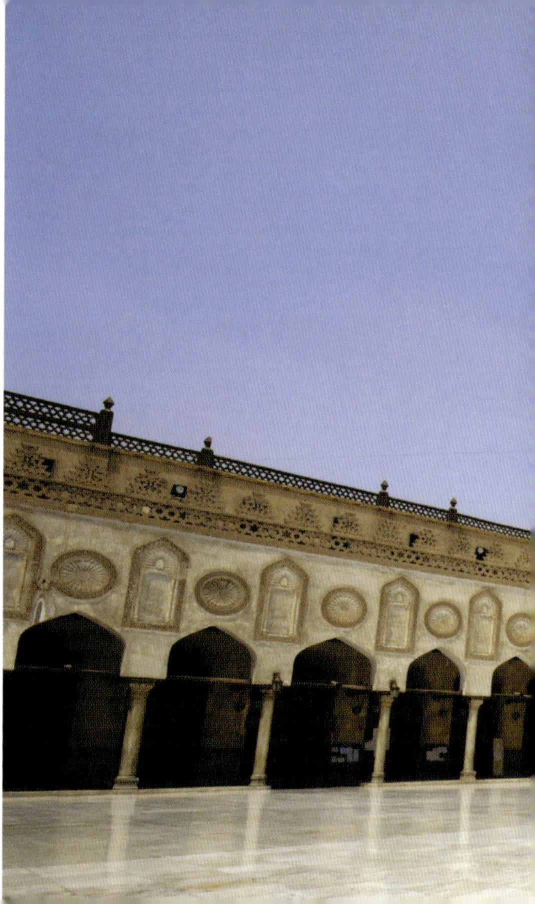

ABOVE AND RIGHT:

Al-Azhar Mosque, Cairo

Al-Azhar is one of the most famous mosques in the Islamic world and was commissioned in 970 AD. As the most famous mosque in Cairo, it has developed into the most important centre of study for Sunni theology and sharia (Islamic Law). The mosque has been renovated many times over more than 1000 years. It's five minarets display the changing periods of the mosque's evolution in their differing architecture styles. Students travel from across the world for lessons in Arabic and Quranic interpretation in the two schools connected to the mosque.

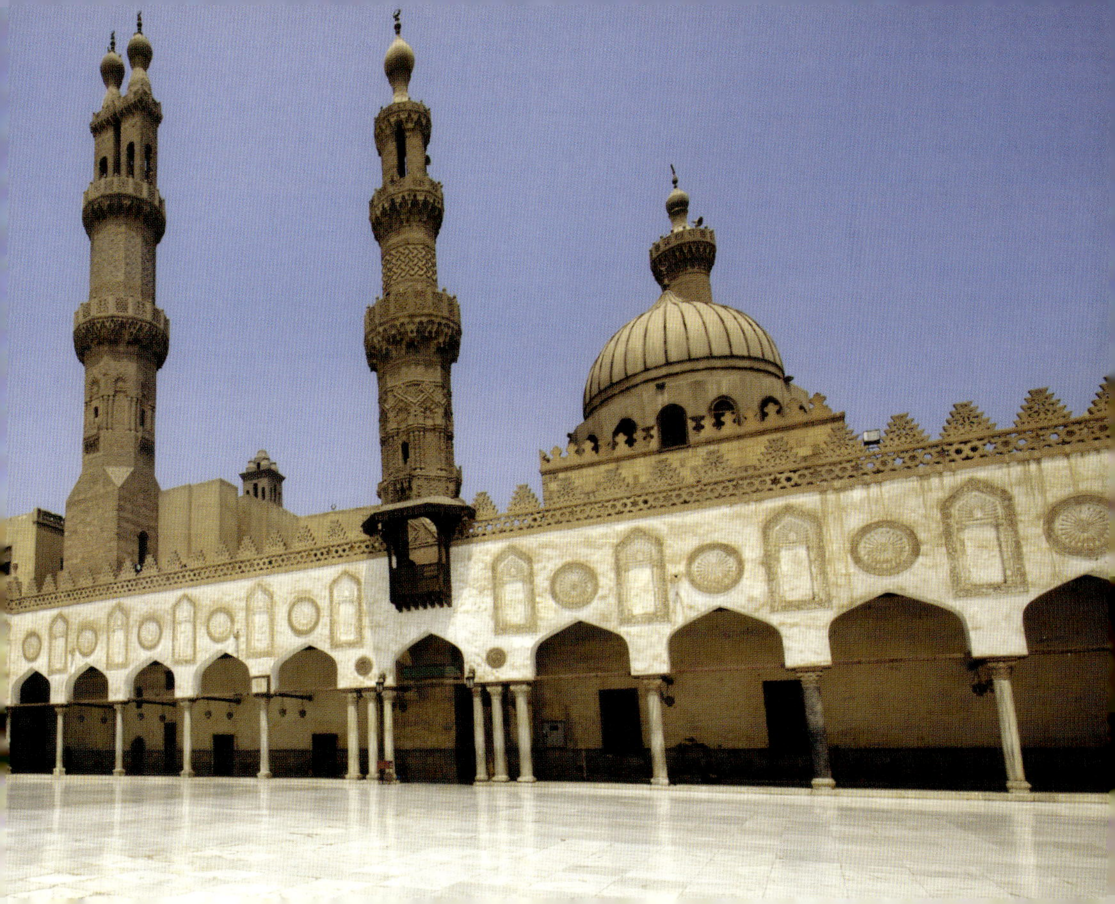

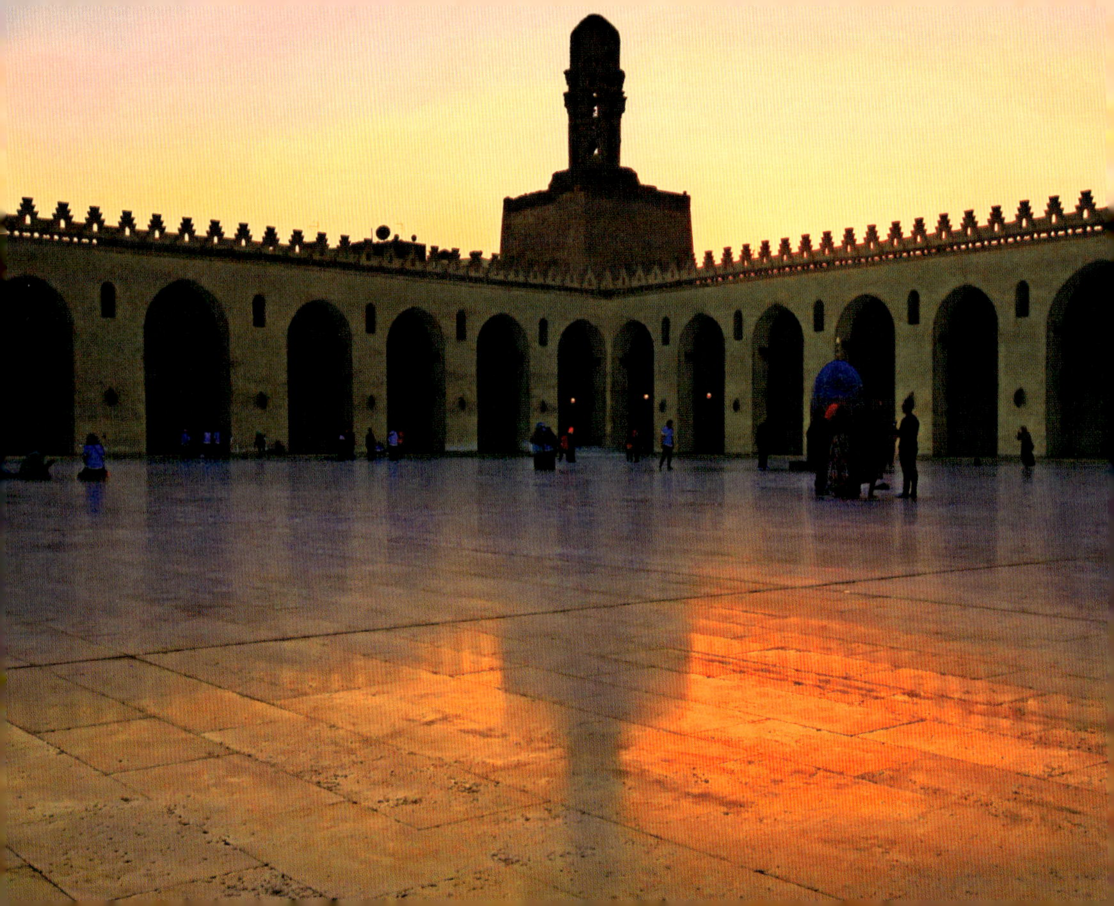

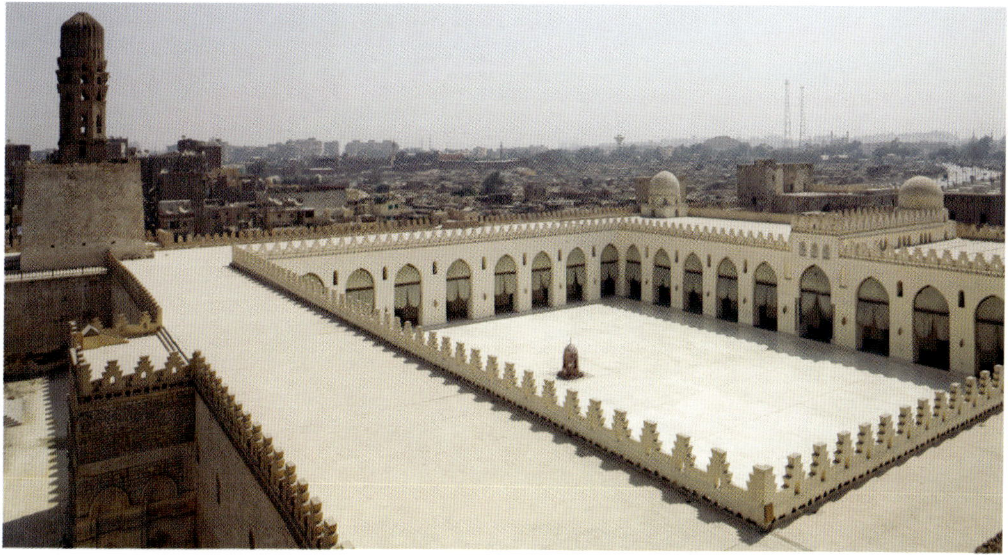

OPPOSITE:

Al-Hakim Mosque, Cairo

This mosque is a major religious site in Cairo. It is dedicated to Al-Hakim bi-Amr Allah, who was both Fatimid Caliph and Ismaili Imam. The mosque has been used for different purposes over time: as a prison during the crusades, as a stable by Saladin and as a fortress for Napoleon.

ABOVE:

Al-Hakim Mosque, Cairo

Starting in 1980, the mosque was entirely refurbished and is now resplendent in white marble and gold, making the mosque today a place of calm and peaceful worship. The two enormous minarets attract local visitors and tourists to this mosque, which would otherwise be hidden in the corner of Islamic Cairo.

Alexandria Sea Front

The harbour and the Corniche of Alexandria represent Egypt's geographic connection with the Mediterranean and classical history, which made Alexandria the greatest city of ancient times.

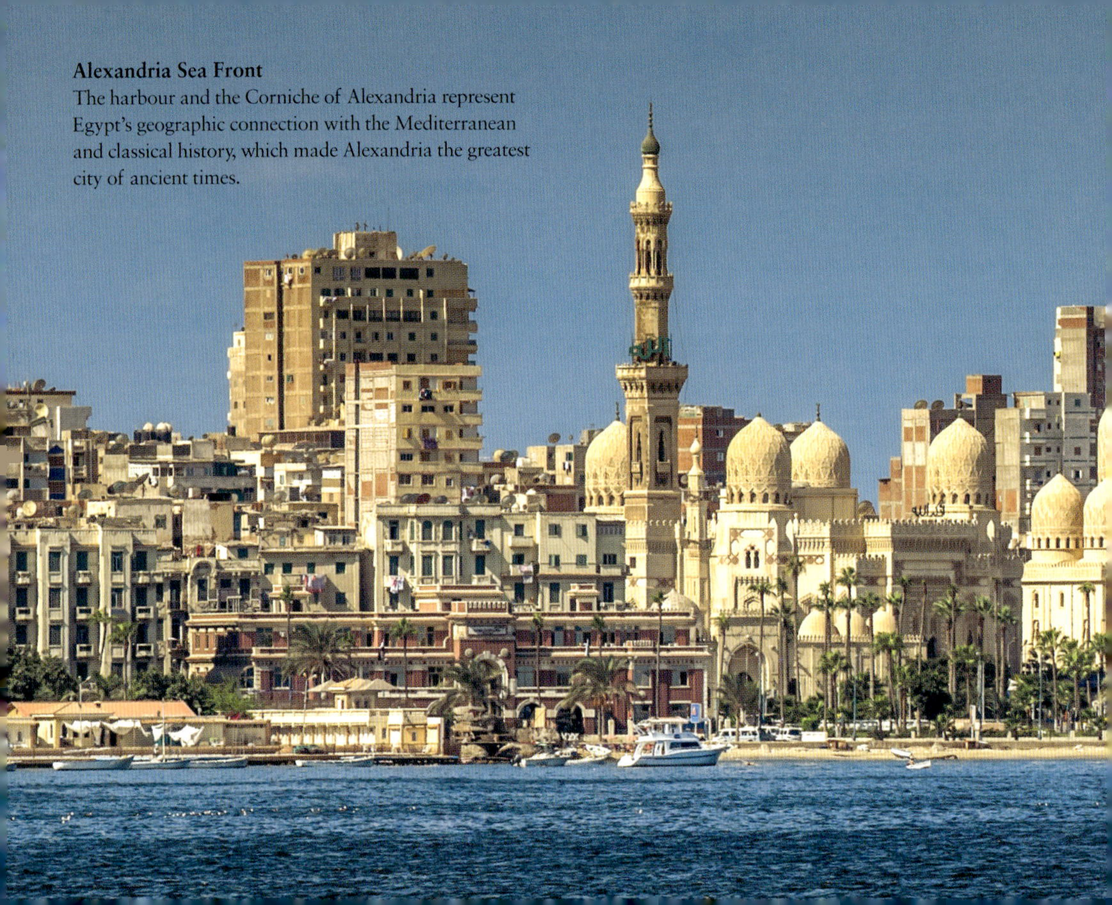

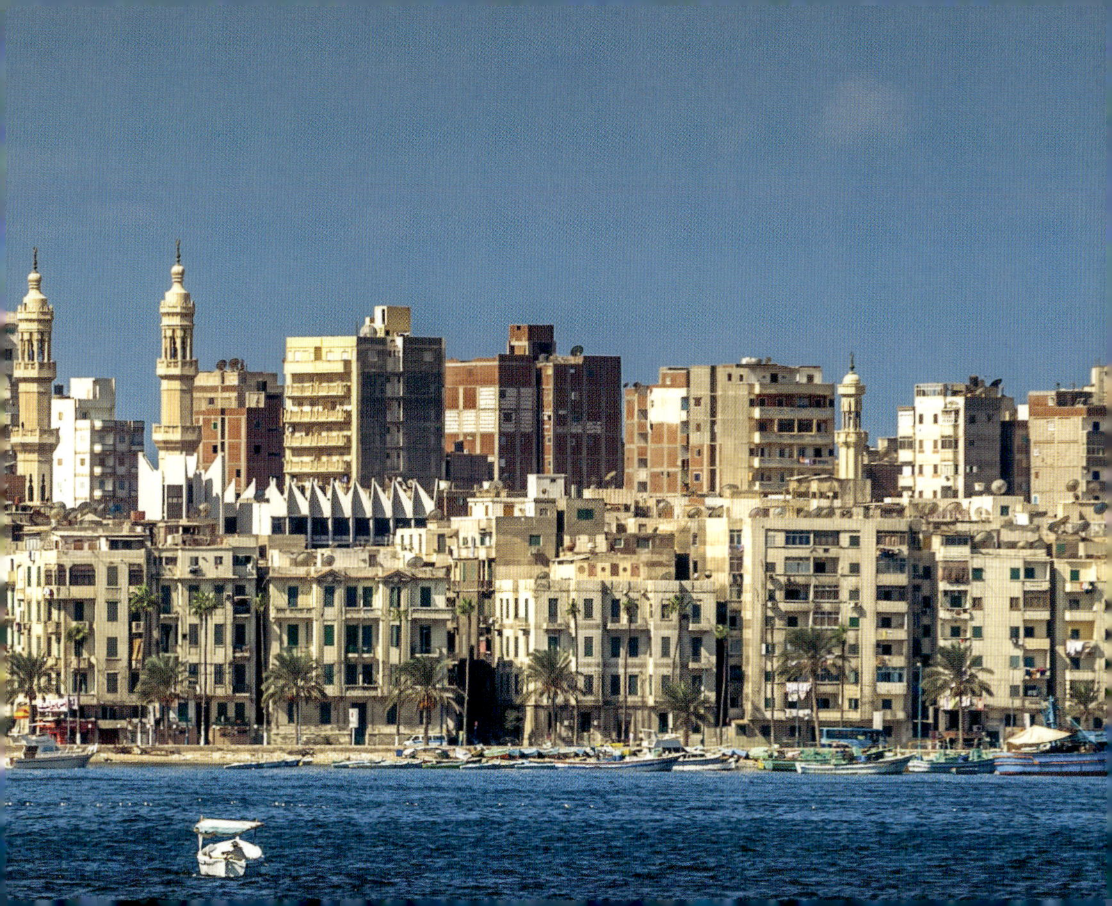

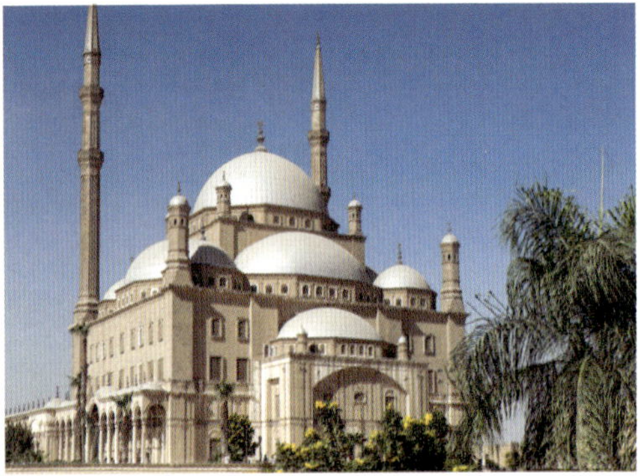

ABOVE:

Mosque of Mohamed Ali Pasha, Cairo

The Mosque of Mohamed Ali Pasha was built in the early 19th century and is more in keeping with the skyline of Istanbul. This is a reflection of the heritage of the Ottoman Albanian commander, Mohamed Ali Pasha.

RIGHT:

Mosque of Amr ibn al-As, Cairo

Better known as Mosque of Amr, Mosque of Amr ibn al-As was the centre of Fustat, the newly founded capital of Egypt, declared in 1641. This location was the site of the original tent of Amr ibn al-As when he arrived as the general of the Muslim army that conquered Egypt and saw the end of Roman influence in Egypt in the 7th century AD.

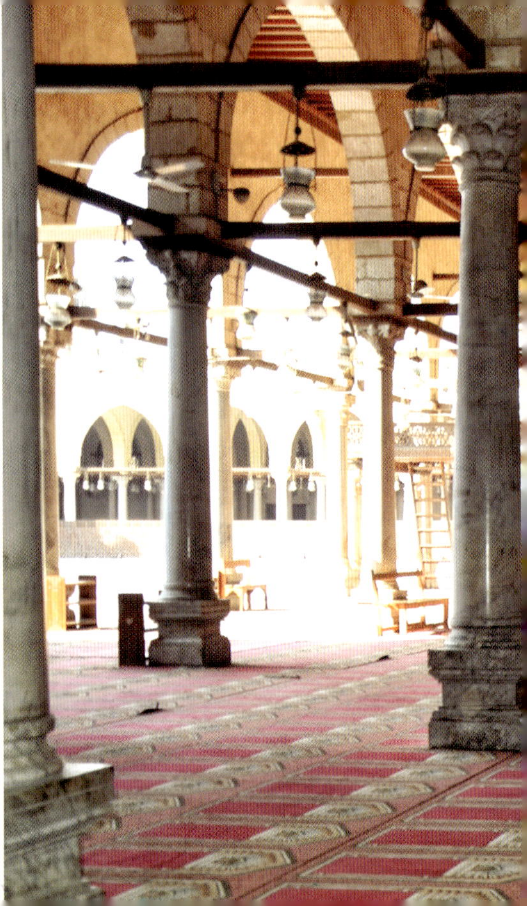

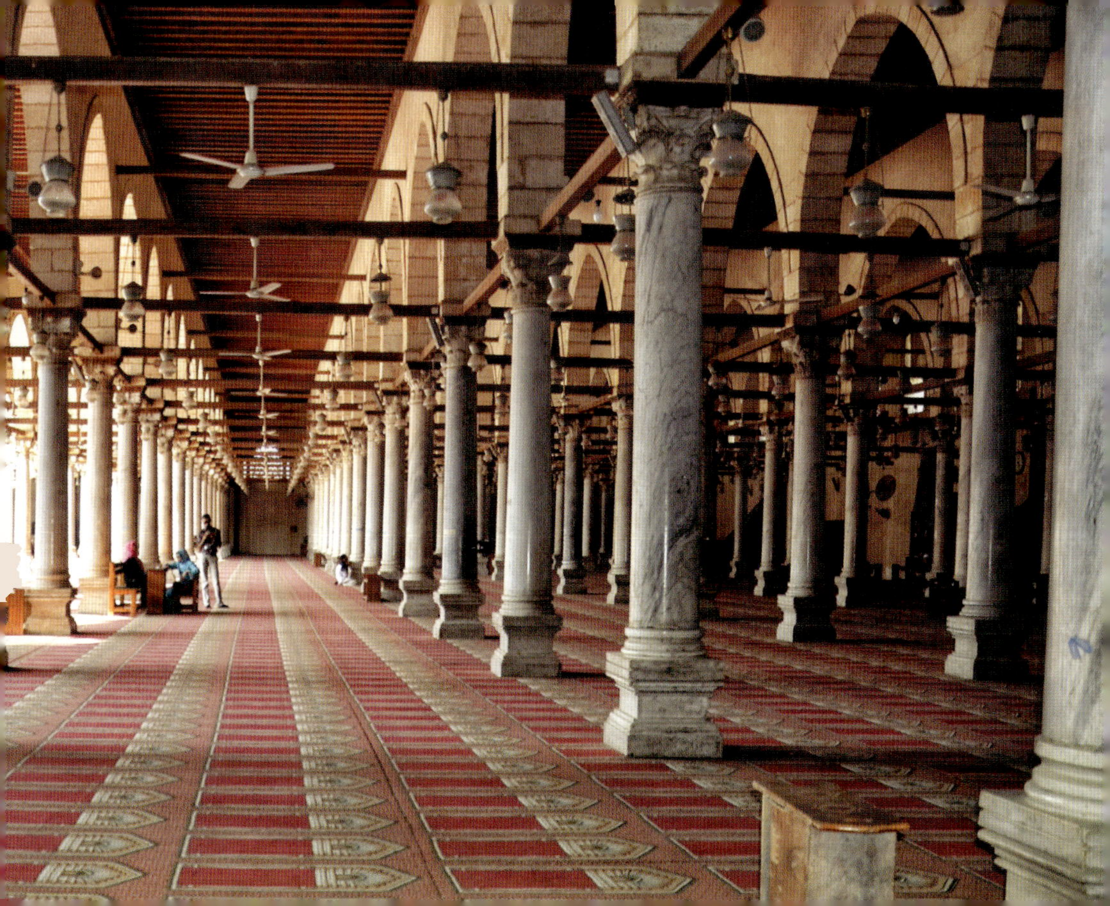

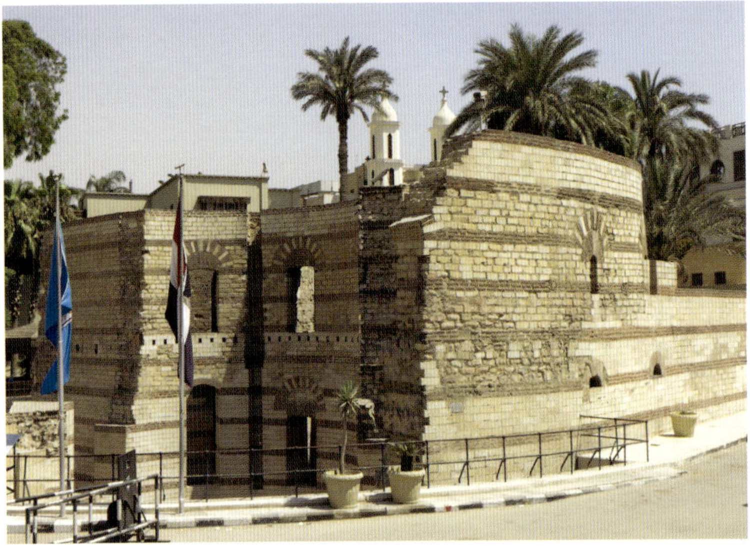

OPPOSITE:

Bab Zuweila, Cairo

One of three of the last surviving gates to Medieval Cairo, Bab Zuweila stands out as a dominating shape above the hectic streets below. Climb to the top of these minarets and take in a sweeping view of the oldest part of today's Cairo. The hectic streets below are full of life, in contrast to the former use of Bab Zuweila as a site of execution.

ABOVE:

Babylon Fortress, Cairo

Situated in Old Cairo are the remains of a fortress known as Babylon. This fortress area was first developed by the Persians when the course of the Nile was different from today. When the Romans came, the position of the fortress changed to its current location. The fort extends over an area which now includes several of Egypt's oldest churches. Here we see part of the Roman fort called Qasr Al Shamah 'Fortress of the Beacon' which today sits by the entrance to the Coptic Museum.

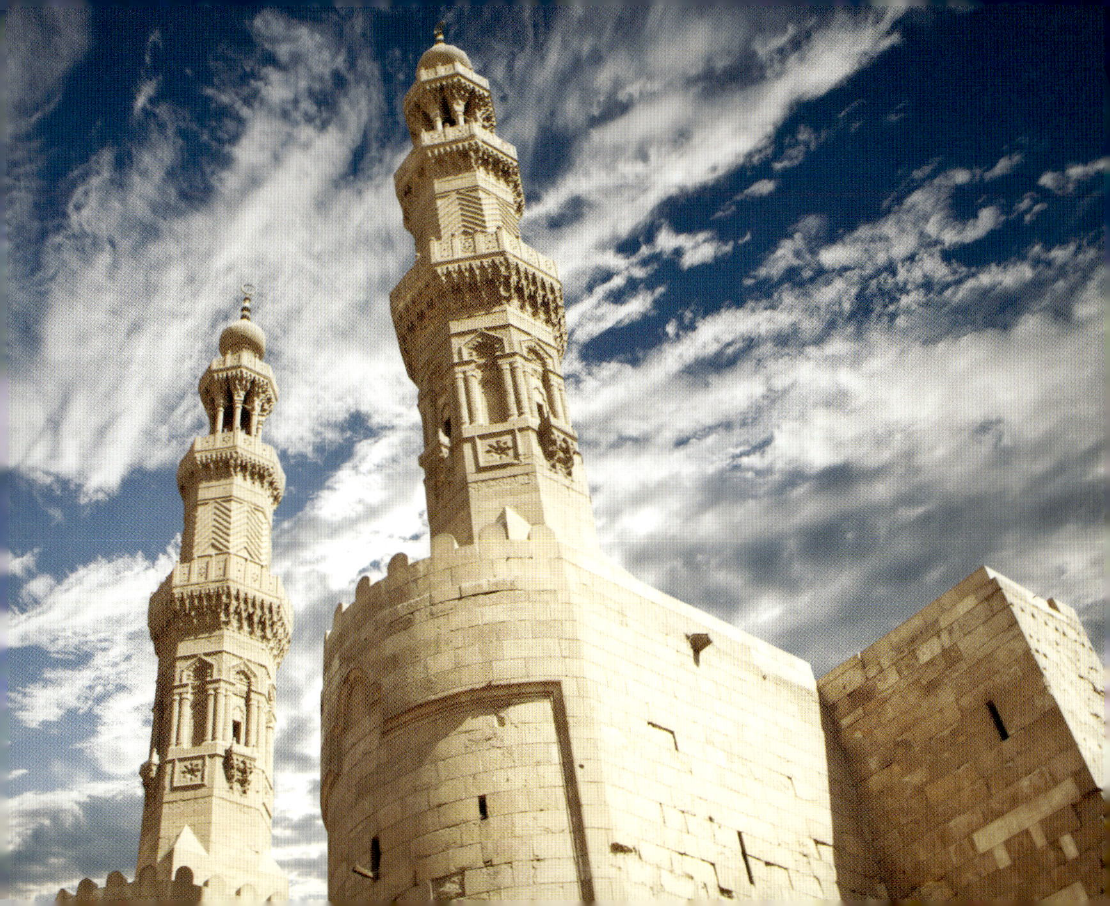

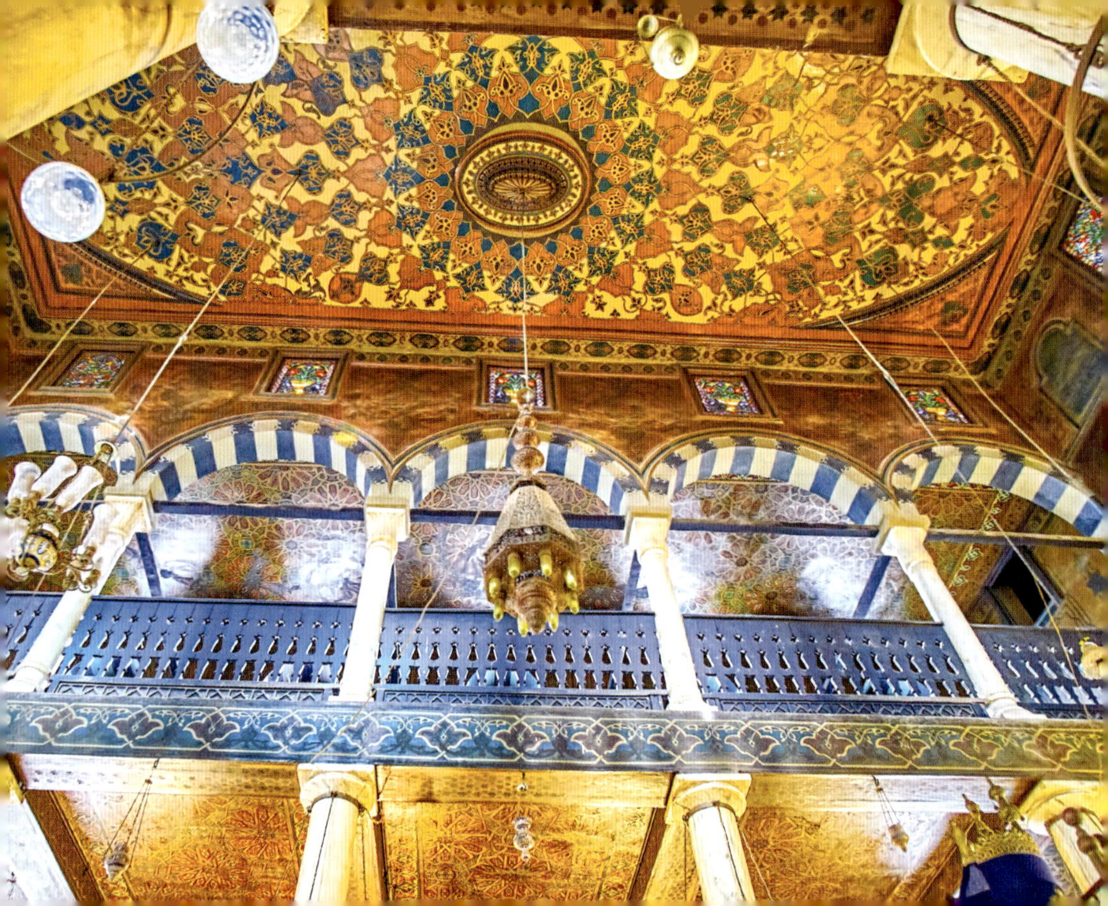

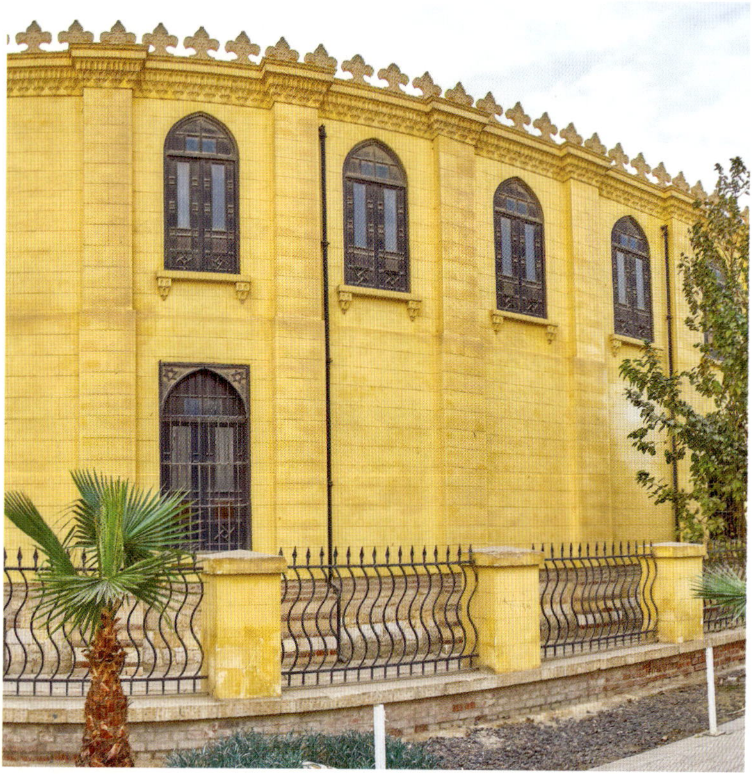

LEFT:

Ben Ezra Synagogue, Cairo

Originally a church of the 4th century, this building became a synagogue in the 9th century and was rebuilt in its existing form by Abraham bin Ezra, a rabbi of Jerusalem in the 12th century. It was rebuilt in the 19th century.

OPPOSITE:

Ben Ezra Synagogue, Cairo

The Christian and Jewish heritage of this site is also shared in stories that surround it. Here in a nearby spring, Moses was found in the reeds of the Nile, and it is also a spot where Mary drew water to wash the baby Jesus.

BELOW:

Bibliotheca Alexandrina

The original library of Alexandria was the centre of knowledge of the ancient world. Having taken centuries to build, it is thought to have been destroyed during several events between the era of Julius Caesar in the 1st century BC and the Muslim conquest in the 7th century AD. In 2002, a new library opened. Below is the Planetarium, part of the new library complex.

OPPOSITE:

Bibliotheca Alexandrina

The façade of the main building of the library is a huge wall decorated in the scripts of more than 120 ancient and modern languages from across the world and from world history.

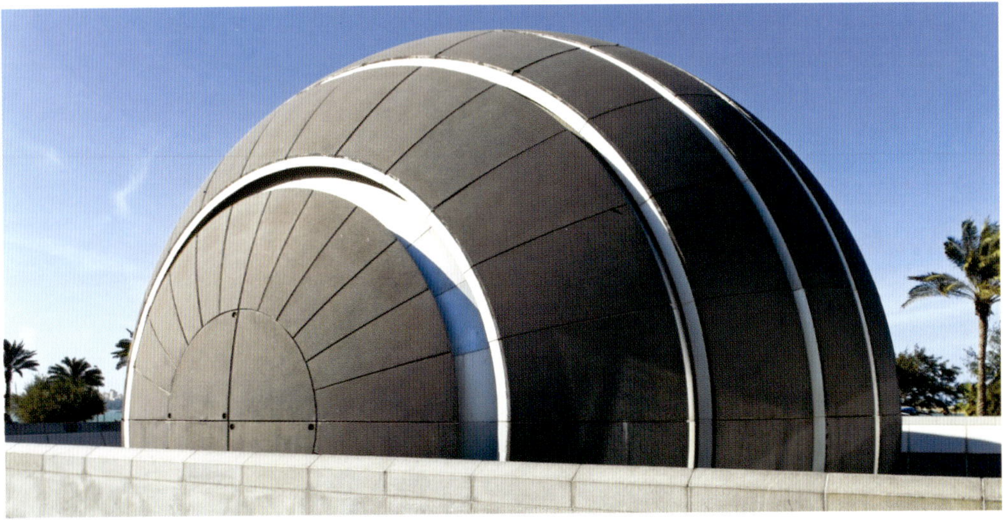

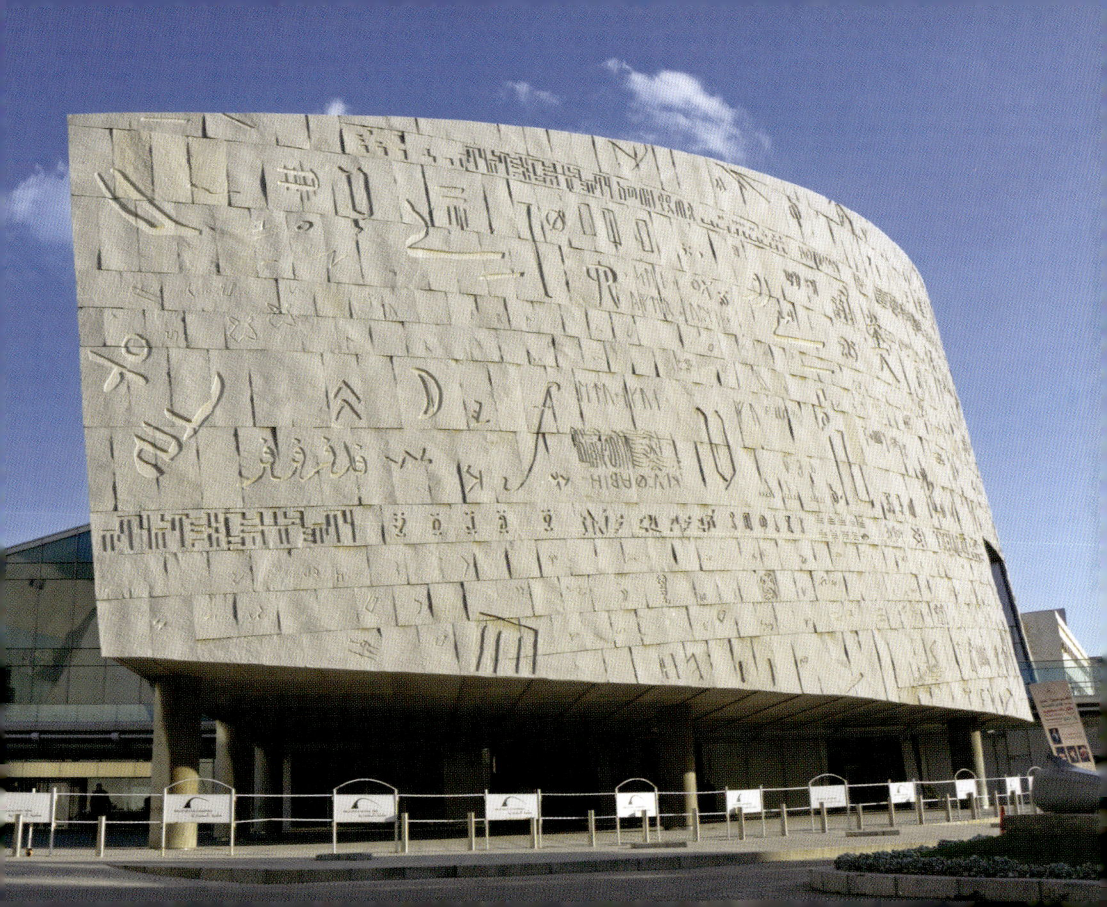

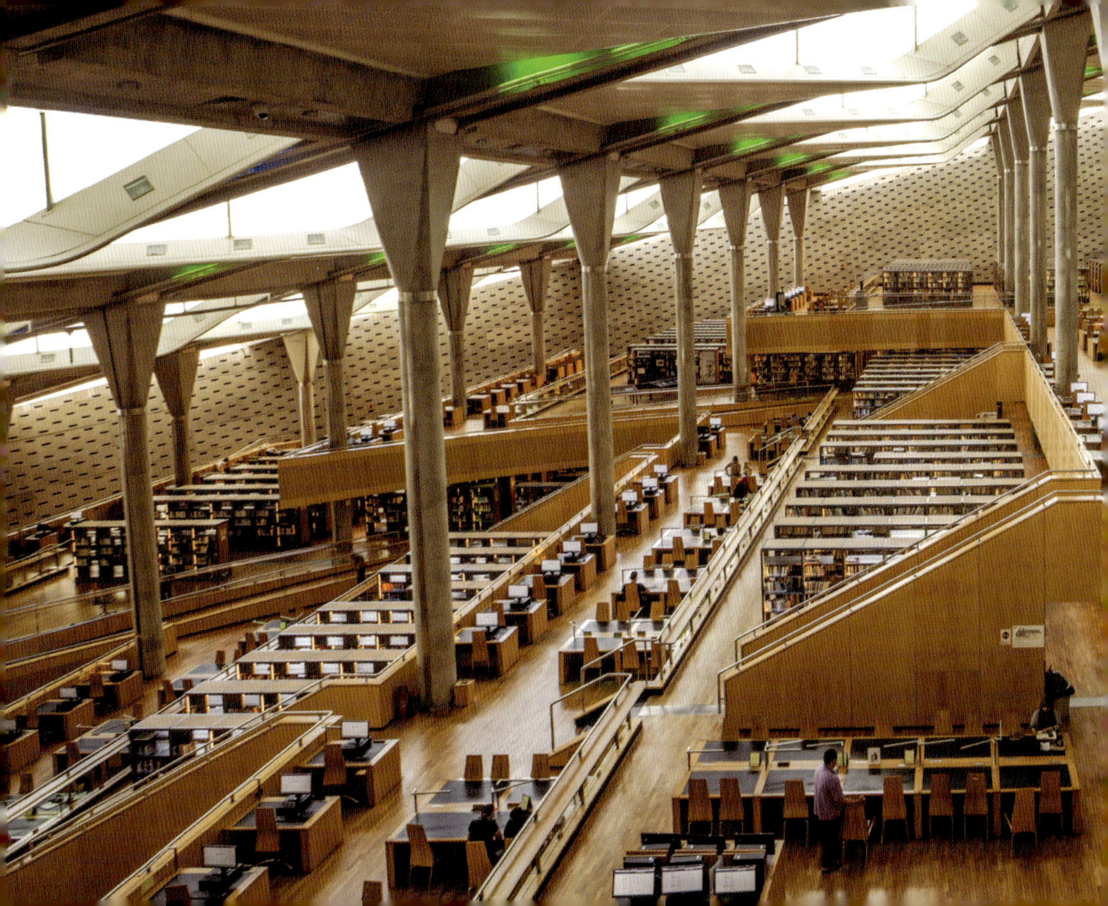

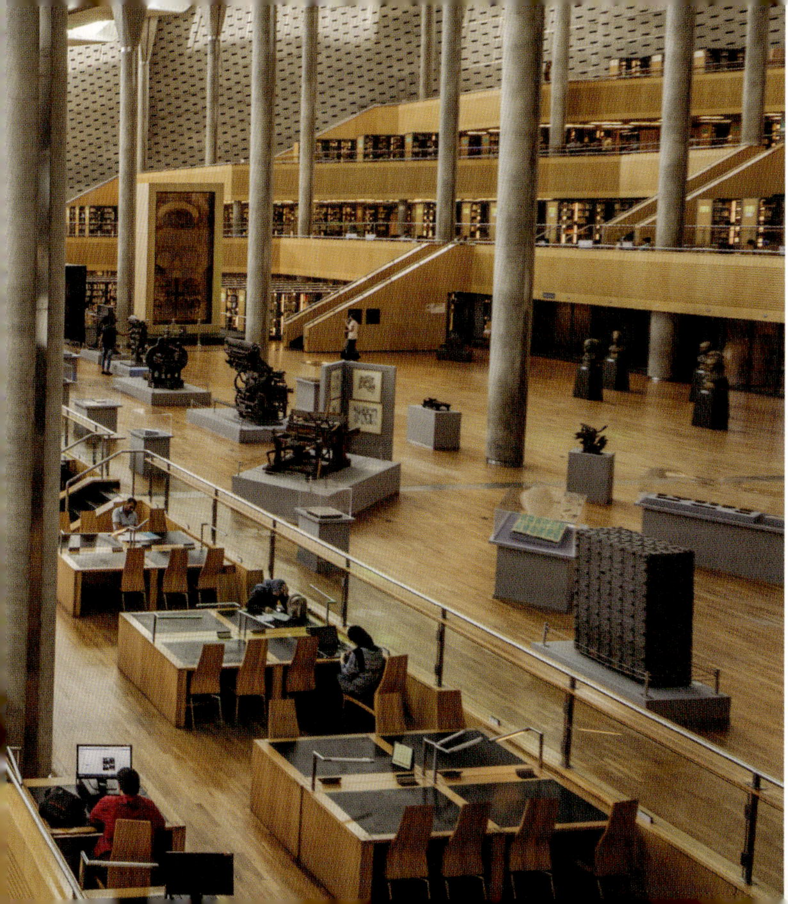

Bibliotheca Alexandrina
When seen from the waterfront, the sloping roof of the new library is designed to resemble the rising sun. The light which shines through this striking feature illuminates the vast main reading room which lies at the heart of the building.

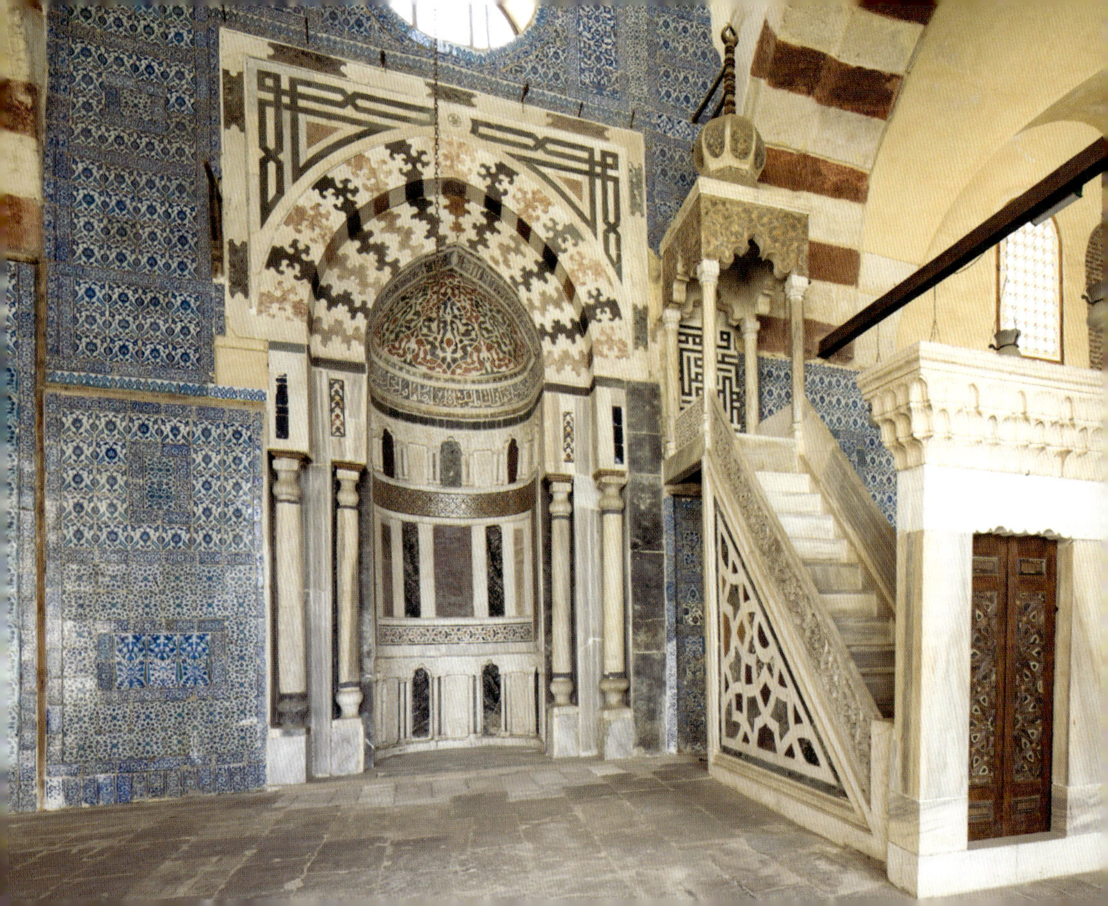

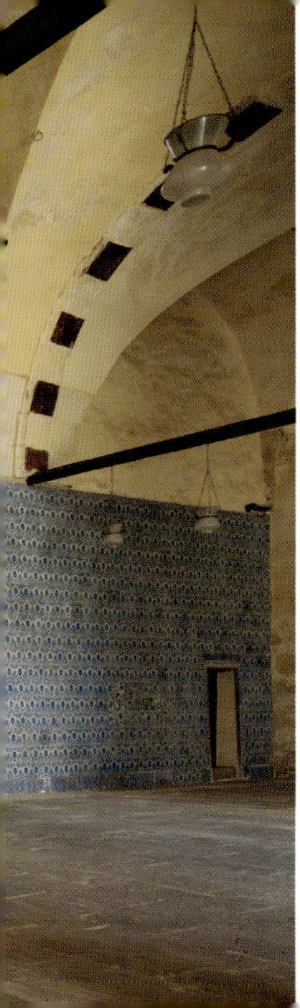

LEFT:

The Blue Mosque, Cairo

The Blue Mosque, or the Mosque of Aqsunqur, is a small secret gem of Islamic Cairo. The wall of Ottoman-style tiles is a delight. The tomb of Turkish governor Ibrahim Agha is at the heart of the mosque, and it was he who introduced the tiles in the 17th century.

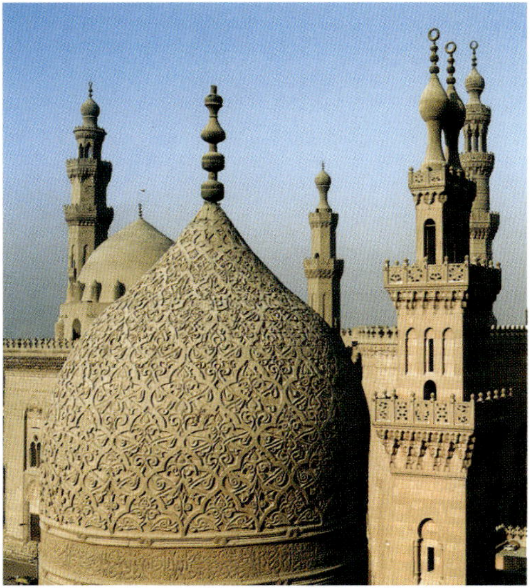

ABOVE:

Domes and Minarets of Islamic Cairo

Historic Cairo was proclaimed a world cultural heritage site in 1979 and as you can see here it fills the skyline with hundreds of minarets and domes. UNESCO described it as: 'One of the world's oldest Islamic cities with its famous mosques, madrasas, hammams and fountains'. It reached its golden age in the 14th century.

RIGHT:

Muizz Street, Islamic Cairo

Muizz Street is named for Al-Muizz li-Din Allah (932–975), Cairo's fourth Caliph of the Fatimid era. This beautifully restored area lies close to the Khan El Khalili bazaar and was pedestrianized in 2008, turning it into an open museum of Islamic architecture.

OPPOSITE:

Sultan Al-Ghuri Complex, Cairo

Sultan Al-Ghuri was known as a cruel despot. He was also a person who enjoyed a love of poetry and music. He built great architecture such as this complex where he hoped to be buried, but he died in battle and his body was never found.

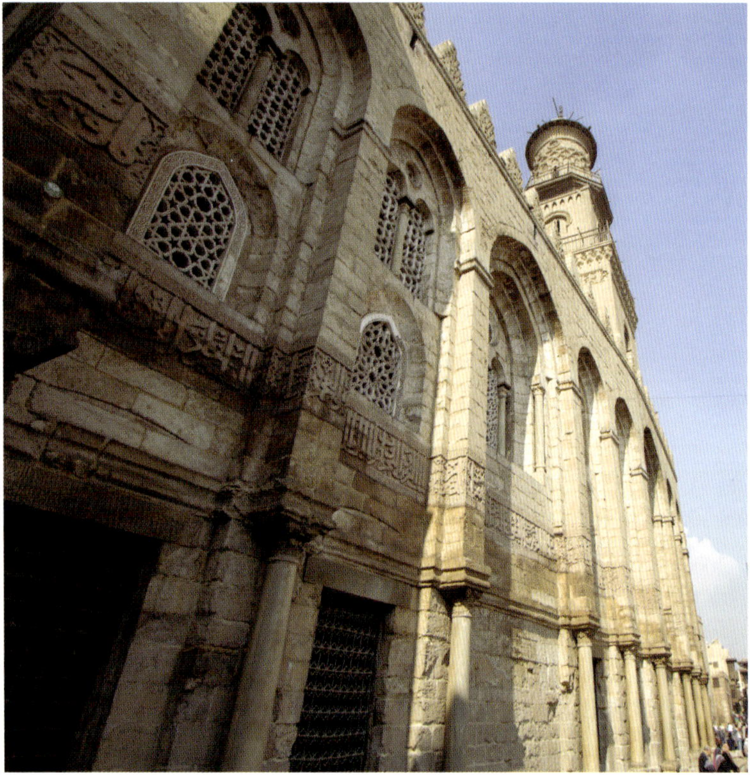

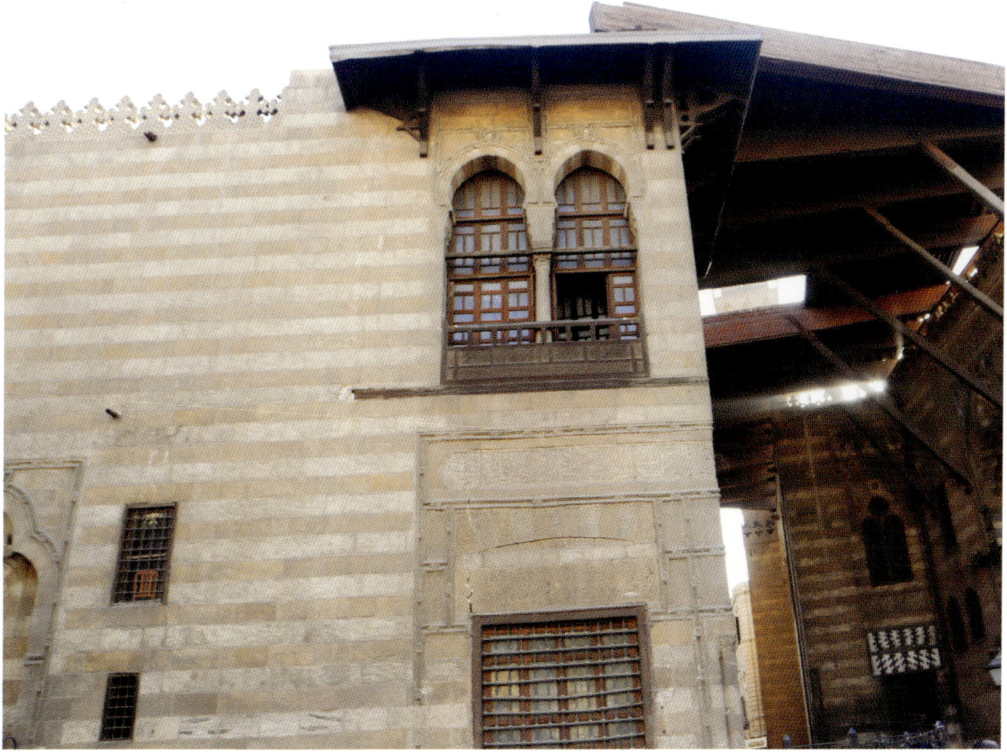

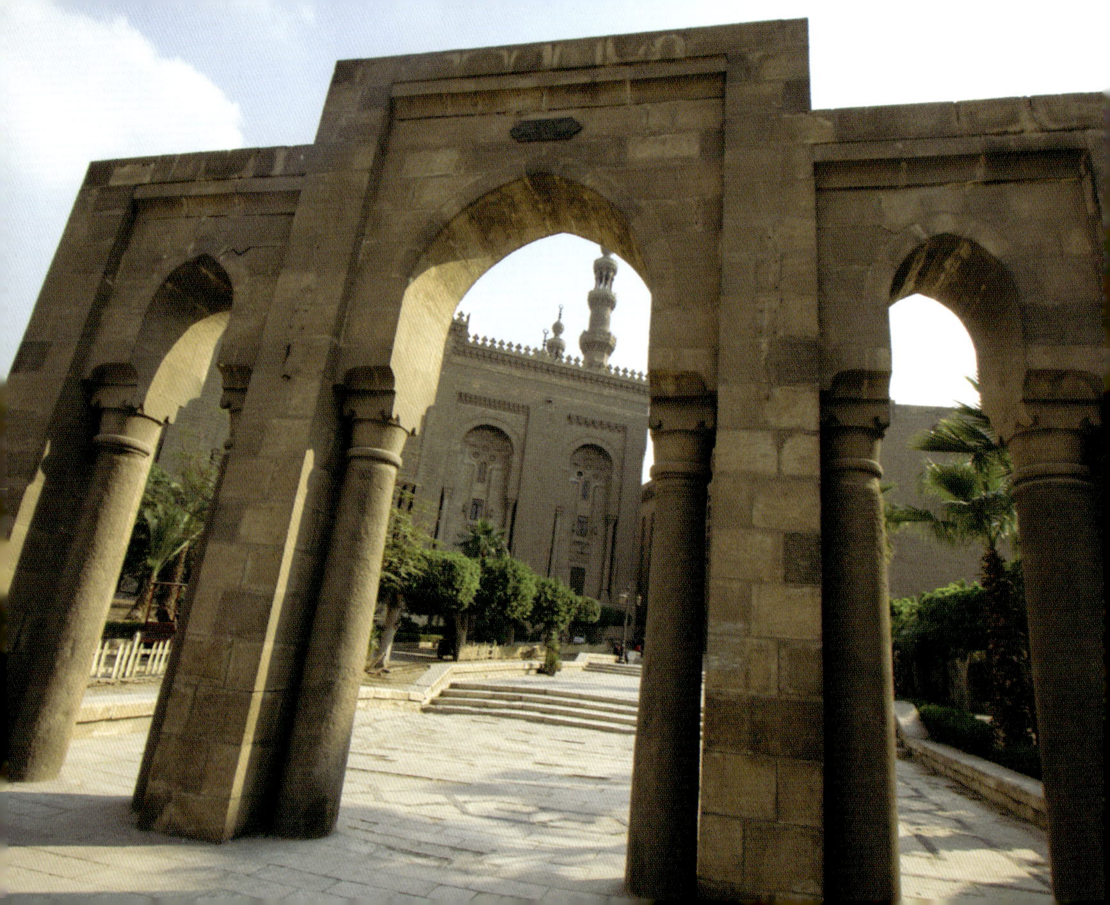

OPPOSITE:

Mosque of Sultan Hassan, Cairo

Situated directly below the citadel is the Mosque Madrassa of Sultan Hassan. This imposing structure is considered one of the finest examples of early Mamluk architecture in Egypt. It contains a mausoleum that was prepared as Sultan Hassan's resting place, but he died in a revolt against him and his body was never found.

RIGHT:

Muizz Street, Cairo

Sabil-Kuttab of Katkhuda, built in 1774. A Sabil is a public fountain, while a Kuttab is a kind of school for teaching children.

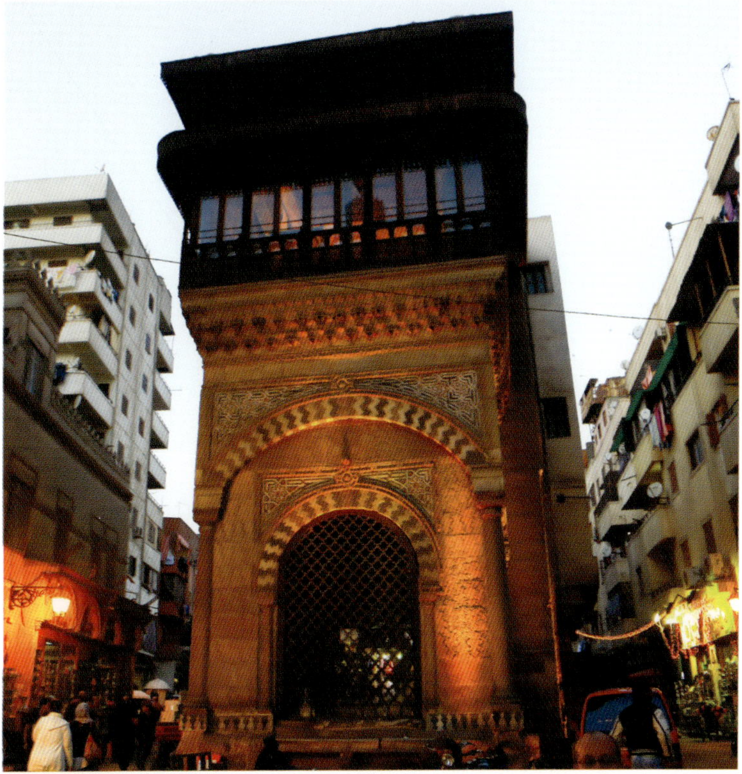

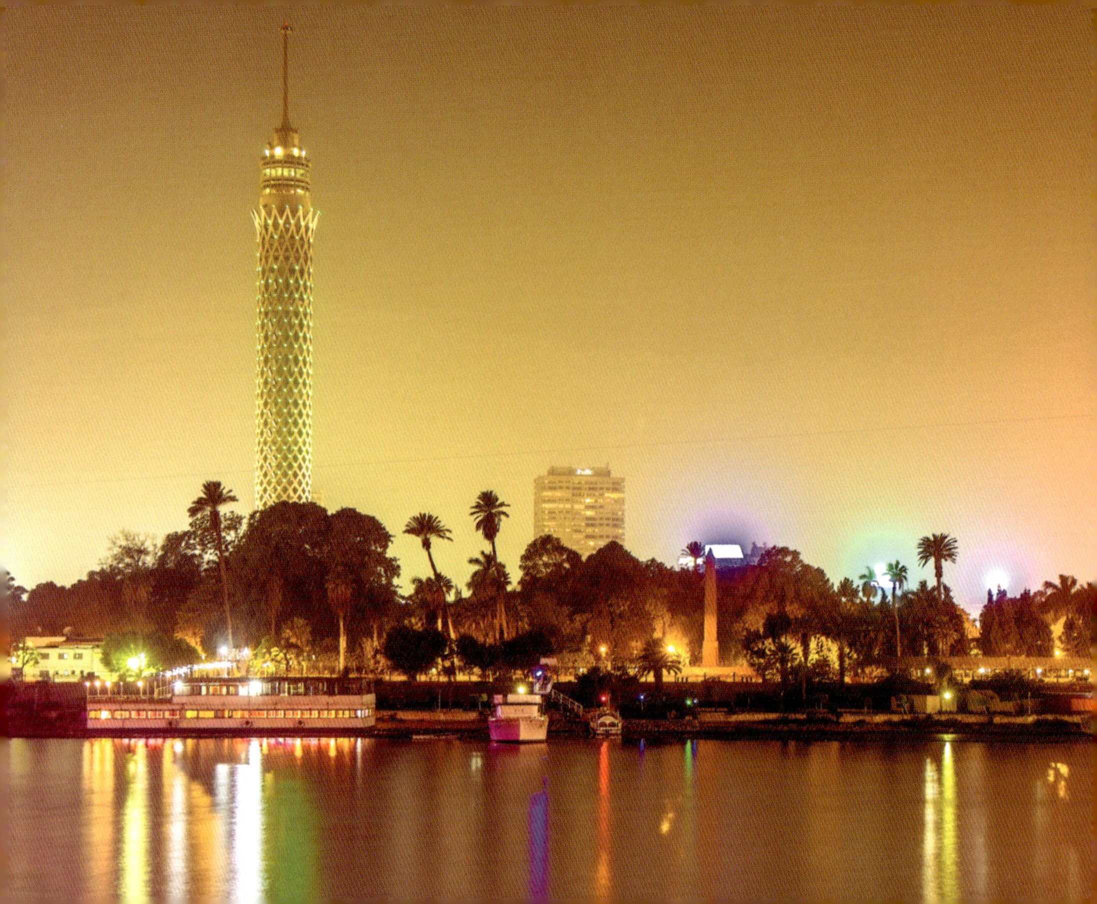

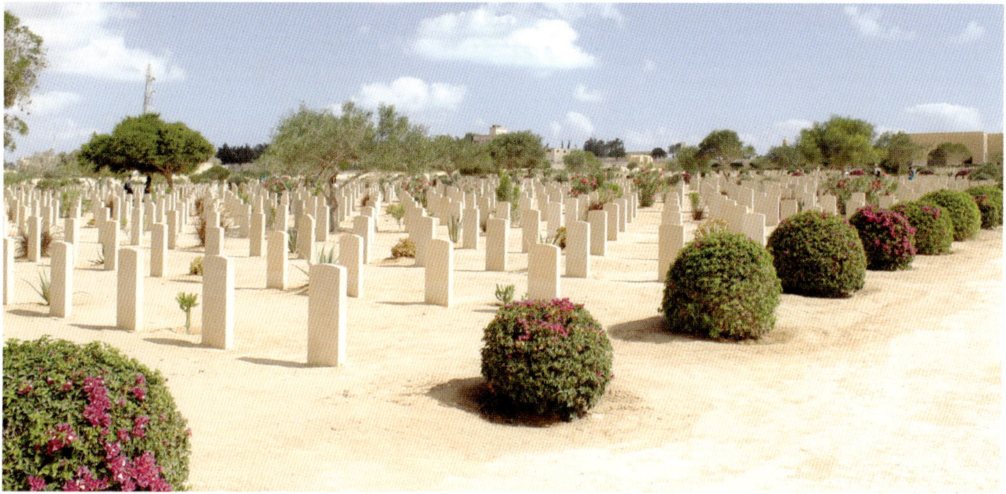

OPPOSITE:

Cairo Tower

Cairo Tower is the most visible landmark of the city, rising more than 180m (590ft) from the centre of Gezira Island. Built in 1961 on the orders of President Gamal Abdel Nasser, it was constructed using funds supplied by the USA in order to buy American arms. In the late afternoon, it provides a stunning all round view of Cairo, to the pyramids and beyond.

ABOVE:

Al-Alamein cemeteries

The decisive battles fought in this isolated spot turned the course of World War II in favour of the Allied forces. There are several cemeteries in the area today marking the many dead who fought for both sides. Above we see the Commonwealth graveyard which includes bodies of soldiers from many countries, a large number of whom were never identified.

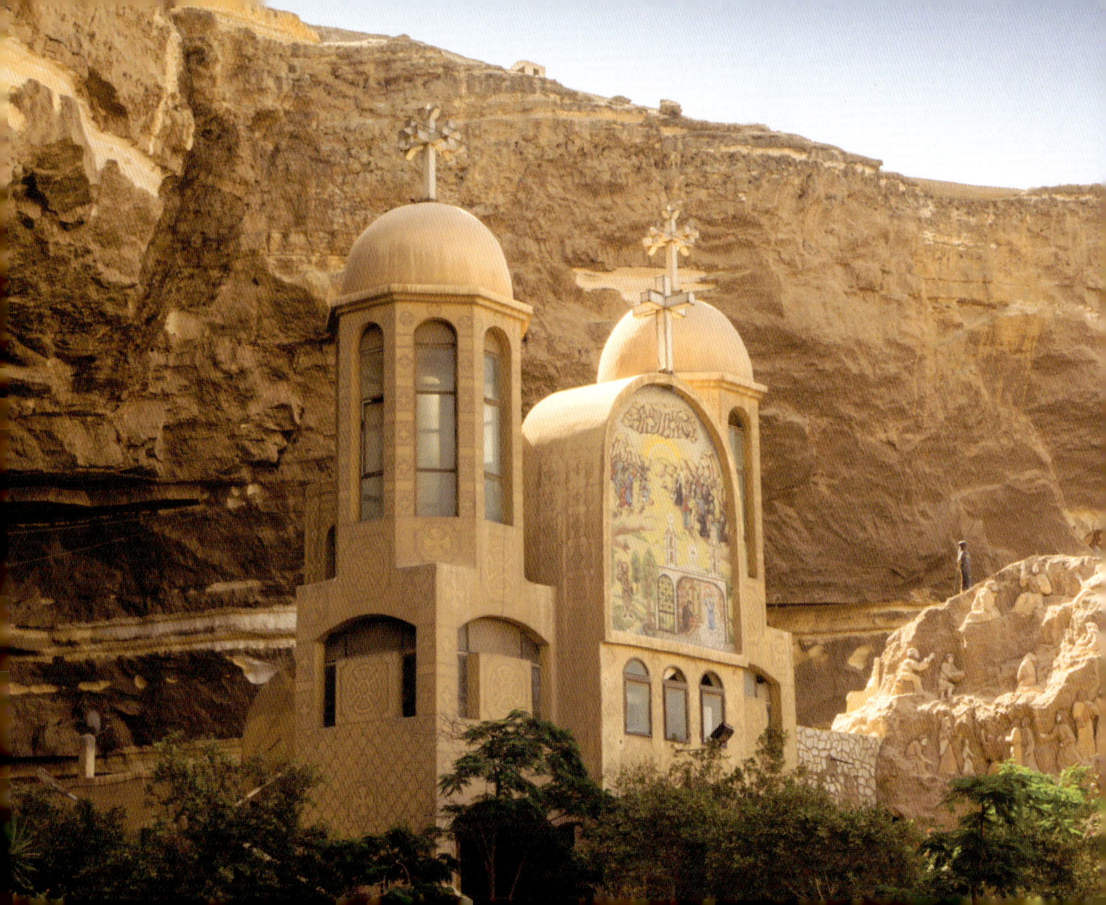

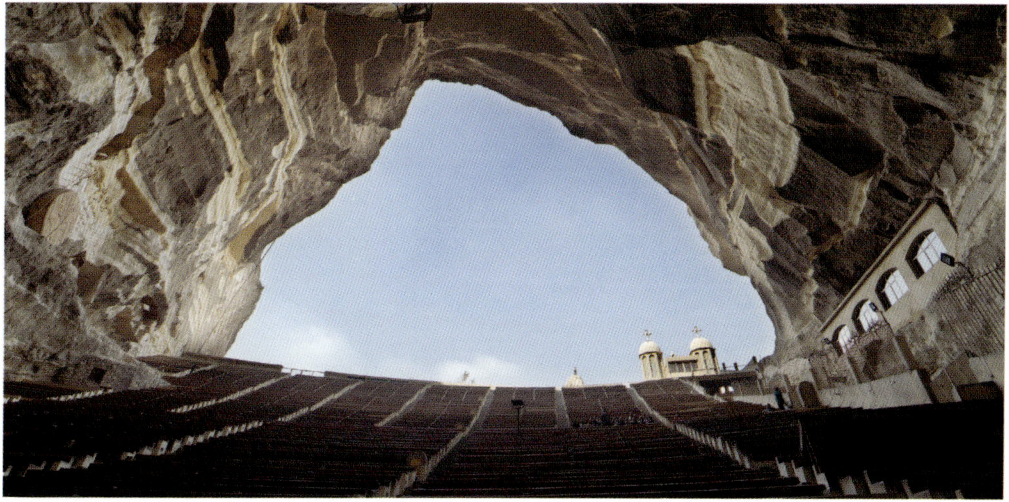

OPPOSITE:

Monastery of Saint Simon the Tanner, Cairo

Established in the 1970s after the original church of the zabbalin (rubbish collectors) was destroyed by fire, this monastery, dedicated to Saint Simon the Tanner, a craftsman of the 10th century, was built in the side of the Mokattam hills above Cairo. The monastery now lies at the heart of a much larger area of churches and community projects.

ABOVE:

Cave Church of Mokattam, Cairo

This vast cavern was dug from the Mukattam hills through the hard work and commitment of the zabbalin Christian community. It is now the single largest church in the Middle East, hosting congregations of up to 20,000 people. A visit to this area involves a complicated drive and steep climb, but it is more than worth the effort to see this fine example of pure devotion.

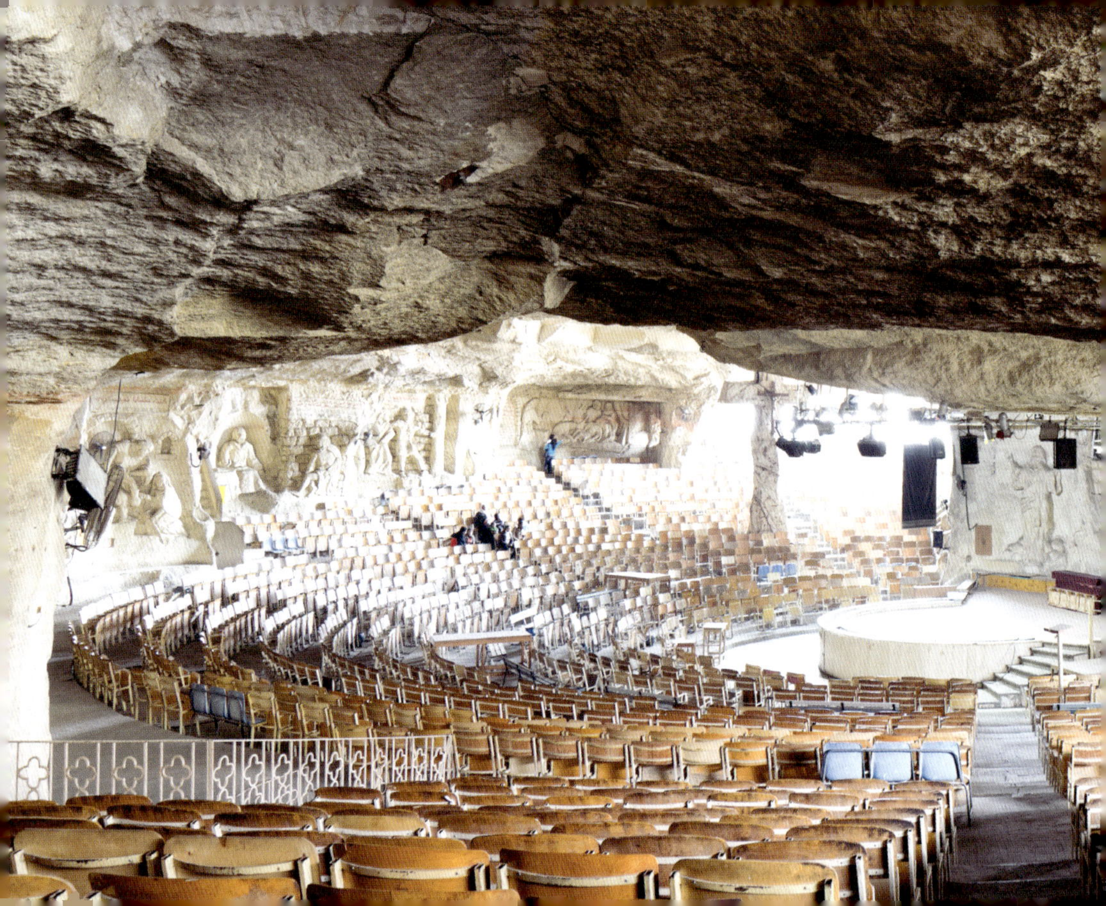

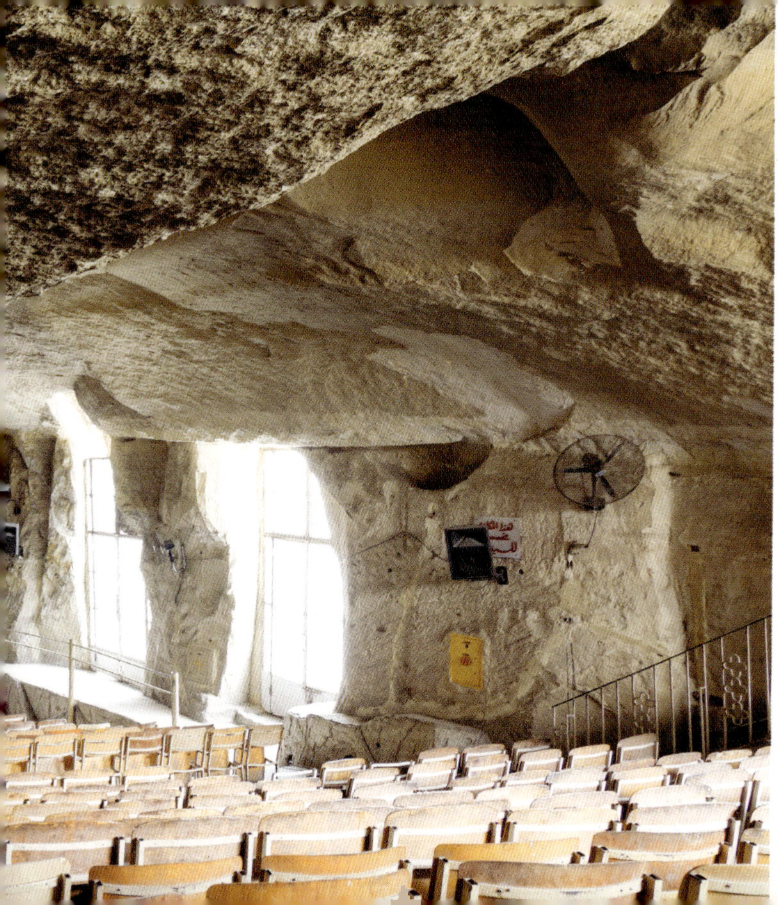

Cave Church of Mokattam, Cairo
The auditorium and the stage of this enormous church can be seen here and it is easy to imagine the atmosphere created by thousands of voices singing together in praise. Important ceremonies are frequently broadcast internationally.

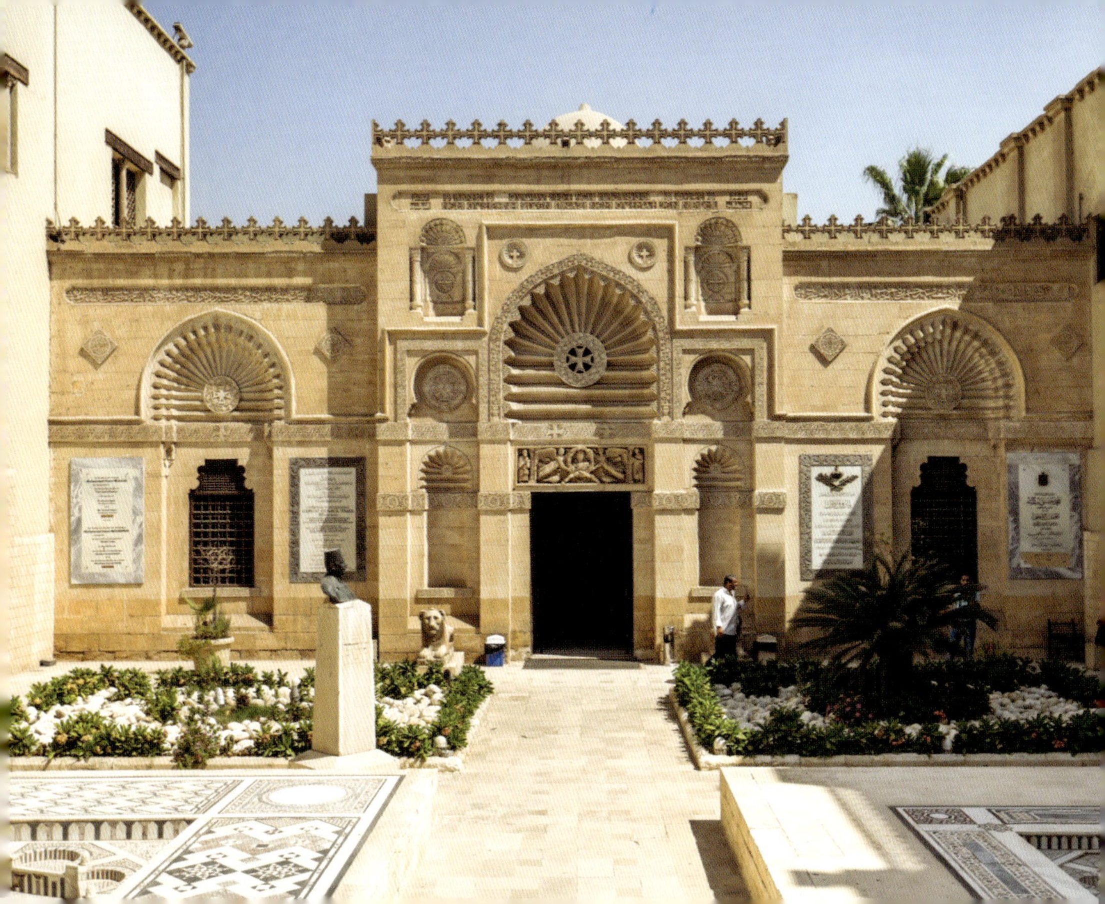

OPPOSITE:

The Coptic Museum, Cairo

The Coptic Museum houses both masterpieces and symbolic work from the dawn of Christianity in Egypt up to the beginnings of the Islamic period. The collection is curated in a way that takes the visitor on a journey through time, from the influence of late Pharaonic art onwards.

RIGHT:

The Coptic Museum, Cairo

The richly coloured ceiling is part of the original wing of the museum founded in 1908. The museum today is much larger, with more than 15,000 pieces in their collection. There are artifacts and art from all media from wood to precious objects and early manuscripts.

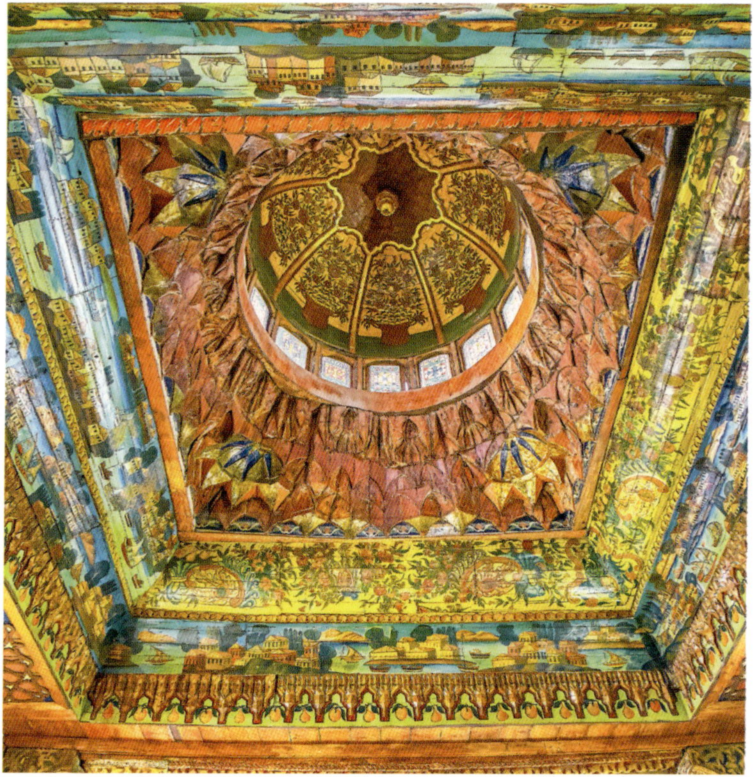

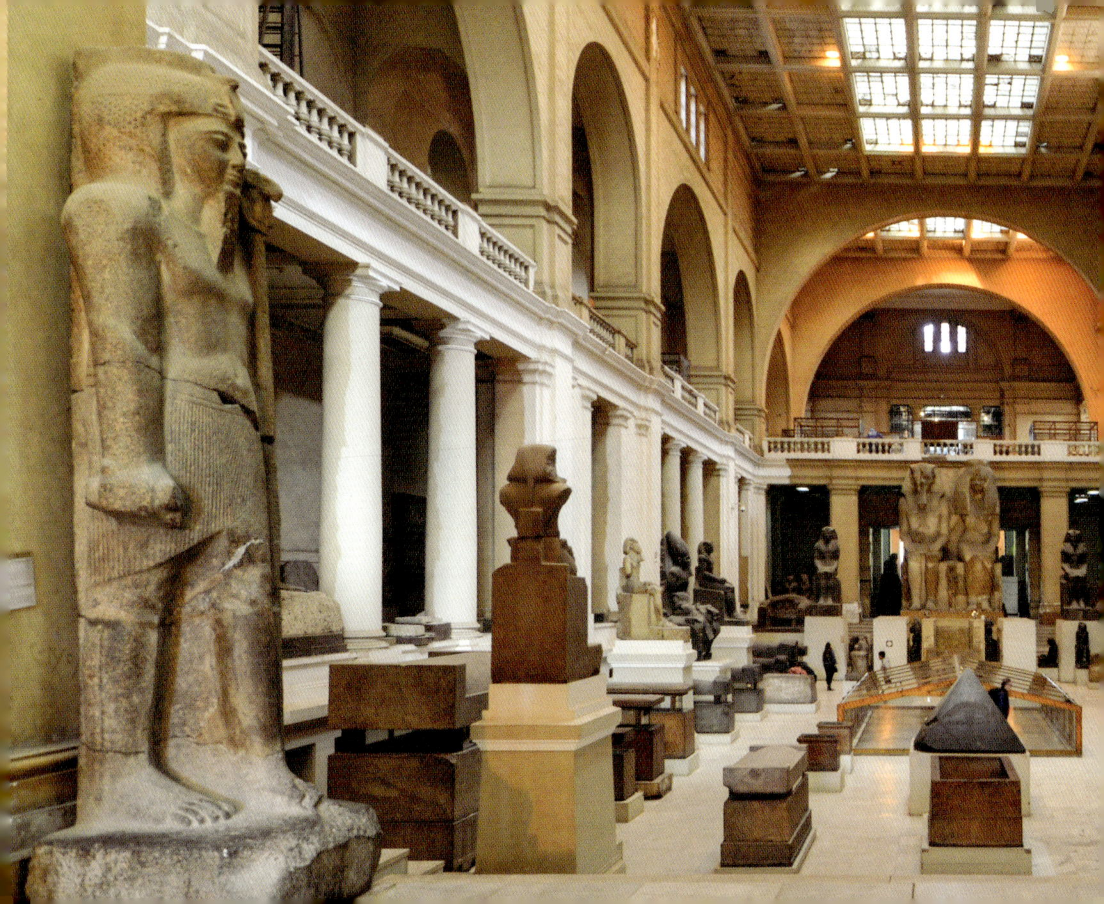

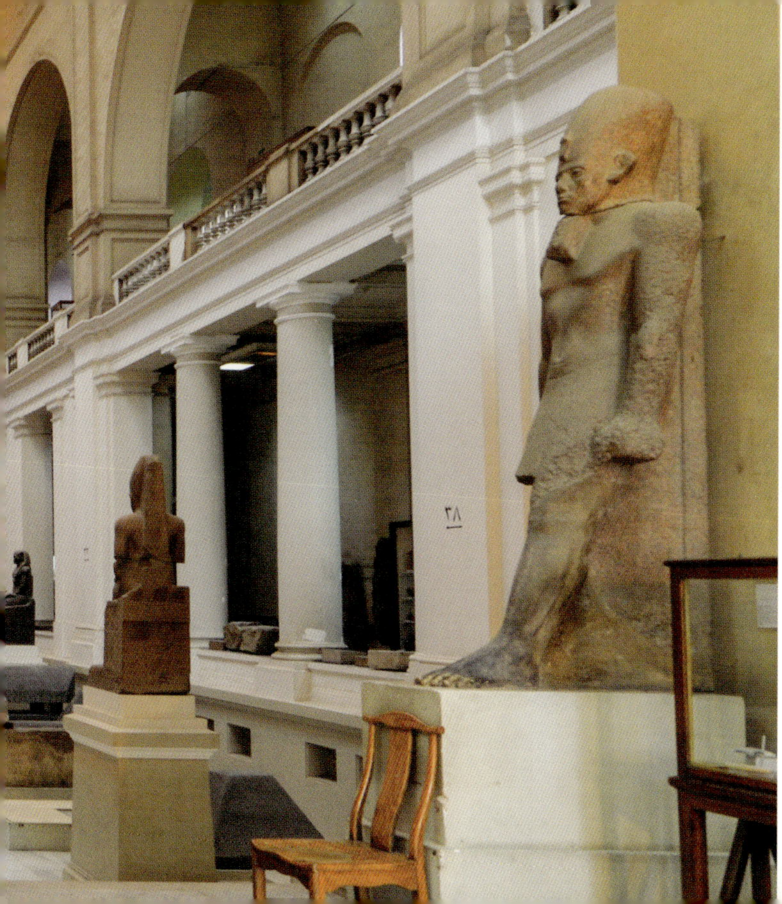

Egyptian Museum, Cairo
The Egyptian Museum, situated in Tahrir Square, is a giant store house of Egypt's ancient heritage, spread over two floors and many different rooms. Here we see the central atrium which houses a mixture of both giant and miniature objects, principally from the periods leading up to and including the Old Kingdom (up to 2150 BC).

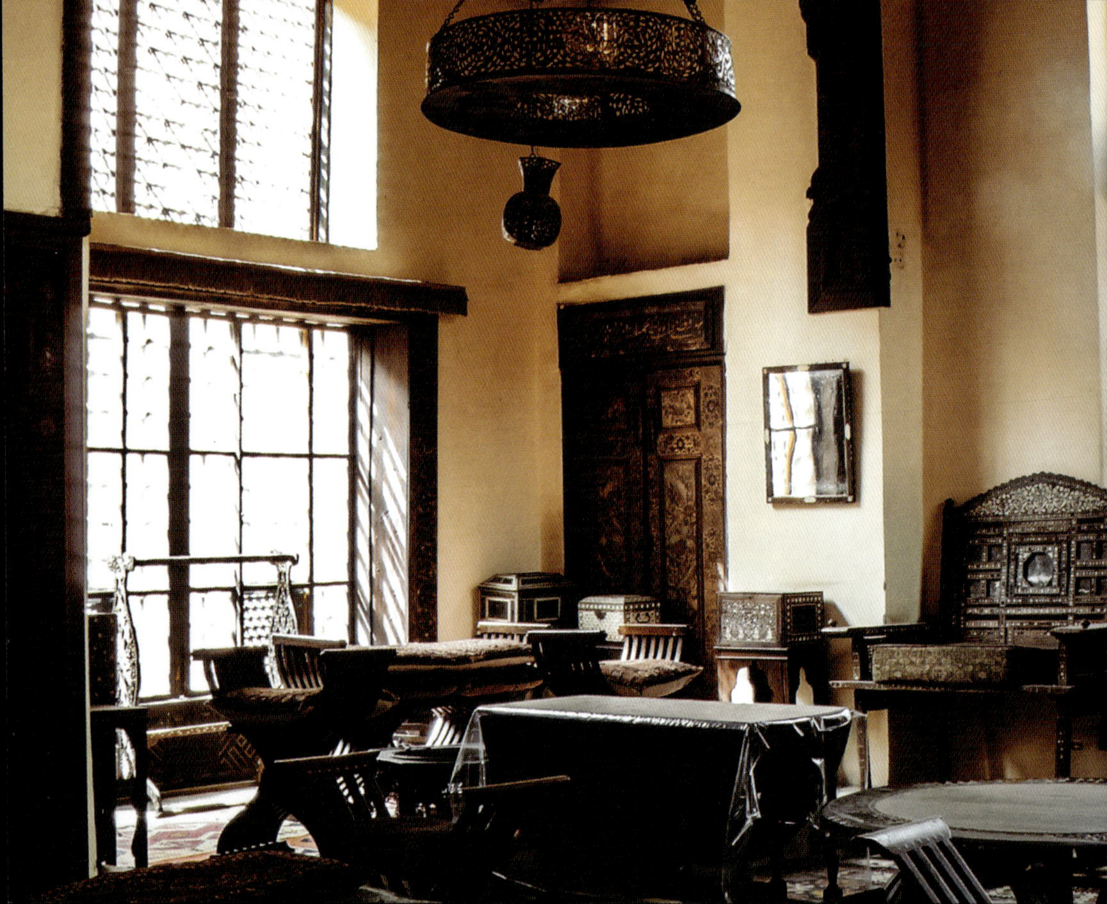

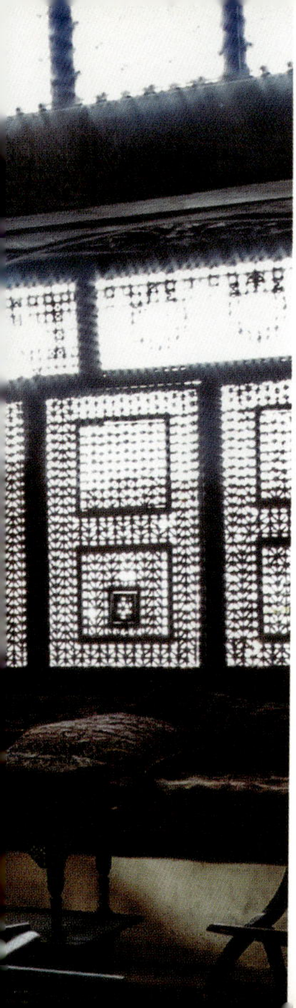

LEFT:

Gayer-Anderson Museum, Cairo

Tucked away by the entrance of the Mosque of Ibn Tulun is this delightful small museum, comprising two 16th-century houses. The rooms are full of objects collected by Major R.G. Gayer-Anderson Pasha in his travels around the Middle East whilst working for the British army. Gayer-Anderson restored the houses in the 1930s and left his collection to Egypt on his death in 1945.

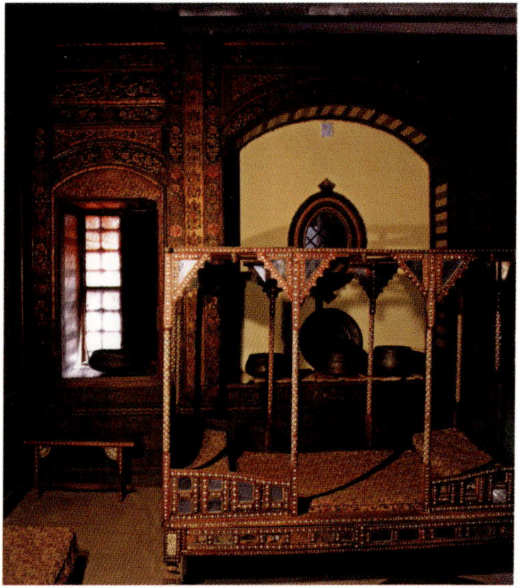

ABOVE:

Gayer-Anderson Museum, Cairo

The atmosphere of British orientalism pervades this museum. In preserving such times, Gayer-Anderson managed to pinpoint the West's fascination with the East. This acute sense of history was perhaps behind the museum's use as a location in the James Bond film, *The Spy Who Loved Me*.

Mosque of Ibn Tulun, Cairo

Arguably the most impressive Islamic monument in Cairo, the Mosque of Ibn Tulun was built in 879 AD and is architecture on its grandest scale. On entering the mosque, its sheer size and architectural simplicity dwarf the visitor. It was built on the orders of the Abbasid Caliph Ibn Tulun, who had come from Baghdad to govern Cairo. His home influences are clear in this mosque's design. The huge courtyard was built to contain the whole population of the area and the governor's soldiers for Friday prayers.

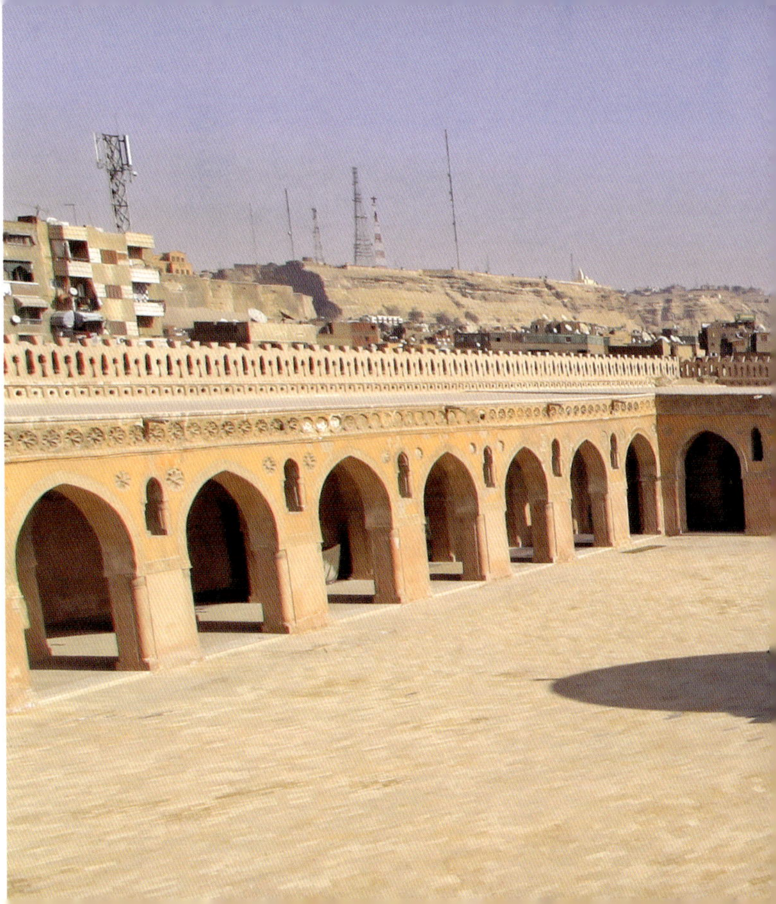

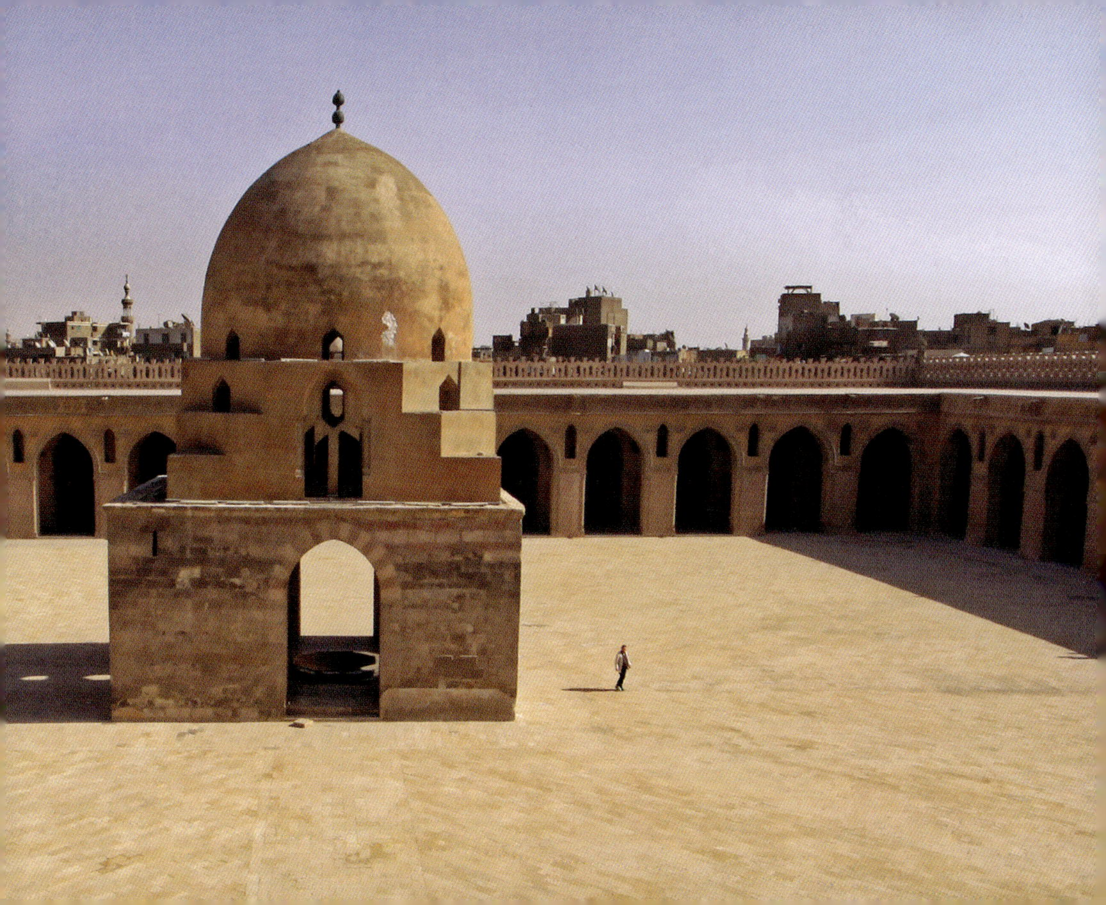

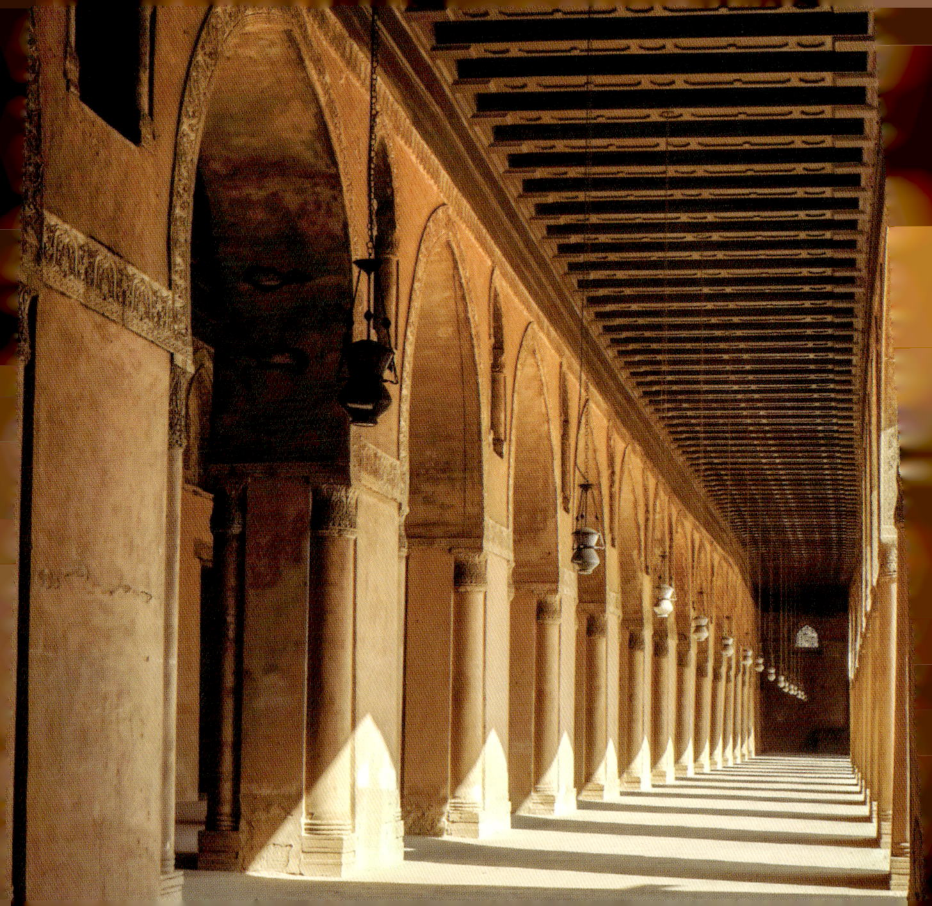

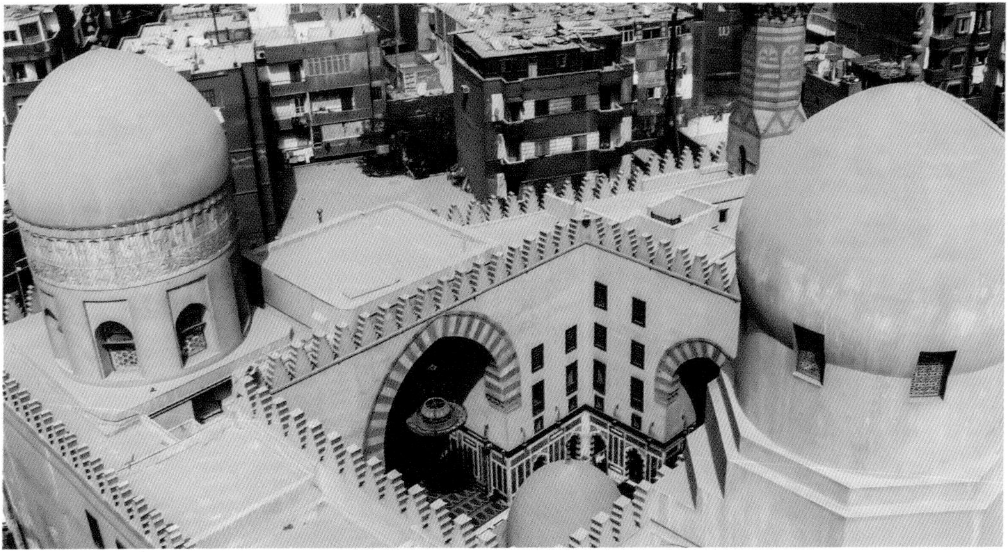

OPPOSITE:

Mosque of Ibn Tulun, Cairo

Although only one section of the mosque is regularly used today for prayer, it is still one of the most impressive of Cairo's devotional spaces.

ABOVE:

Madrasa of Sarghatmish, Cairo

The view from the minaret of the mid-14th-century Mosque of Ibn Tulun. This school, mosque and mausoleum were built on the orders of Sarghatmish, a Mamluk soldier who became the most powerful man in Egypt during the reign of Sultan Hassan in the 14th century. Ultimately he was jailed and murdered.

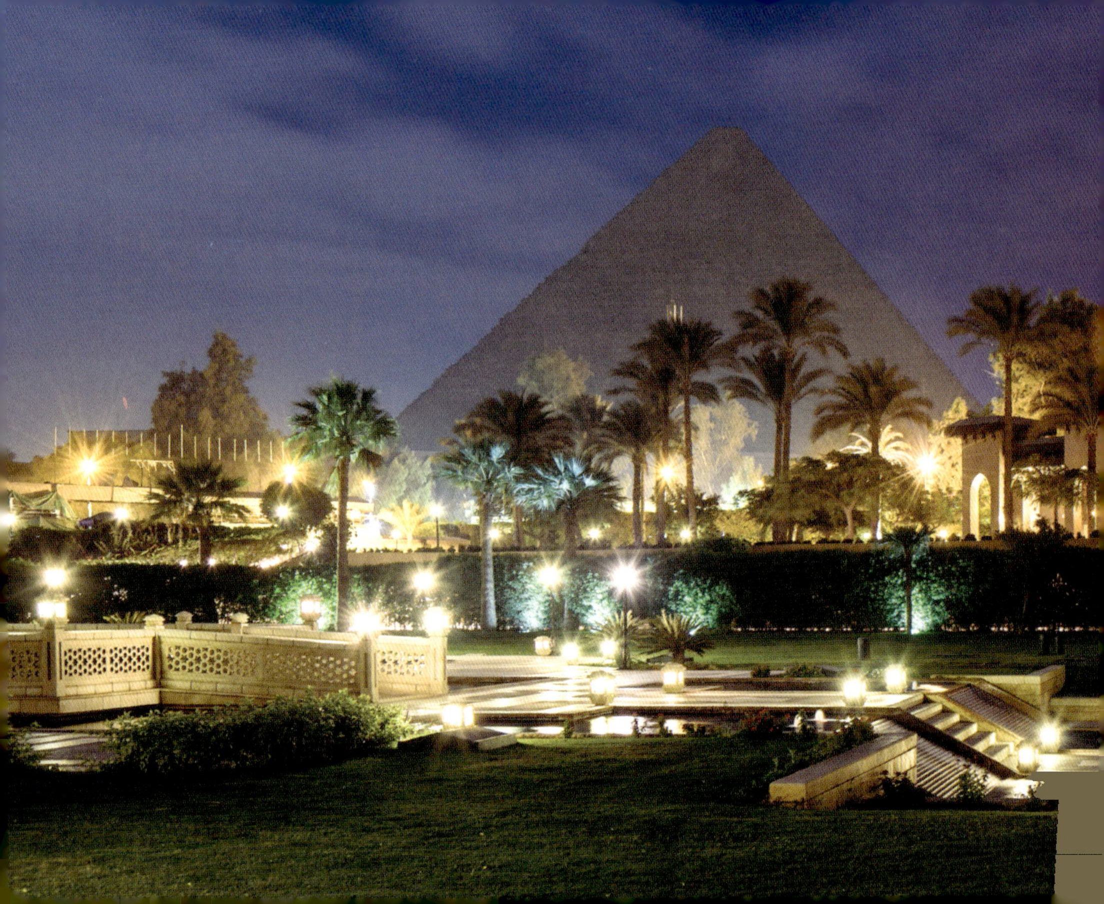

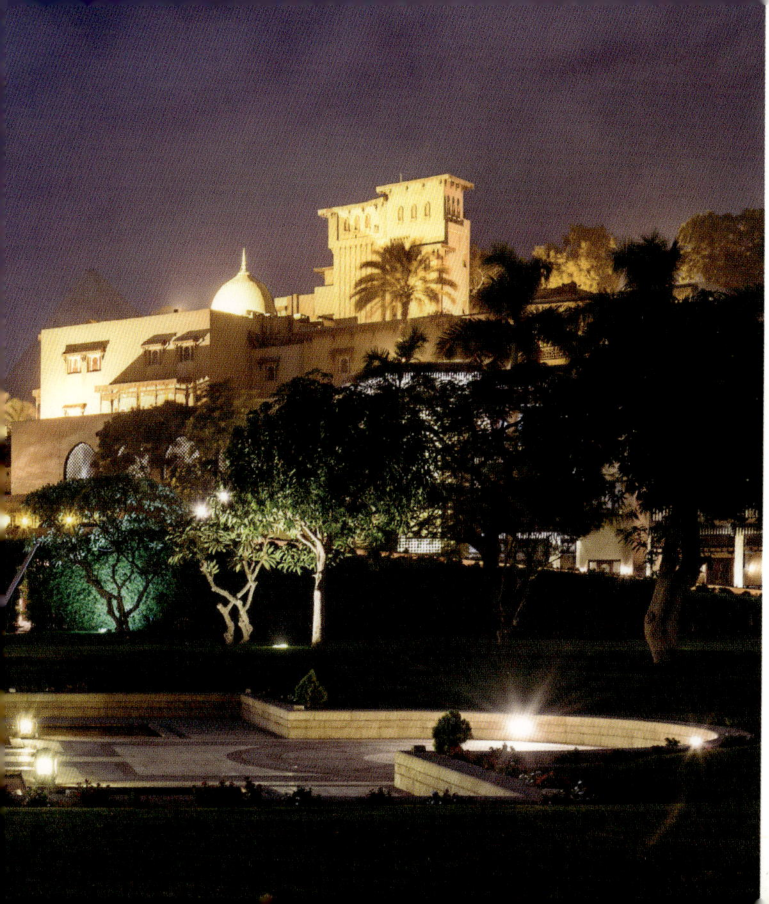

The Mena House Hotel, Cairo

This most perfectly placed hotel was a hunting lodge until 1869. The original building forms the old wing of what is now a larger resort complex. The stylishly decorated antique rooms include a bar surrounded with gold and dark wood. There is also a sumptuous restaurant in which royalty, the rich and the famous have dined overlooking the pyramids, from the golden age of travel until today.

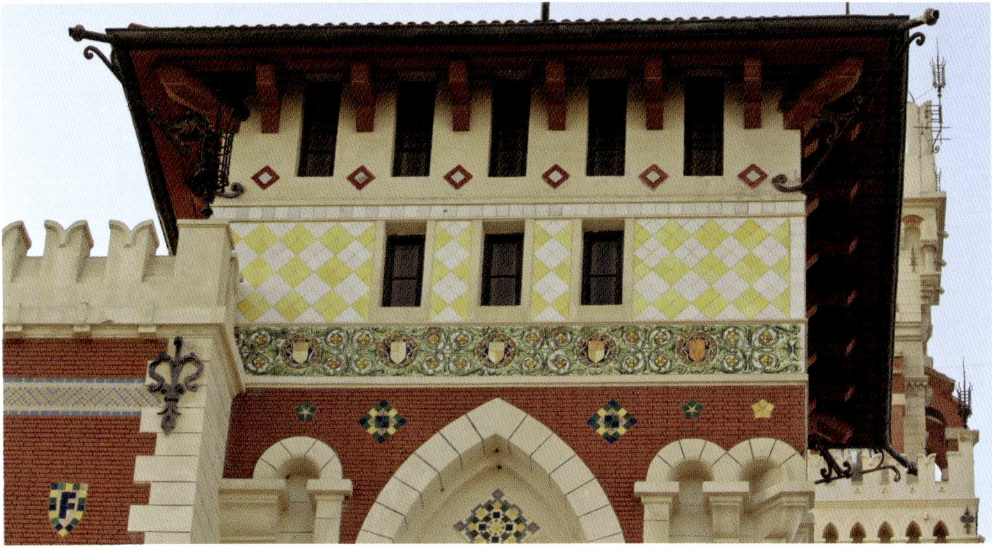

ABOVE:

Montaza Palace, Alexandria

The Montaza Palace, situated to the far east of Alexandria, was built in the 19th century. It was designed as the summer home of the Khedive Abbas Helmy II. Its mixture of North African and Italianate styles creates a fun summer sensibility.

OPPOSITE:

Montaza Palace, Alexandria

The palace itself is closed to the public but its gardens provide a popular escape for Alexandrians. With an attractive mixture of European, tropical and sub-tropical plants, trees and flowers, the gardens create an ideal getaway for picnics and family time.

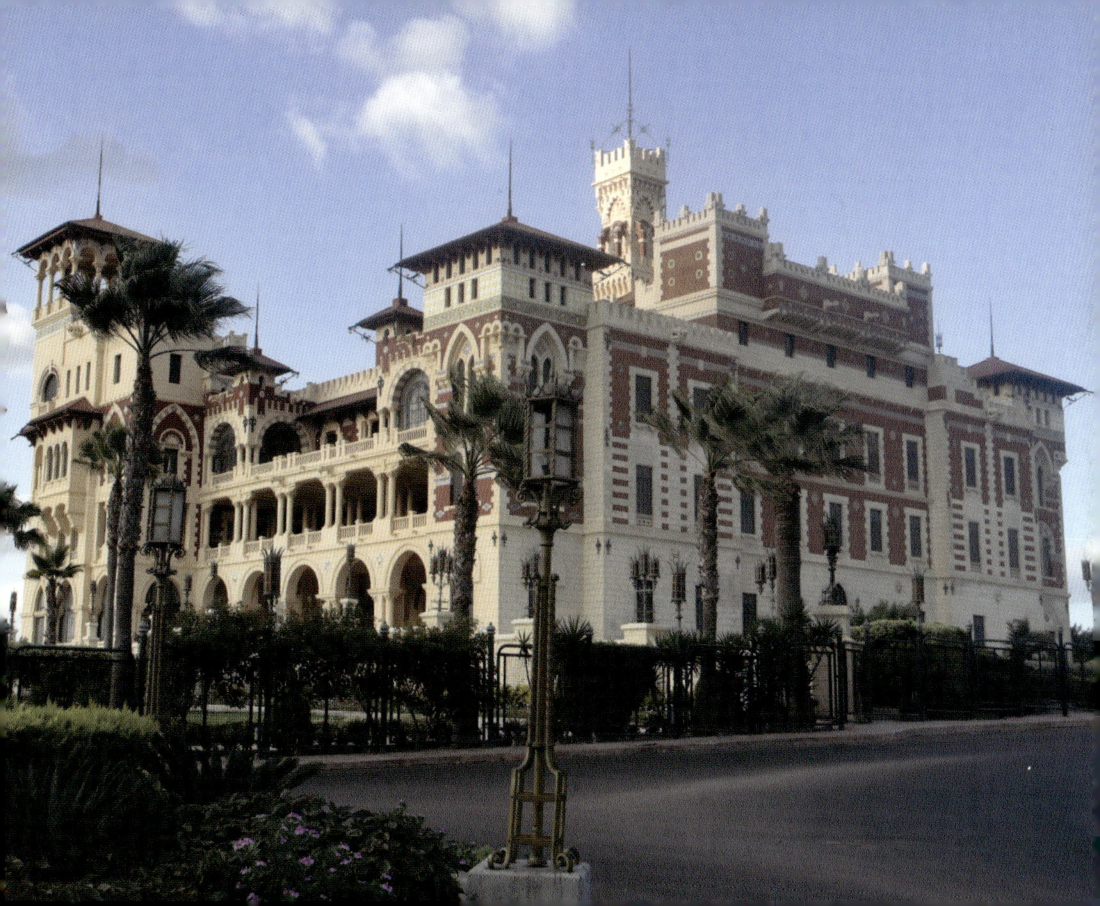

Fort Qaitbay, Alexandria

Looking out across the eastern harbour of Alexandria, a fort of the Mamluk Sultan Qaitbay dominates the horizon. It was built on a site of the lost Pharos of Alexandria, the legendary lighthouse which was one of the Seven Wonders of the Ancient World. This imposing fortress, designed to protect Alexandria's harbour, was built in the late 15th century. It is believed that some of the walls include material from the Pharos itself.

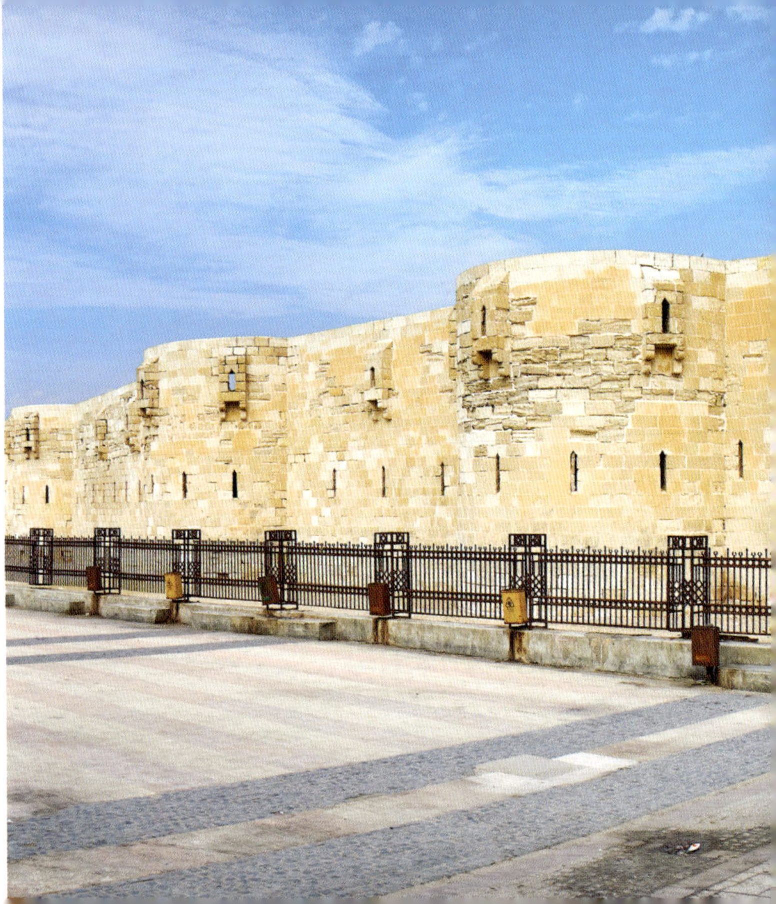

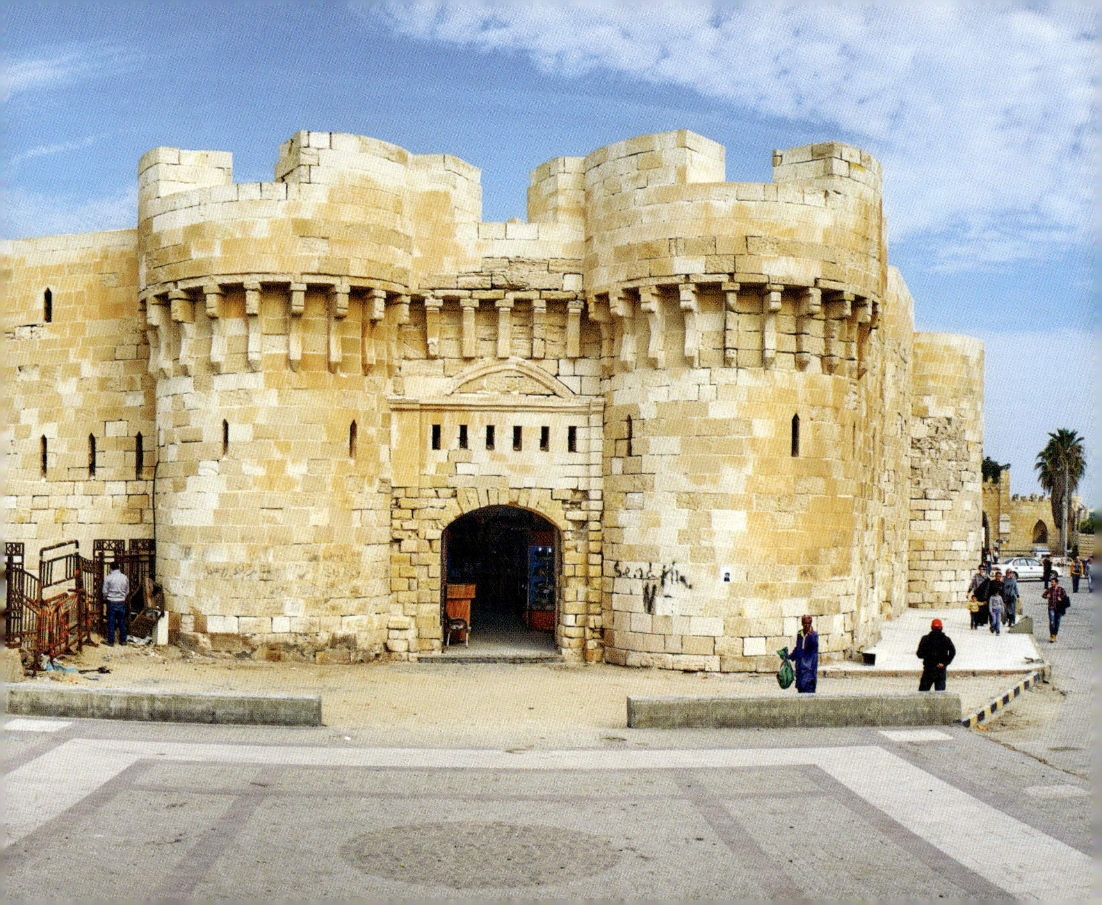

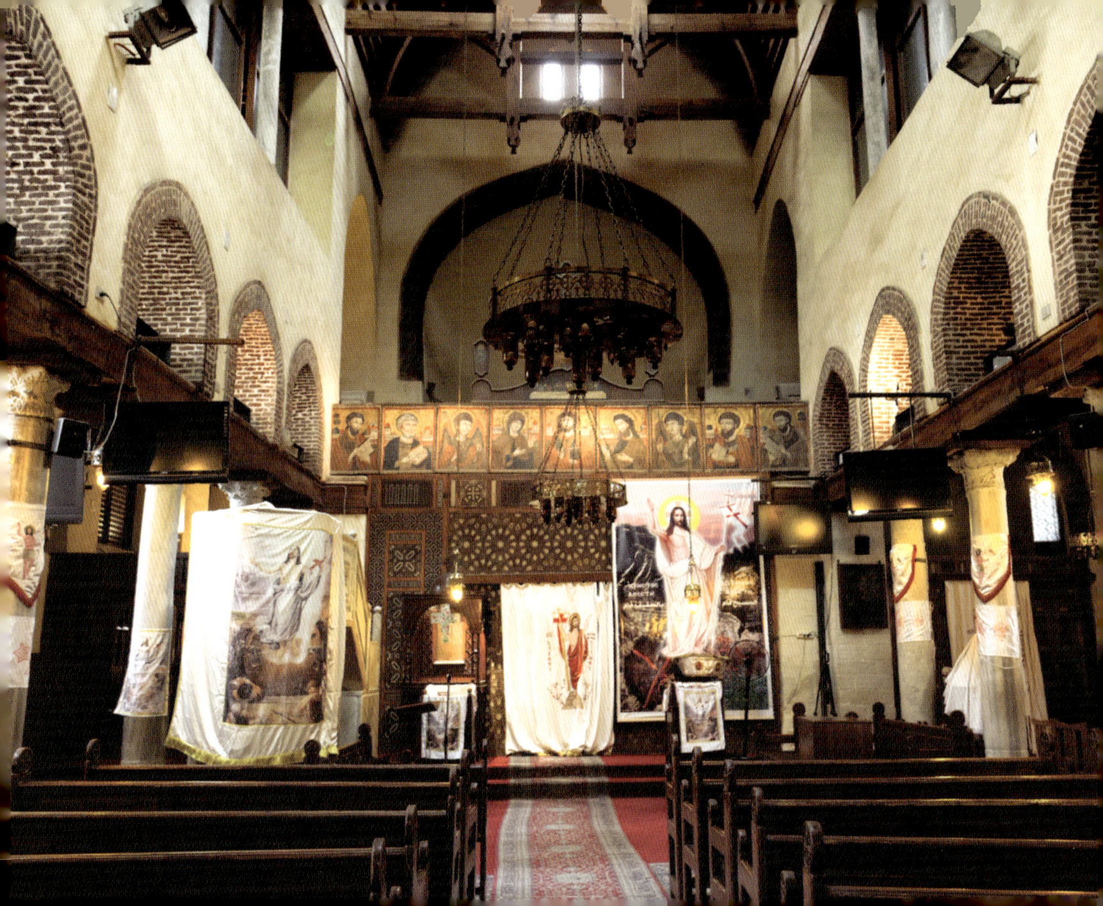

LEFT:

Church of Saint Barbara, Cairo

The Coptic Orthodox Church of Saint Barbara is at the heart of Old Cairo and its original building dates to the 5th or 6th century. Saint Barbara was a Christian martyr killed by the Romans. Her relics lie within. The church is the home of several rare and beautiful icons and remains a busy place of worship.

RIGHT:

Coptic Cairo, Crypt

Many of the churches and historical sites in Coptic Cairo have associations with the Holy Family, whose flight to Egypt brought them to this area. Crypts devoted to this time are found in churches and mark spaces where the Holy Family are believed to have found refuge.

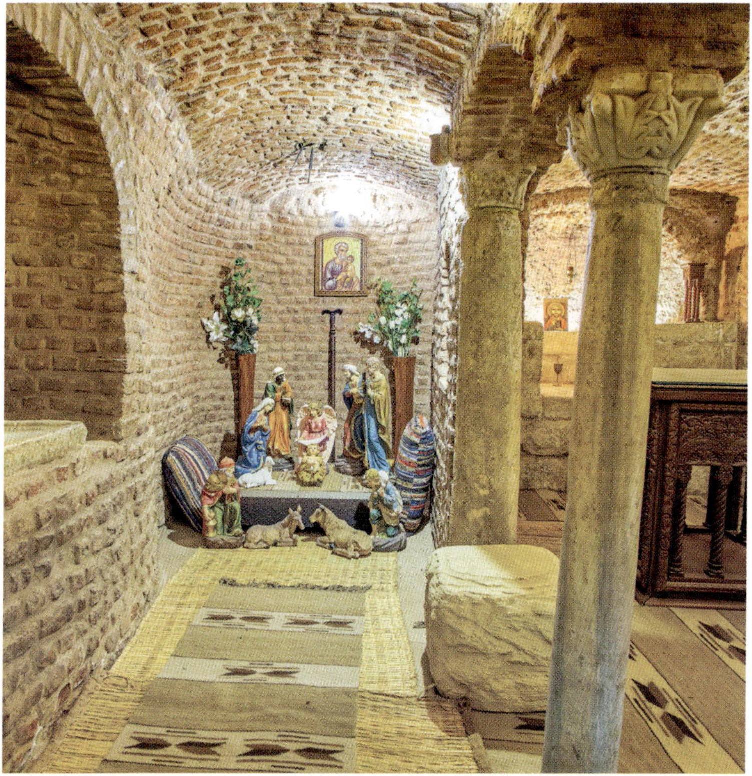

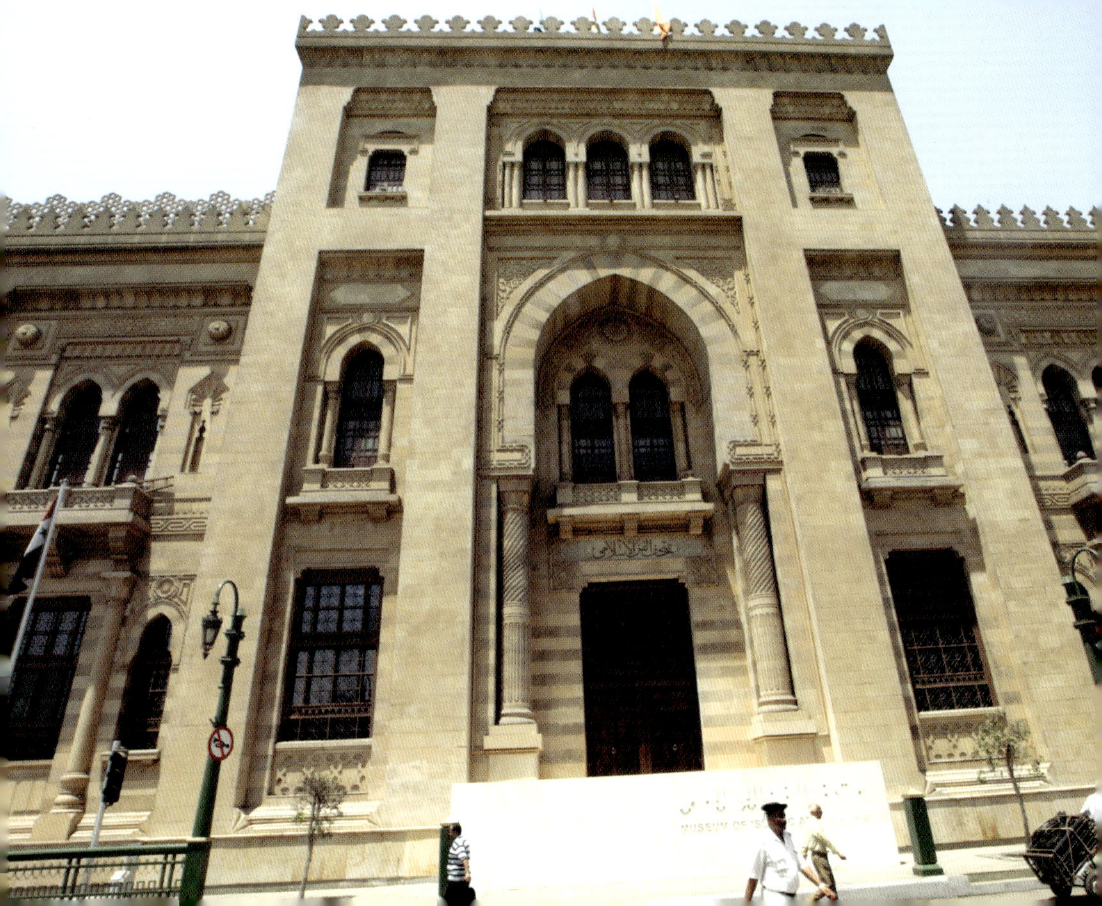

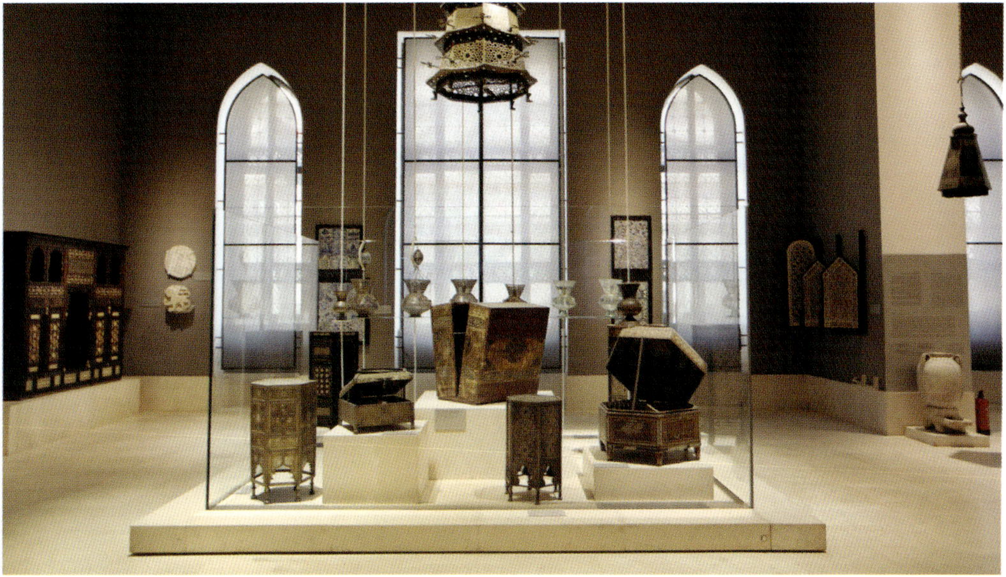

OPPOSITE:

Museum of Islamic Art, Cairo

This recently renovated museum displays Islamic art from the whole Middle East. In the same building is the Egyptian Library, with its archive of more than 750,000 volumes dating back to the Quranic manuscripts of the 8th century AD.

ABOVE:

Museum of Islamic Art, Cairo

In more than 20 rooms, the museum displays and explains the chronology of art – including pottery, carpets or wood work – taking the visitor through the key periods of Islamic history.

The Saladin Citadel of Cairo

The Citadel built by Saladin in the 12th century still dominates the Cairo skyline. Within its walls, there are three mosques and three museums to enjoy, as well as gardens. The Citadel's chief attraction is the stunning view it provides of the city. There is a sweeping panorama of Islamic Cairo which sits below the Citadel and leads the eye to the modern city beyond. On the distant horizon sit the Pyramids.

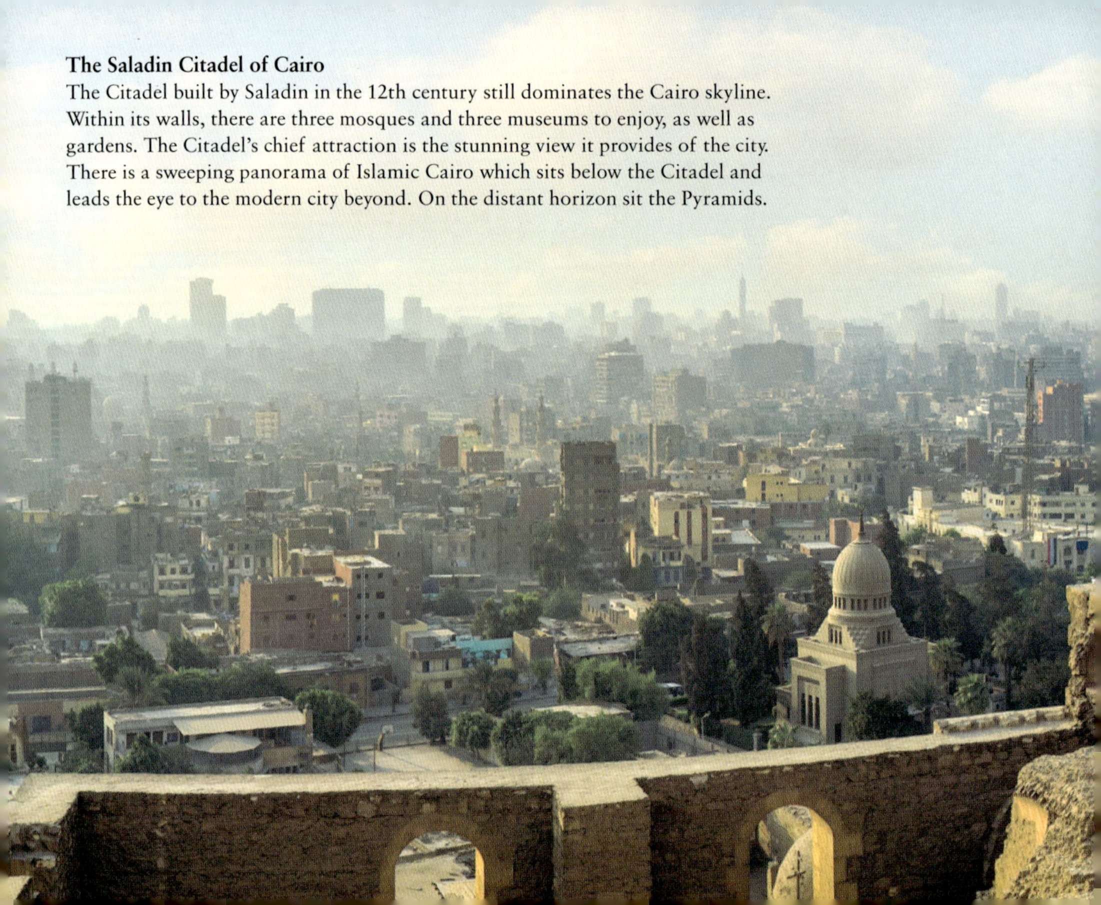

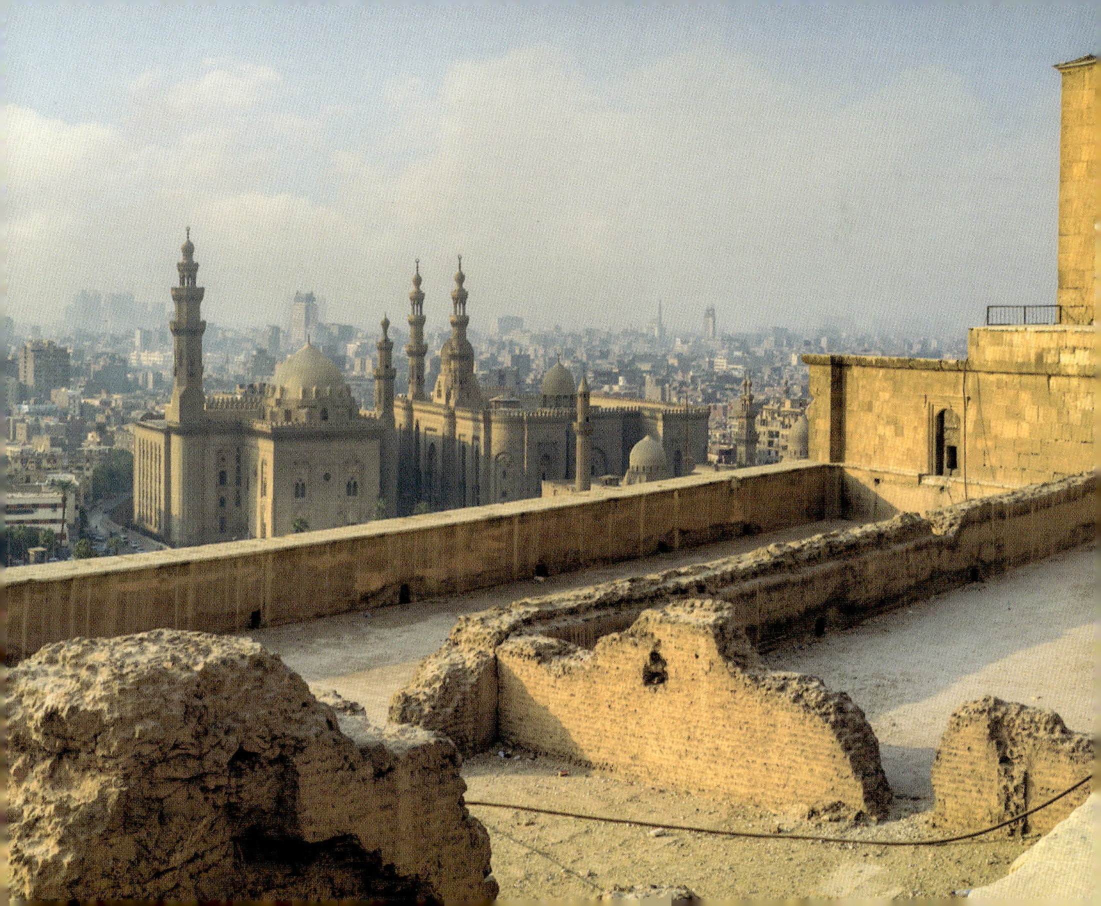

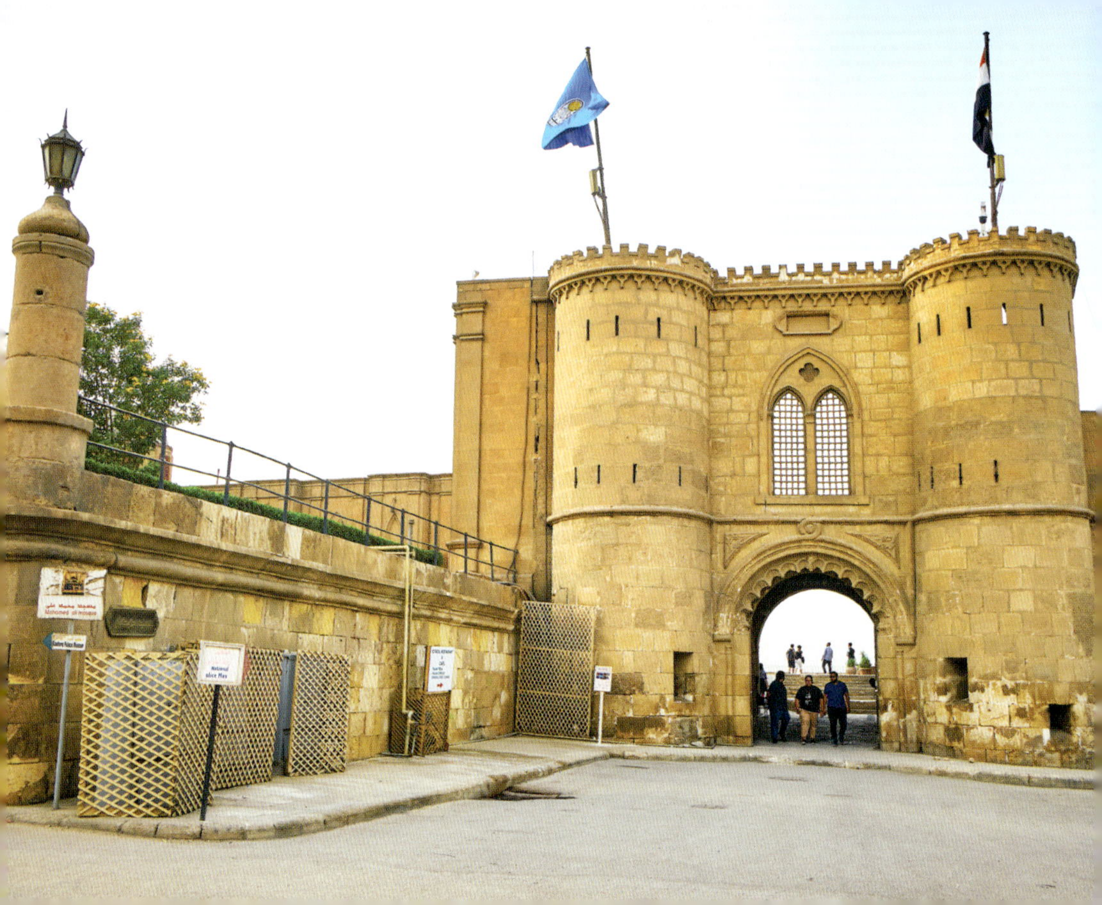
National
olice Mus

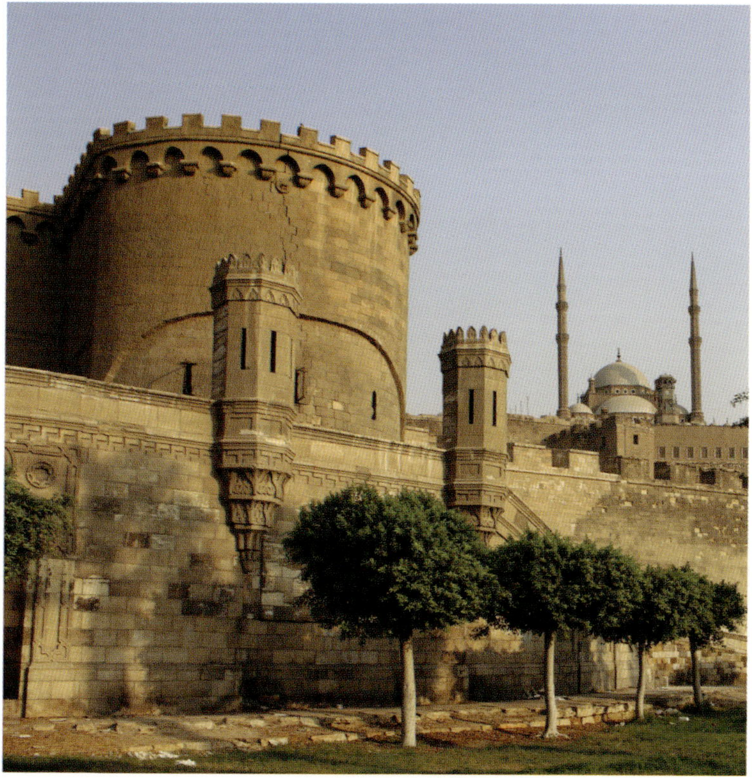

LEFT:

The Saladin Citadel of Cairo

The main gateway and two guard towers may lack beauty, but were a statement of strength for the seven centuries during which the Citadel provided safe haven for Egypt's rulers. In later times, this fortress provided security to the Ottomans and even during the visit of Napoleon. In World War II, the Citadel served as a barracks for the British Army.

OPPOSITE:

The Saladin Citadel of Cairo

The distant Mosque of Mohamed Ali – on the right of the photograph – lies at the heart of the Saladin Citadel.

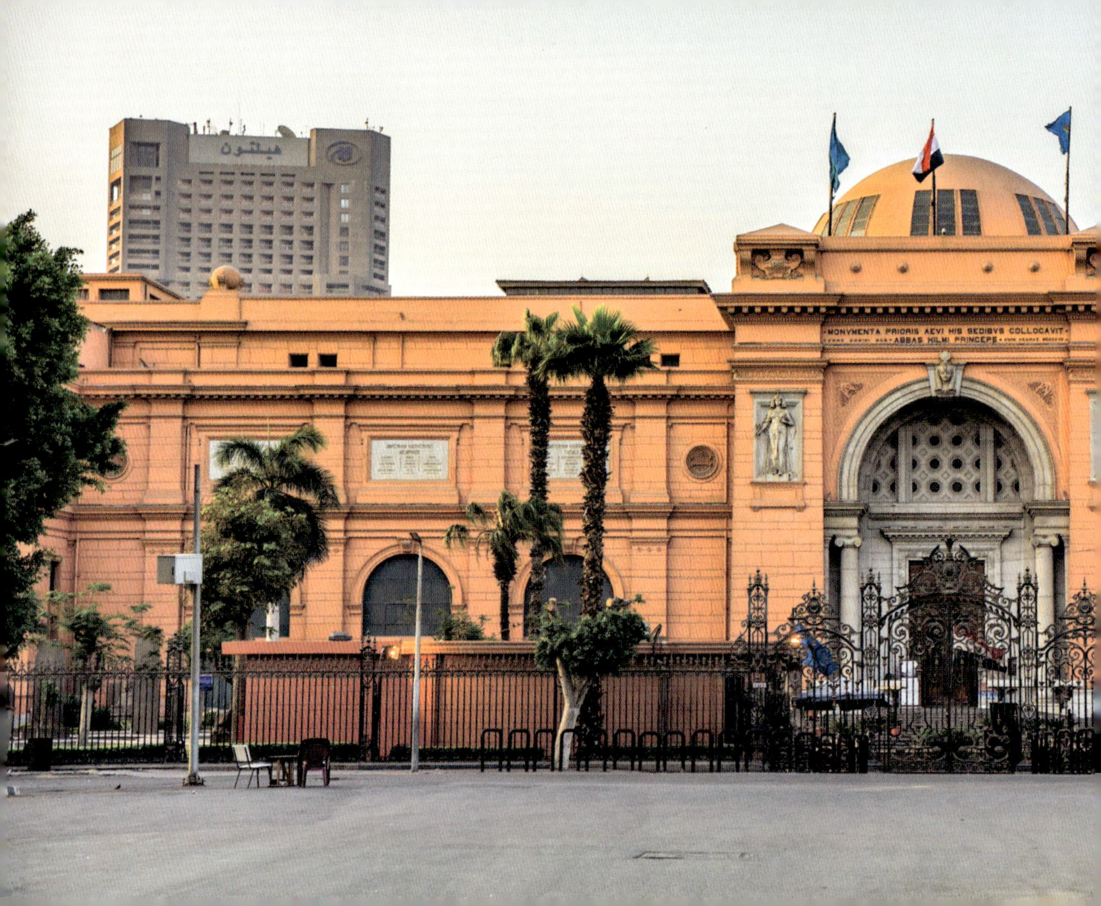
هيلتون
MONVMENTA PRIORIS AEVI HIS SEDIBVS COLLOCAVIT
ABBAS HILMI PRINCEPS

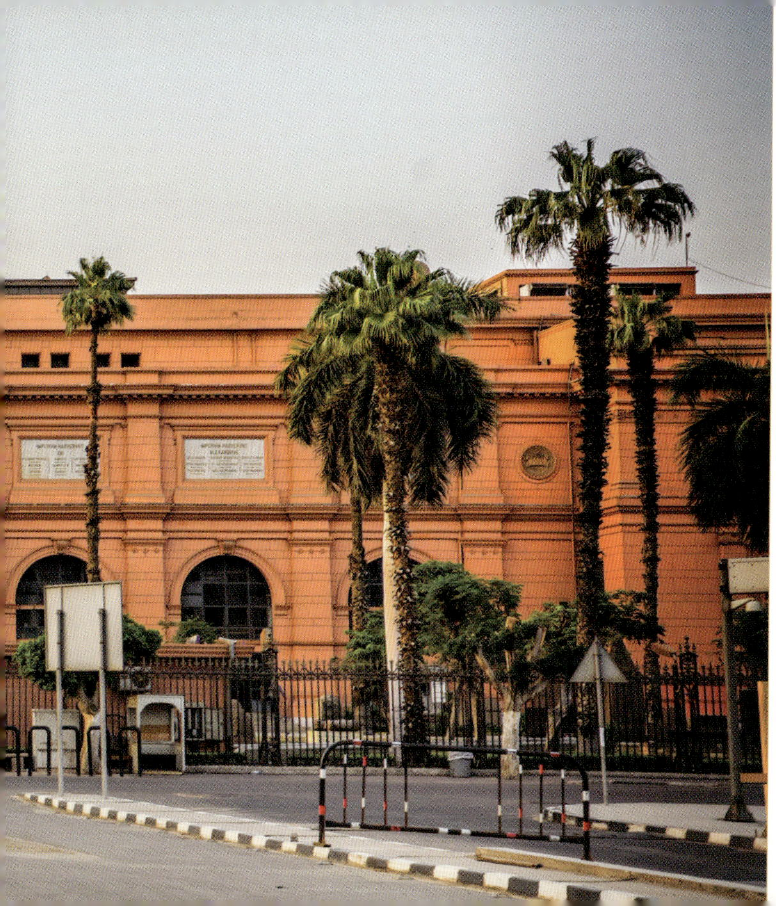

The Egyptian Museum, Cairo

Built in 1901, the Museum of Egyptian Antiquities houses the world's largest collection of pharaonic antiquities. It sits proudly in Tahrir Square in the heart of Cairo. As you enter the Museum's garden from the main gate, you find yourself in a space filled with trees and statues, including a series of busts portraying many of the great early archaeologists who rediscovered Ancient Egypt in the 19th century. Most importantly you see August Mariette, the founder of the Egyptian Antiquities Service and Jean-François Champollion, famed for deciphering hieroglyphics.

RIGHT:

The Hanging Church, Cairo

This famous church is so-called due to its position. It sits suspended above one of the gates of the Babylon Fortress in Old Cairo. Visitors climb a stairway to the entrance, seen here. The modern façade and bell towers are from the 19th century but hidden within is a church packed with Coptic history.

OPPOSITE:

The Hanging Church

The small interior of the Hanging Church features a wide range of geometric patterns and intricate decoration, collected over more than 1000 years. The pulpit seen here forms a centrepiece. However, the true riches of the church are in its icons and painted scenes of the lives of saints.

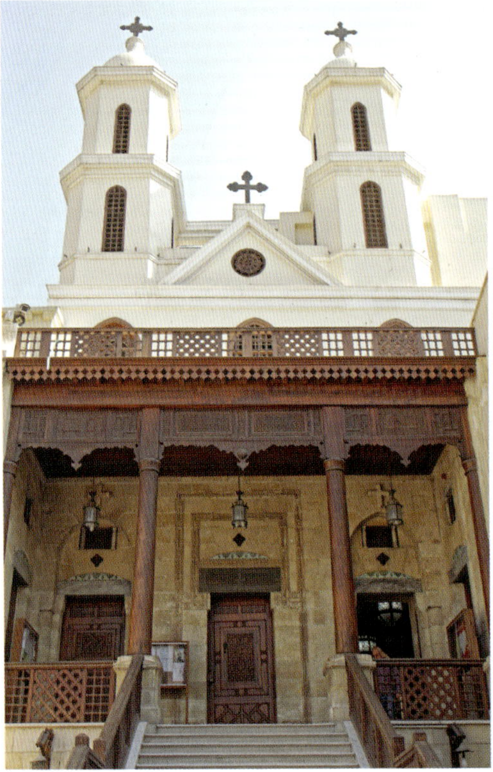

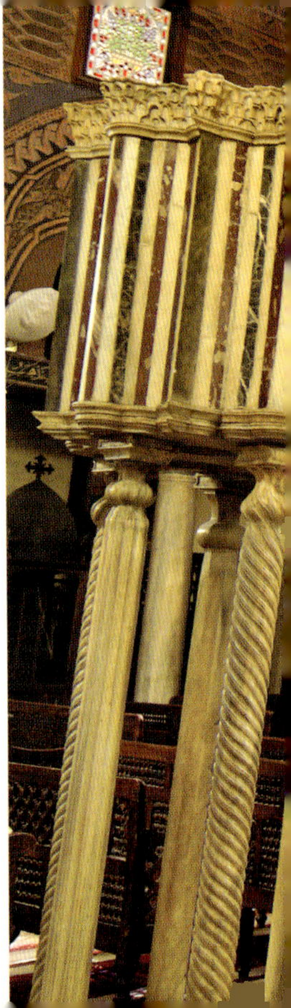

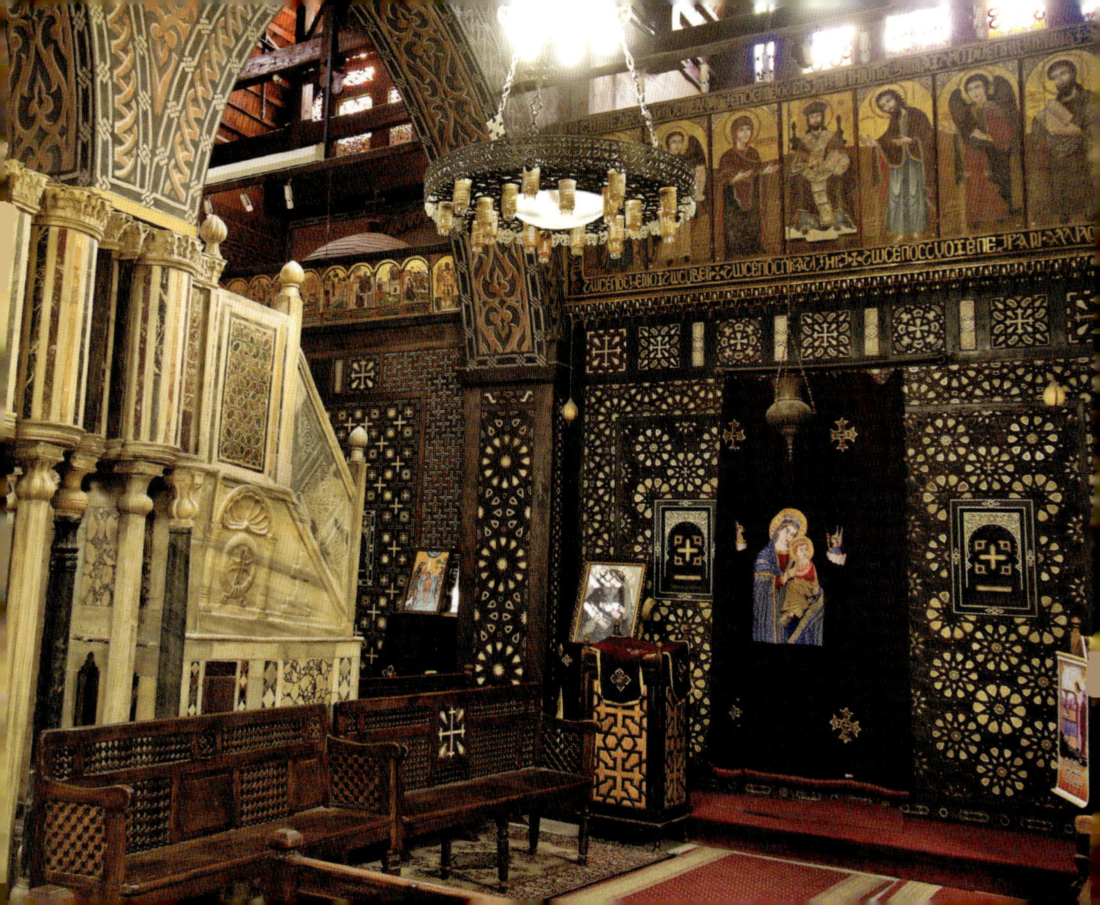

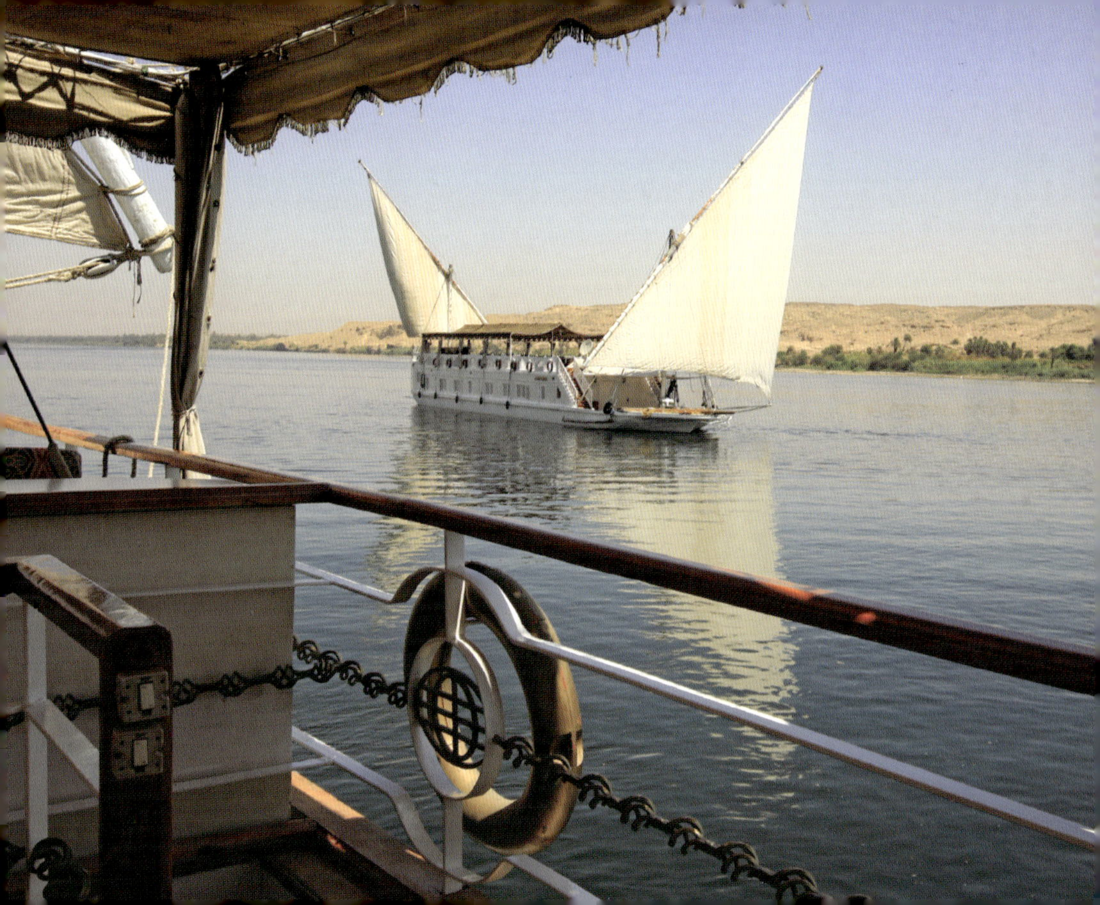

Waterways

Despite being 90 per cent desert, with the Western Desert (or Libyan Desert) and the Eastern Desert (also known as the Arabian Desert) comprising most of the country, Egypt is still very much a country which is built around water. Whether on the Mediterranean in the north or the Red Sea in the east, the sea shore has brought prosperity. In the past, the Mediterranean was crucial in linking Egypt with the Levant and the rest of the ancient world. Even more vital, however, is the Nile, dividing these vast desert spaces and providing everything necessary to build a prosperous civilization. When you travel through Egypt today, from Aswan to Alexandria, the ongoing dependence of Egypt on the Nile is clear. It plays a vital role in tourism as it provides the perfect way to see monuments, whilst learning how Ancient Egypt prospered and grew, based on the annual flooding and fertility brought by the mighty river.

As much as it plays a role in the economic life of the country it also plays a vital social role. Taking a boat ride is all part of a family gathering, be it a felucca, ferry boat or water taxi.

OPPOSITE:

Dahabiyas on the Nile

These traditional Egyptian sailing boats had disappeared from the Nile for many years until recently. There are now many such boats offering cruises between Luxor and Aswan.

The River Nile

The Nile is the world's longest river and as it flows through Egypt, its waters play as vital a role today as they did for the people of Ancient Egypt. The fertile valley which runs from south to north can be seen here outlined by the barren desert beyond. Egypt's dependence on this river has been recognized and recorded by many writers and historians. Visiting Egypt more than 2500 years ago, Herodotus called the country 'The Gift of the Nile'.

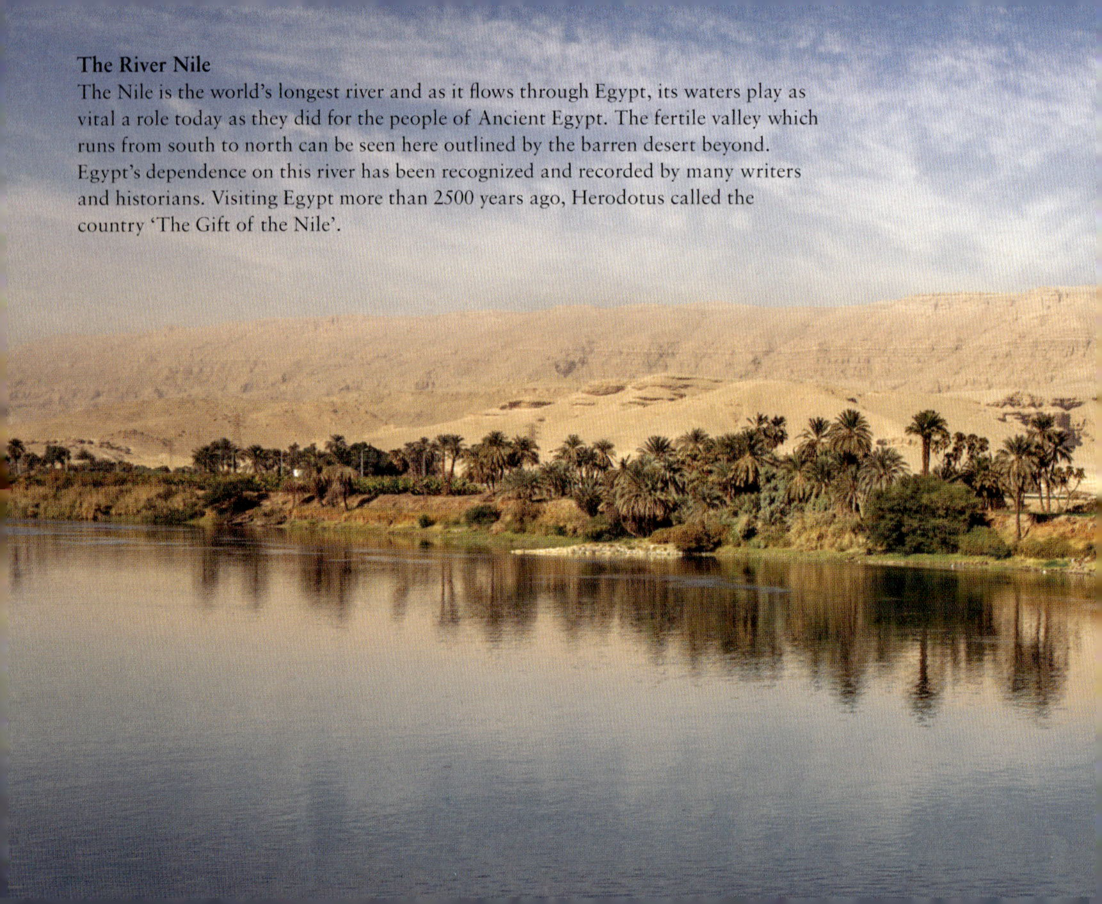

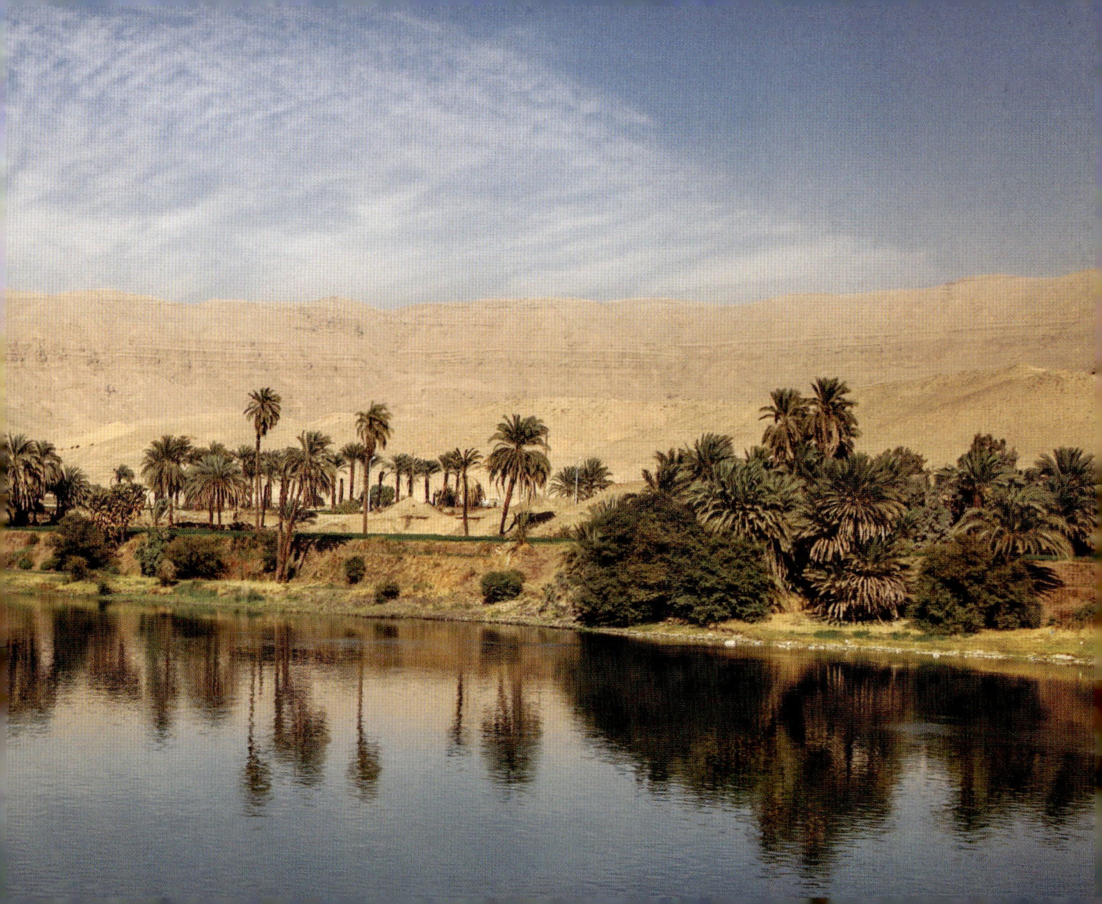

The Nile Delta
Above Cairo, the Nile Delta is a vast cultivated region fed by the two main branches of the Nile and extensive irrigation. This lush green area contains a range of potential day trips for the visitor, including several interesting monasteries.

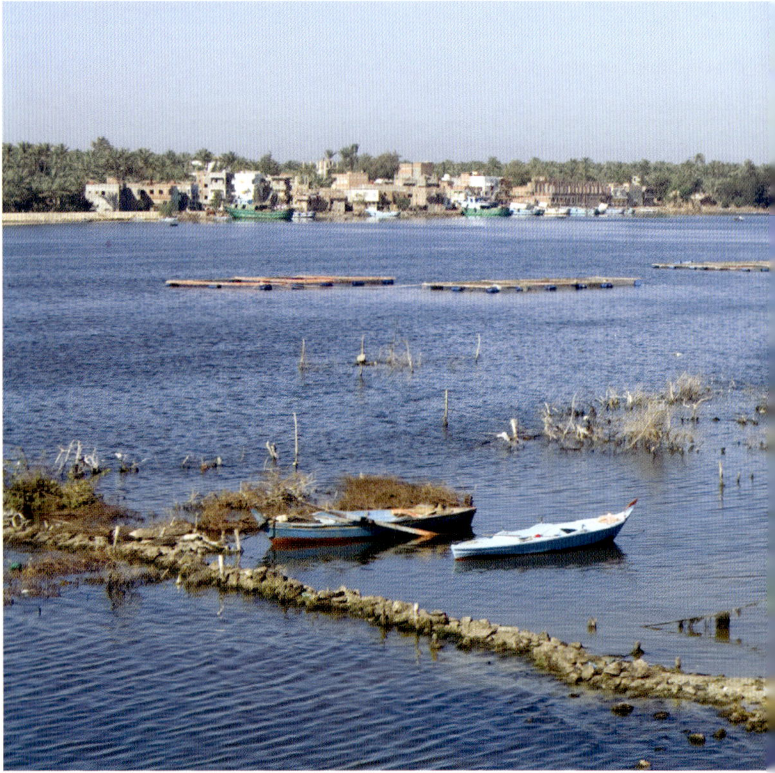

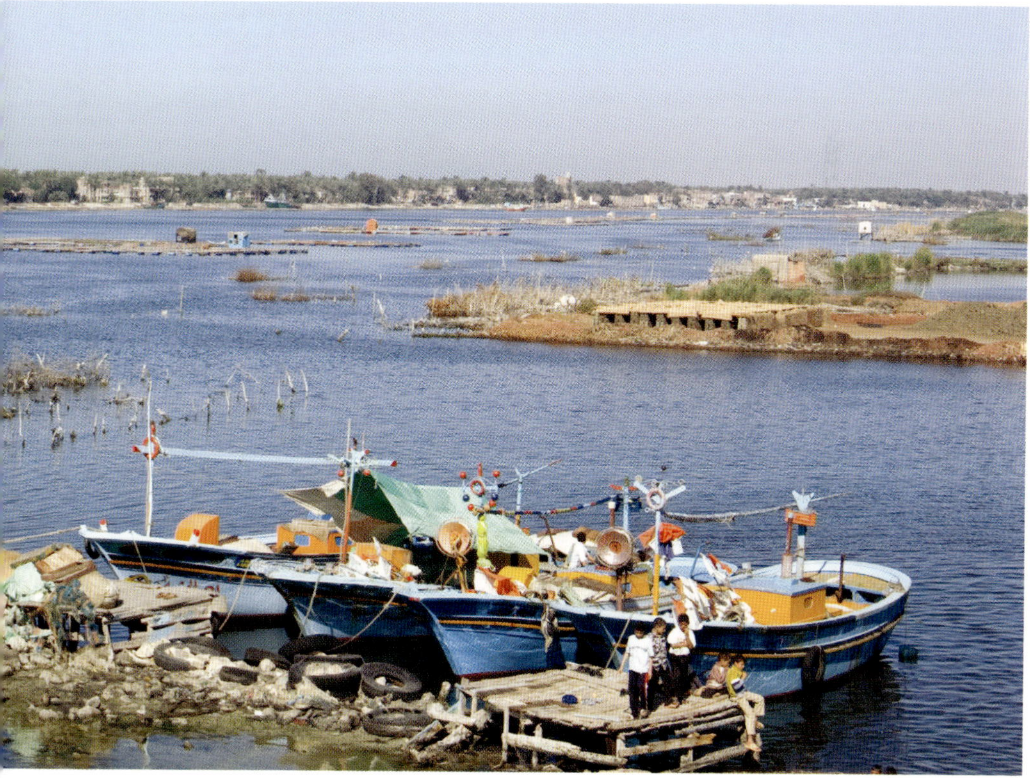

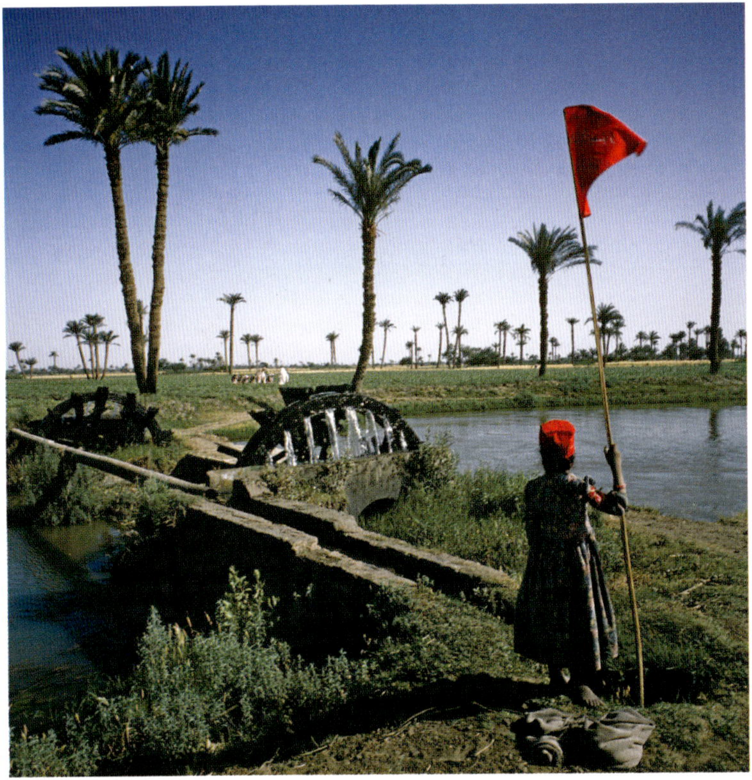

LEFT:

The Nile Delta

Waterwheels are still a feature of the irrigation of the delta region, as they have been for thousands of years. As water passes from section to section, red flags and red hats are used as bright visual communication tools between workers to ensure the correct flow of water through the canal and onto the fields.

OPPOSITE:

Great Bitter Lake

This large expanse of water sits alongside the Suez Canal and provides a wide waterway which allows shipping to change position as needed before passing through the actual canal. It was formerly a dry salt flat and due to the high salinity it lacks vegetation or birdlife.

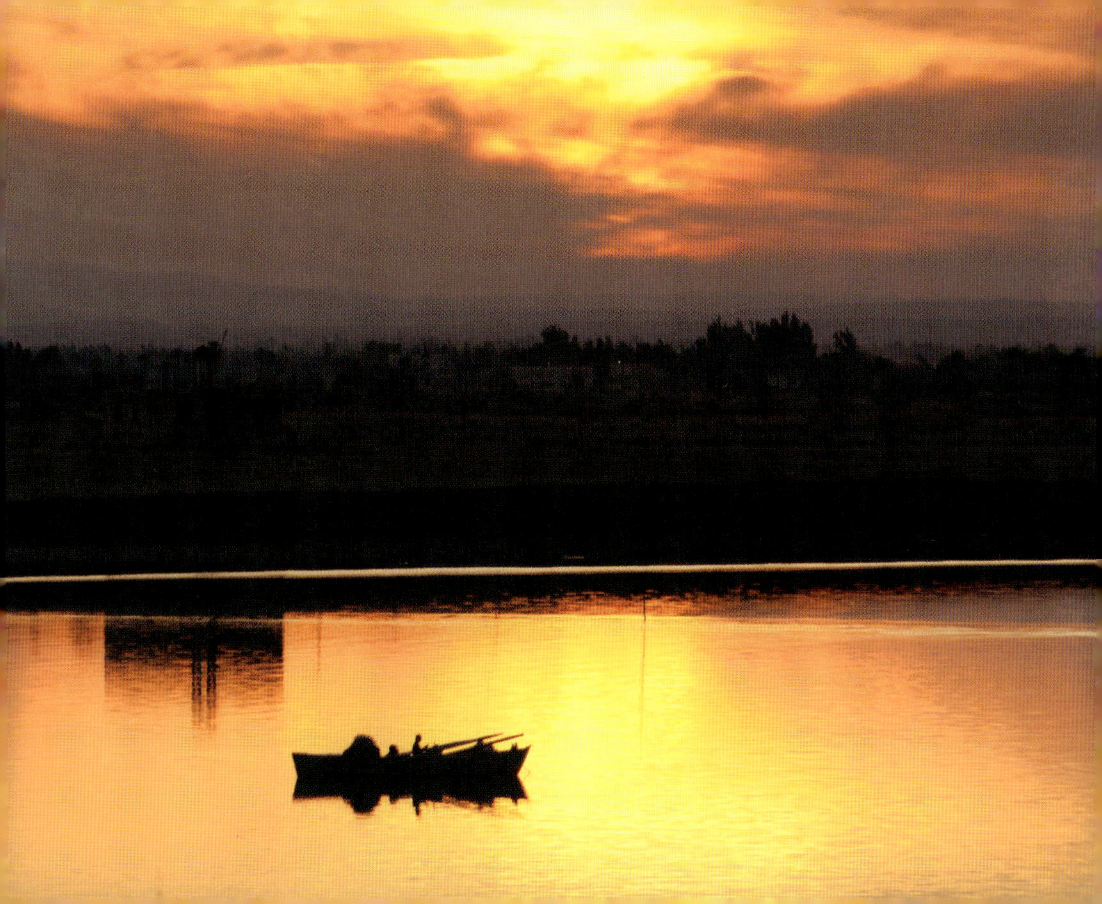

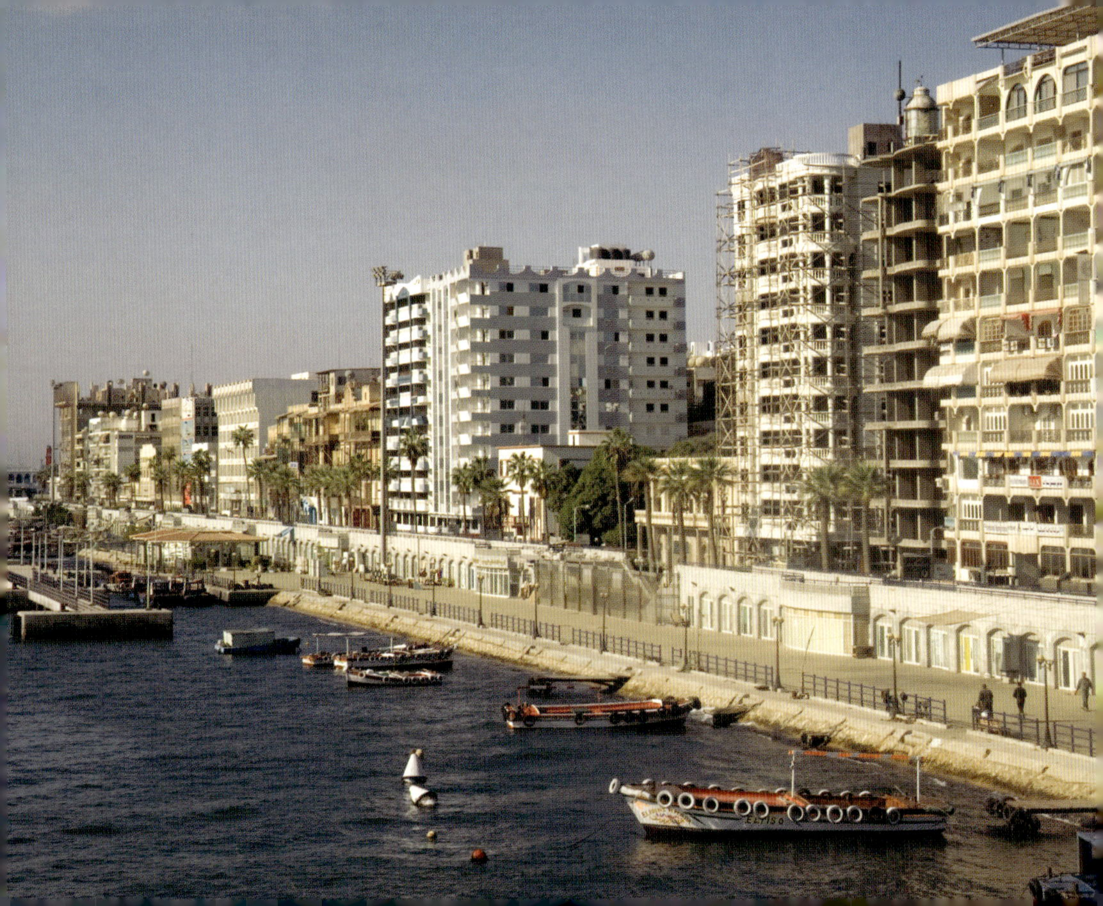

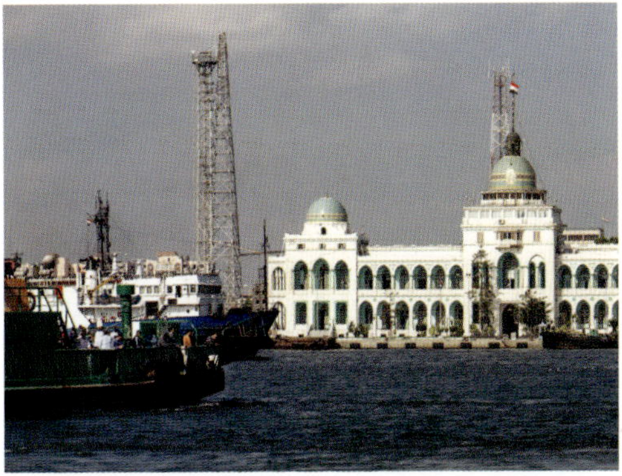

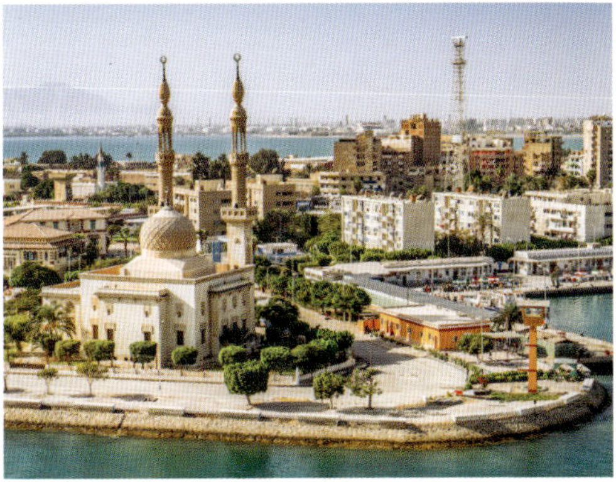

OPPOSITE:

Waterfront, Port Said

The waterfront of this once great seafarers' city has lost the lustre of the famous days when it prospered along with the Suez Canal, the opening of which triggered this city's birth. Despite the decline in its reputation for providing passing sailors and passengers with a good night out, it is still worth visiting, not least to stand by the canal and watch the giant ships pass you by.

TOP LEFT:

Waterfront, Port Said

The Suez Canal Company building, with its distinctive green domes, stands out along the canal front even today. The company and canal came under the management of Britain and France, for many of its early years, until President Nasser nationalized it in 1956 and the Suez Canal Authority was formed to oversee this vital source of foreign currency income. The canal was recently improved and widened.

BOTTOM LEFT:

Waterfront, Port Said

The city provides the visitor with ample opportunity to walk by the waterside in all directions, and to cross the canal to its sister city of Port Fuad by one of the regular ferries. The two cities look out to the Mediterranean and guard the entrance to the canal together.

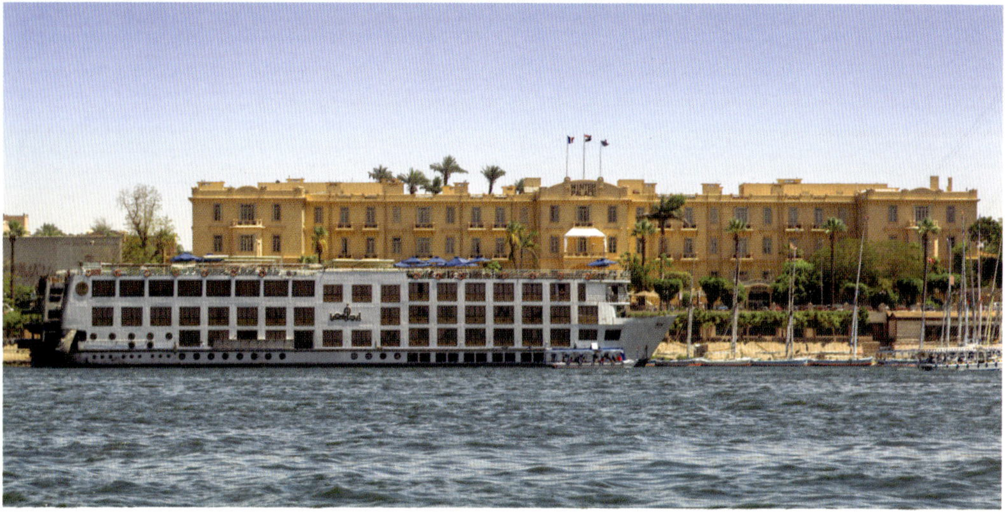

ABOVE:

Winter Palace Hotel, Luxor

This view of the Winter Palace Hotel gives some hint as to its perfect position on the east bank of the Nile at Luxor. The hotel opened in January 1907 to great acclaim and soon established itself as the place to stay and be seen in. Frequently a winter refuge for Egypt's royal family, it also played host to Agatha Christie when she was writing *Death On The Nile*.

FAR RIGHT:

Winter Palace Hotel, Luxor

The discovery of the tomb of Tutankhamum was Luxor's most famous moment and Howard Carter, the archaeologist who found the treasures, announced his find from the staircase of the Winter Palace Hotel.

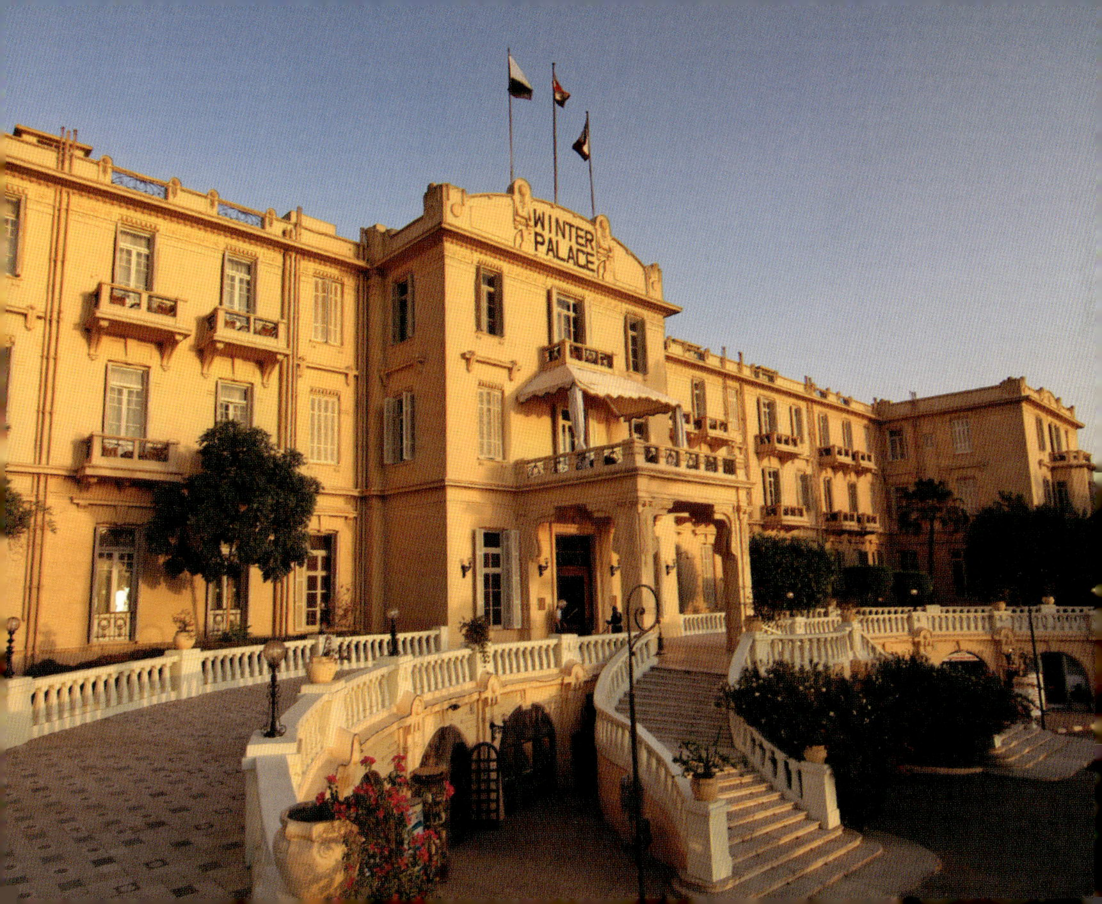
WINTER
PALACE

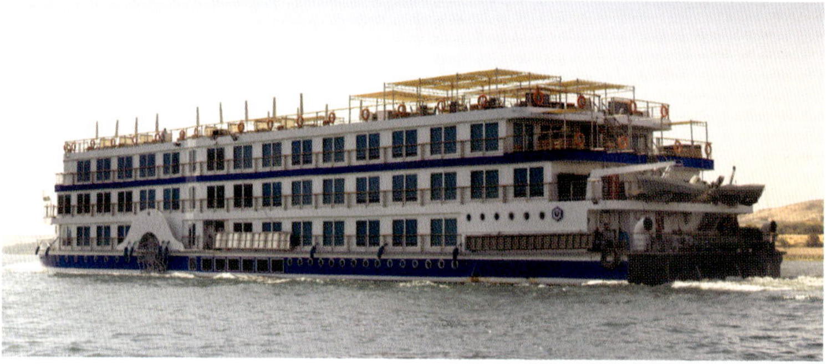

ABOVE:

Cruising The Nile

The idea of cruise holidays may bring to mind gigantic ocean-going ships full of casinos, but on the Nile it remains a much more sedate holiday. Most cruises are on boats such as the one above, offering a peaceful setting between stops at the many temples along the way.

RIGHT:

Cruising The Nile

There is no other landscape like the Nile valley and it's a pleasure to travel along it in this style. Being under sunny skies and with all you need to relax on hand, it is no surprise that a Nile cruise is on many people's wishlist. The trip is usually between Aswan and Luxor and can be in either direction, taking three or four days.

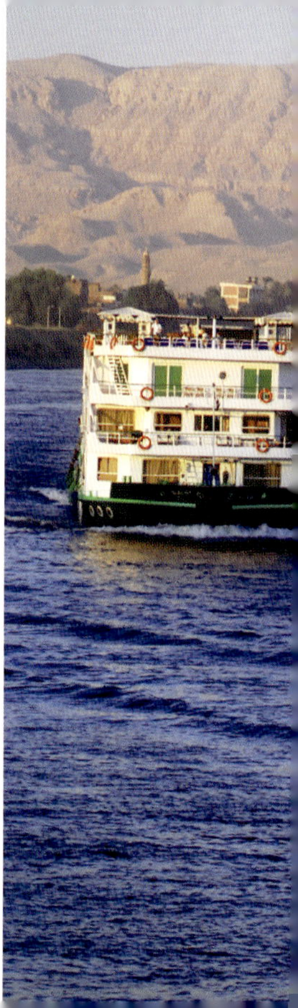

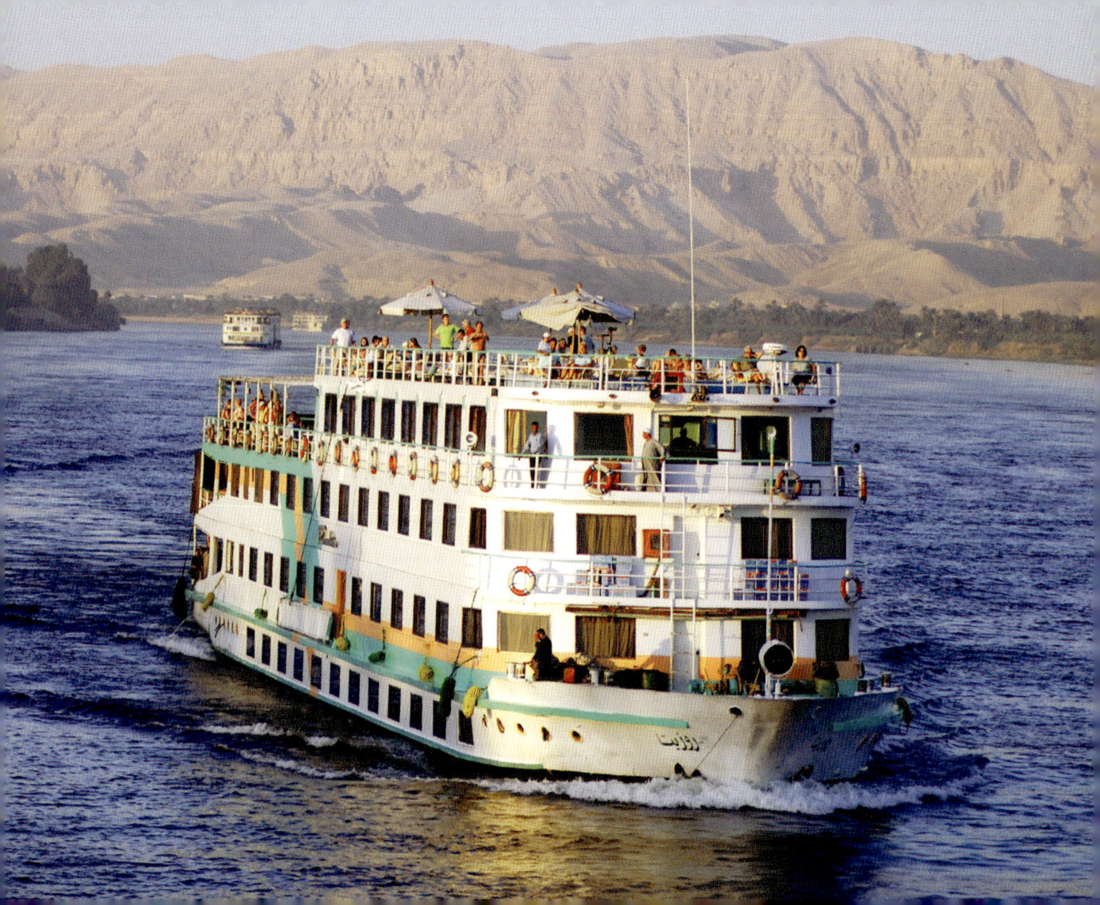

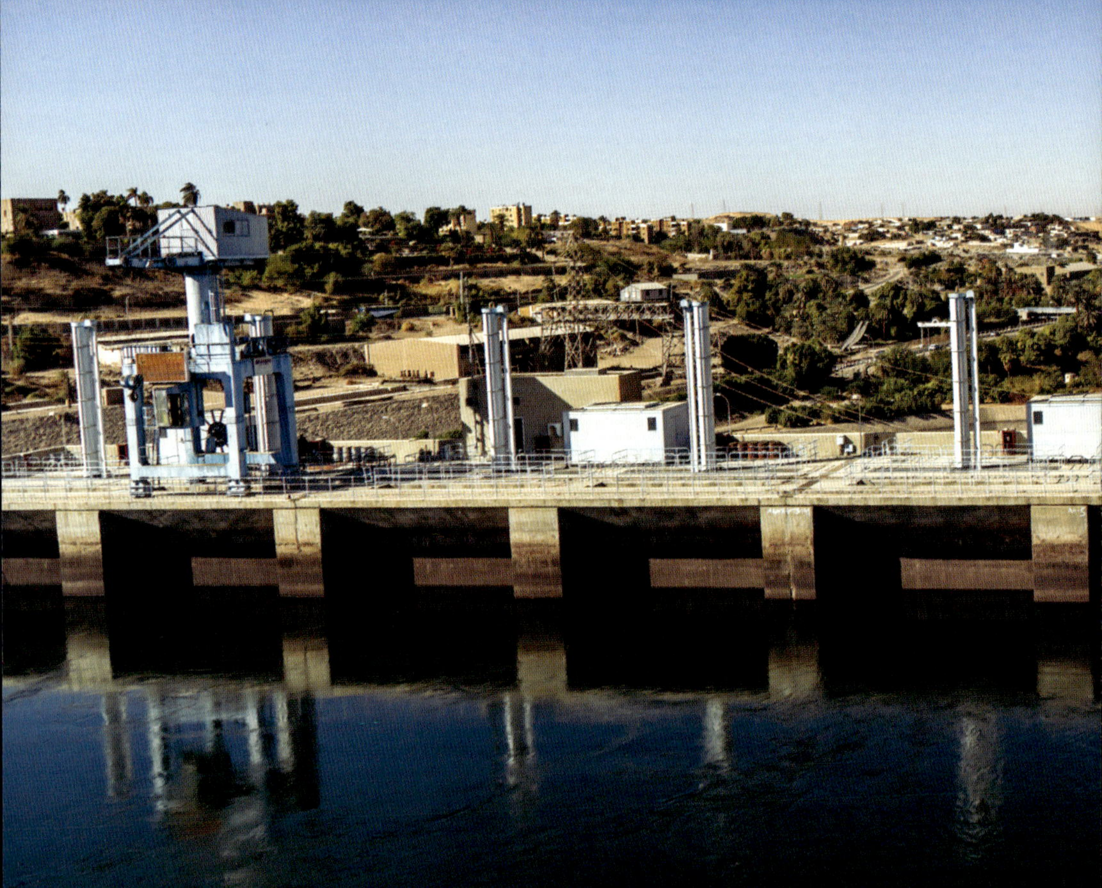

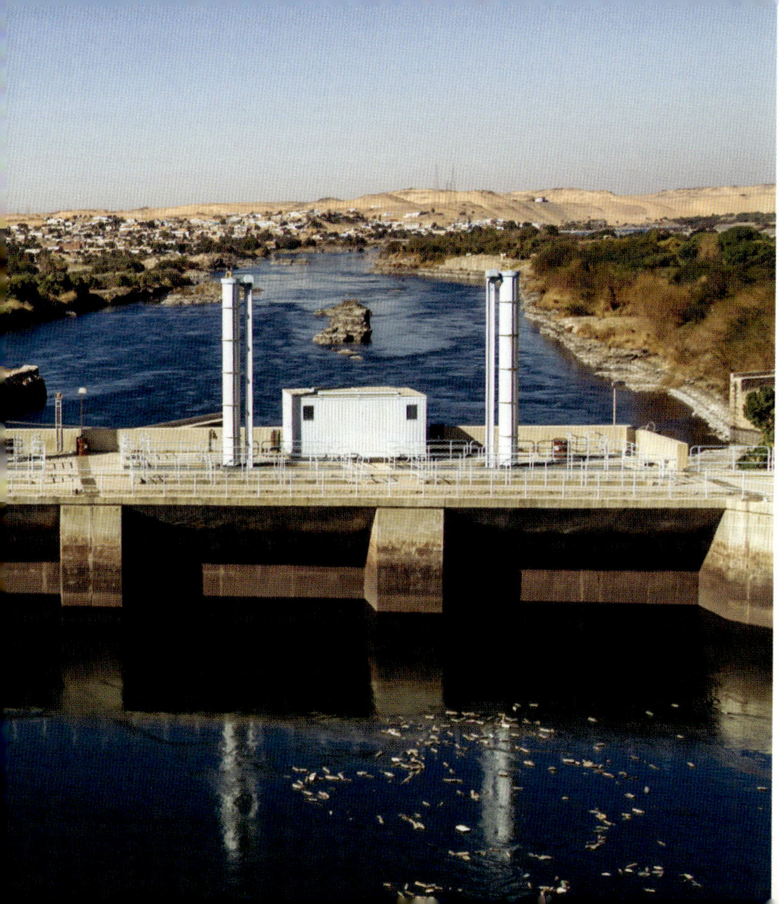

Aswan High Dam, The Nile

Completed in 1971, the High Dam has controlled the flow of the Nile through Egypt ever since. This huge project took ten years to build, the dam itself is almost a kilometre long at its base and 111m (364ft) high. The construction of this dam created Lake Nasser, now a massive reservoir which is some 547km (340 miles) long, and averages 32km (20 miles) in width.

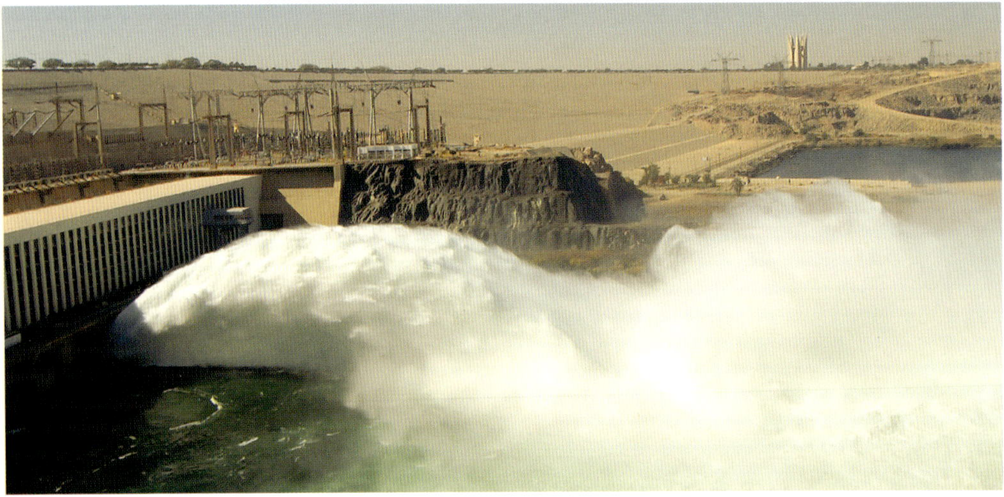

ABOVE:

Aswan High Dam, The Nile

The High Dam controls the flow of the Nile, ensuring even irrigation from the water stored in the reservoir. It also generates hydroelectric power. The importance of these benefits to Nasser's industrial plans were vital in the modernization of Egypt after the overthrow of the monarchy in 1952.

OPPOSITE:

Aswan Low Dam, The Nile

Some 6.4km (four miles) upstream from the High Dam is the original dam which was completed in 1902, and at the time set many construction records for its size and the storage capacity it created. Indeed, it was so successful that within 60 years it was clear a new, bigger dam was needed. Today it provides an attractive place to cross and see the Nile in both directions, including a fine view of Philae Temple.

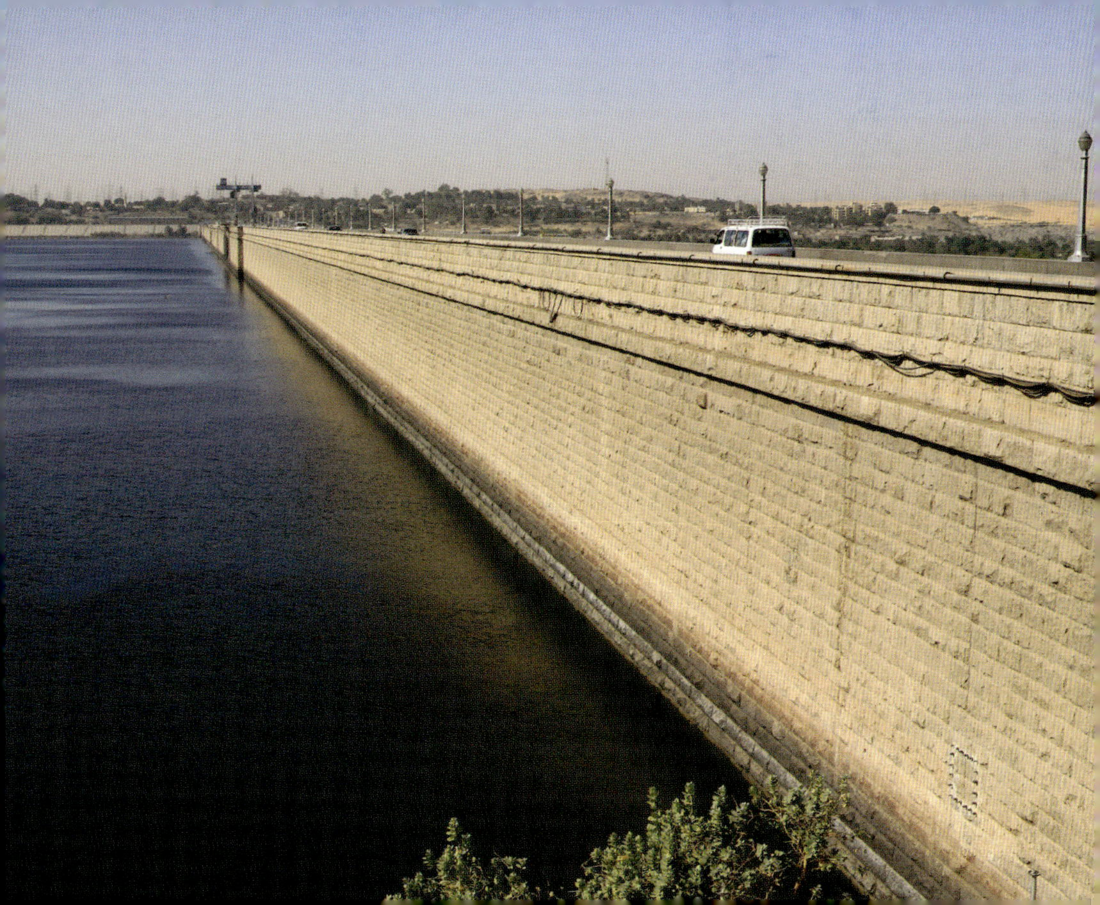

Elephantine Island, The Nile

Aswan sits beside the Nile and among its many charms are the various islands which lie in the river and can be visited by boat with ease. It is a fun and relaxing way to spend a few hours sitting, and watching the world and water go by. In the foreground we see the Botanical Island, a beautiful place of flora first collected by Lord Kitchener. Elephantine Island lies behind and features walks and the charmingly named, but very local, 'Nubian Museum'.

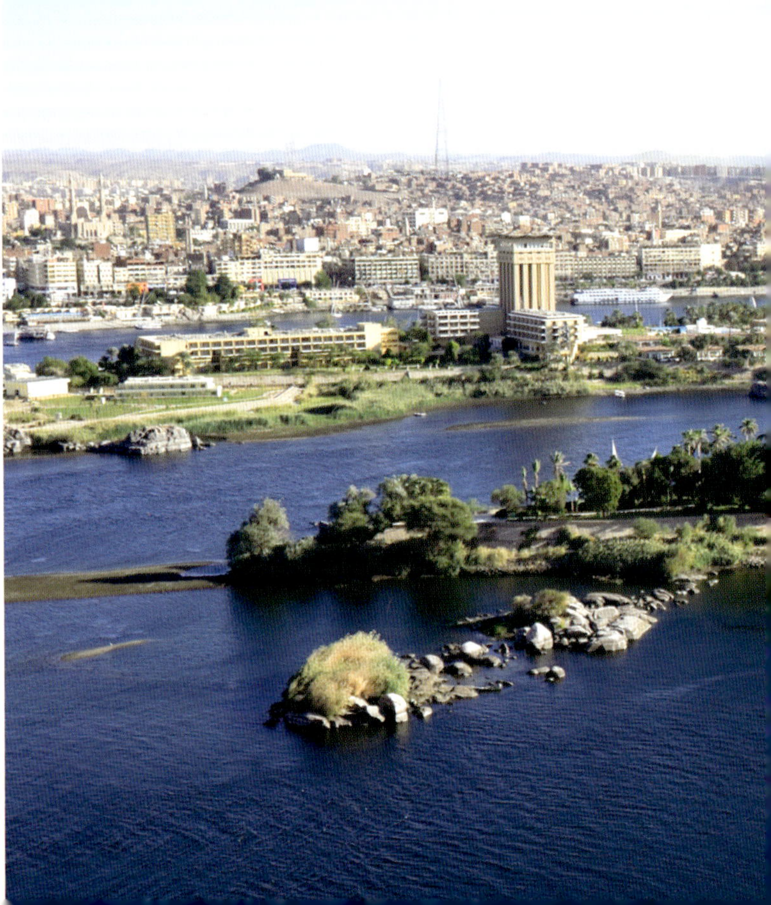

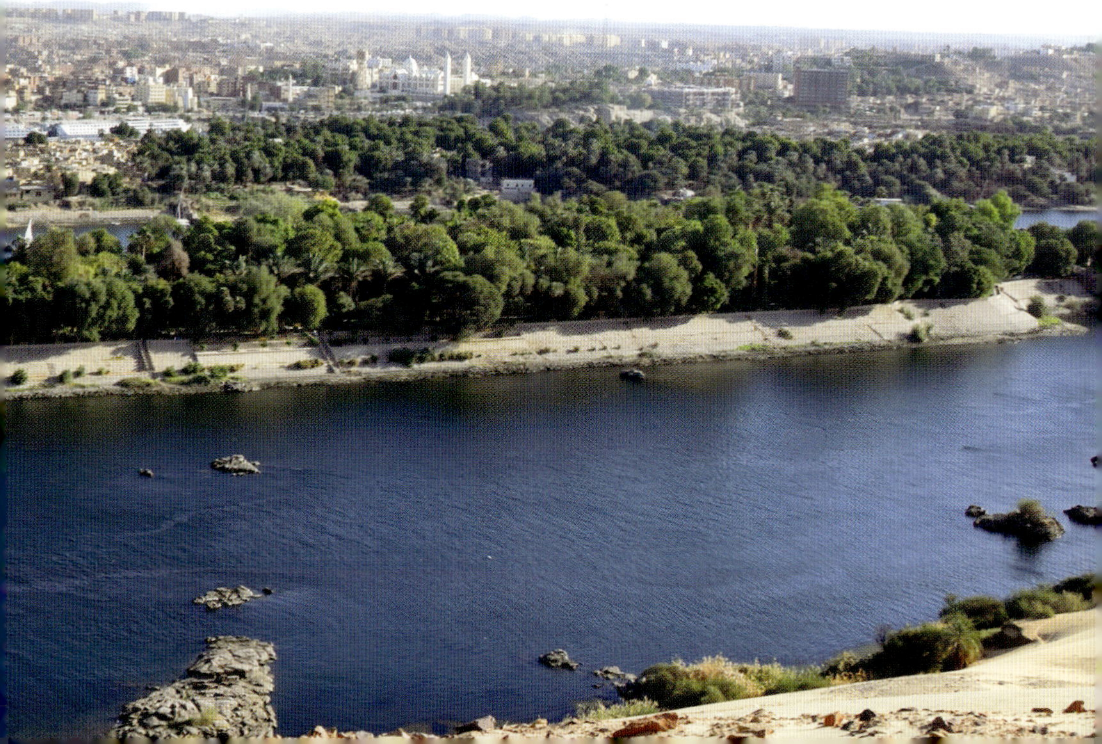

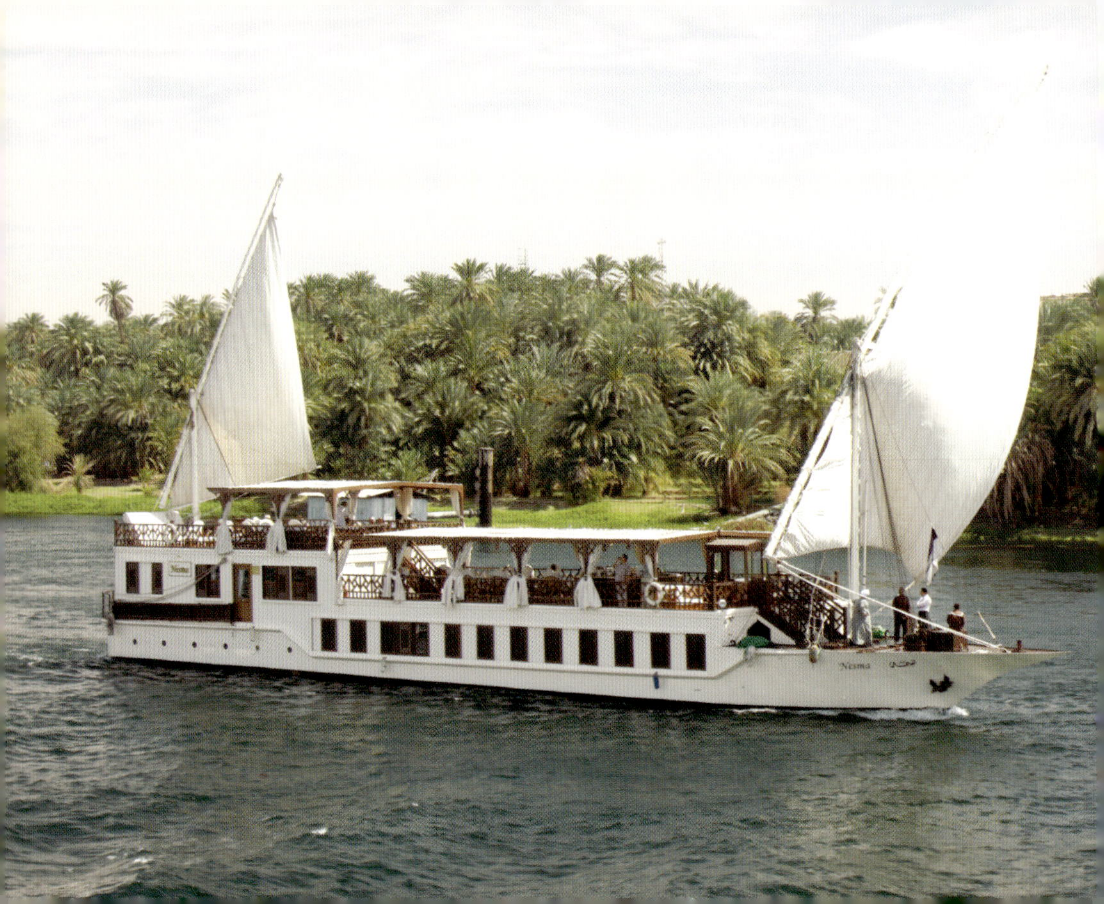
Nesma

OPPOSITE:

Dahabiyas

The return of these shallow-bottomed craft, with their distinctive two (or more) sails has been a welcome sight for those who know the Nile and its history. Such boats are depicted in the art of Ancient Egypt, especially in tomb paintings.

RIGHT:

Feluccas

No visit to Egypt is complete without a trip on a felucca. Travelling on one, you will move in silence and feel at one with the river. Although strongly associated with Egypt, feluccas are also found in the Red Sea area and Eastern Mediterranean as sea-going vessels.

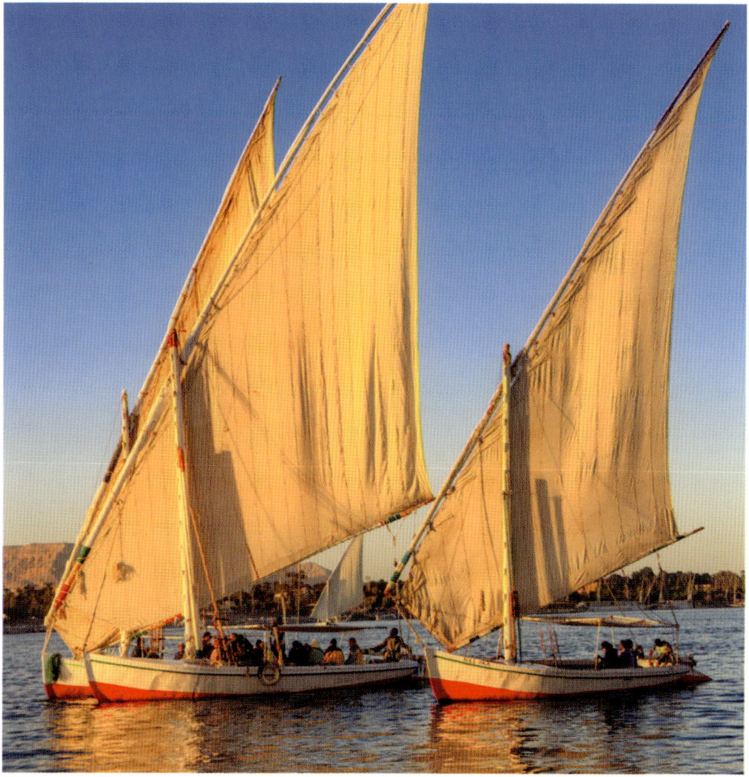

Gulf of Aqaba

This deep, water filled gorge is filled by the Red Sea via the Straits of Tiran. With mountains on either side, the coastline touches Egypt, Jordan, Israel and Saudi Arabia.

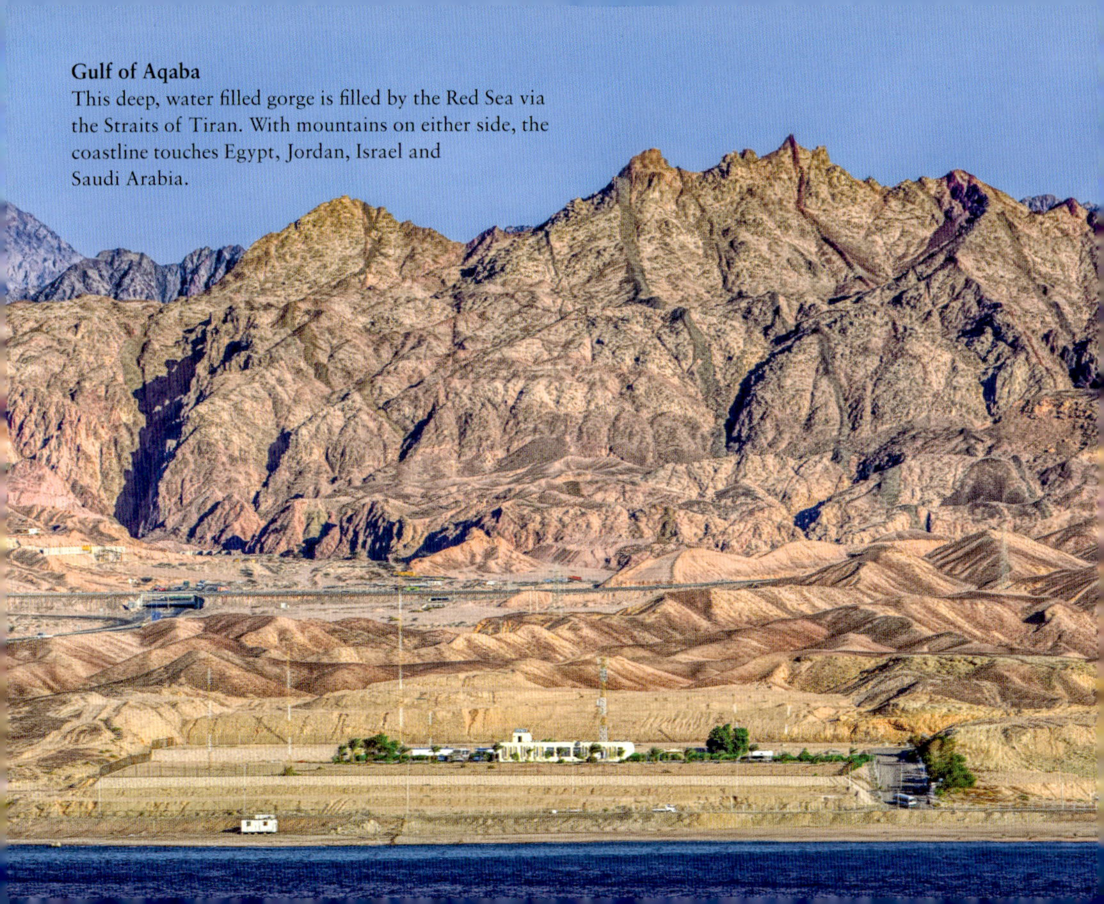

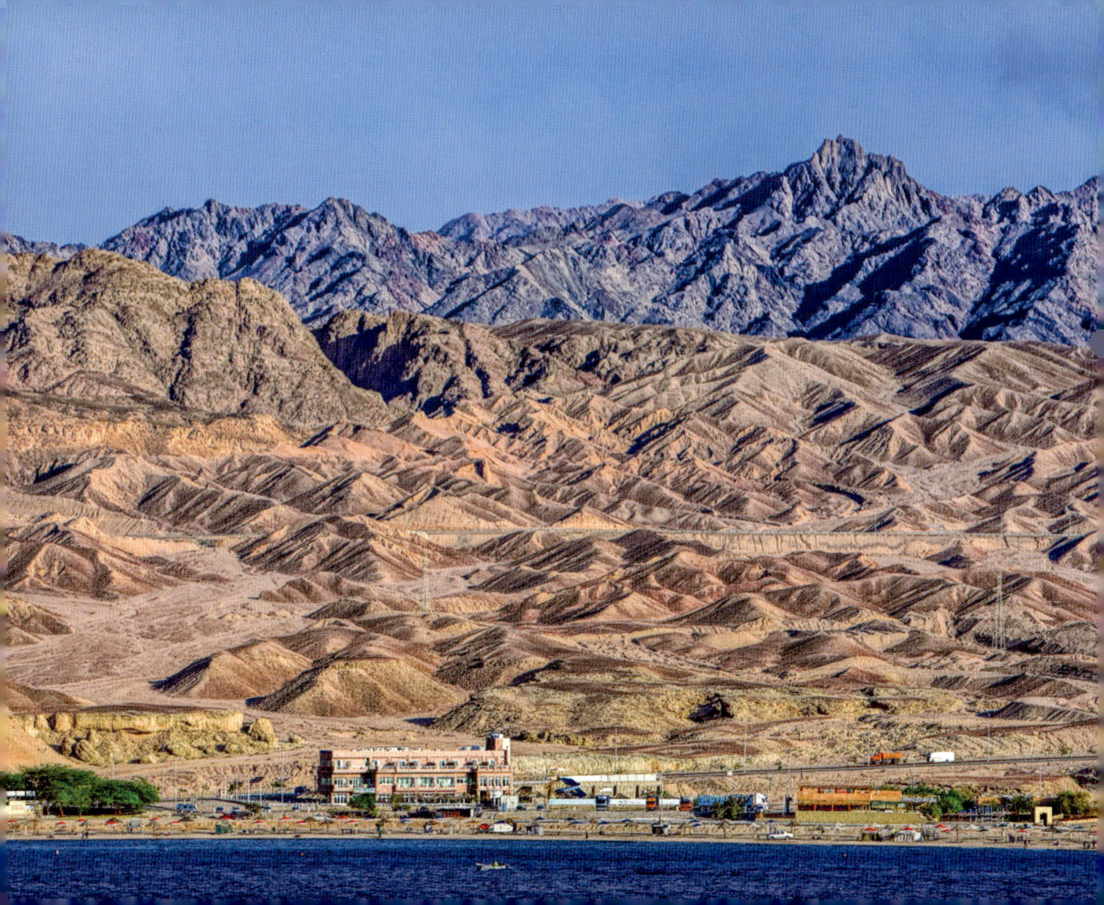

Pharaoh's Island, Gulf of Aqaba

Near the town of Taba is a small granite outpost. It is surrounded by reefs and fine diving sites. Sitting above the outcrop is Saladin Citadel, originally a crusader castle which Saladin then captured in the 12th century. It was later used and expanded in both Mamluk and then Ottoman times.

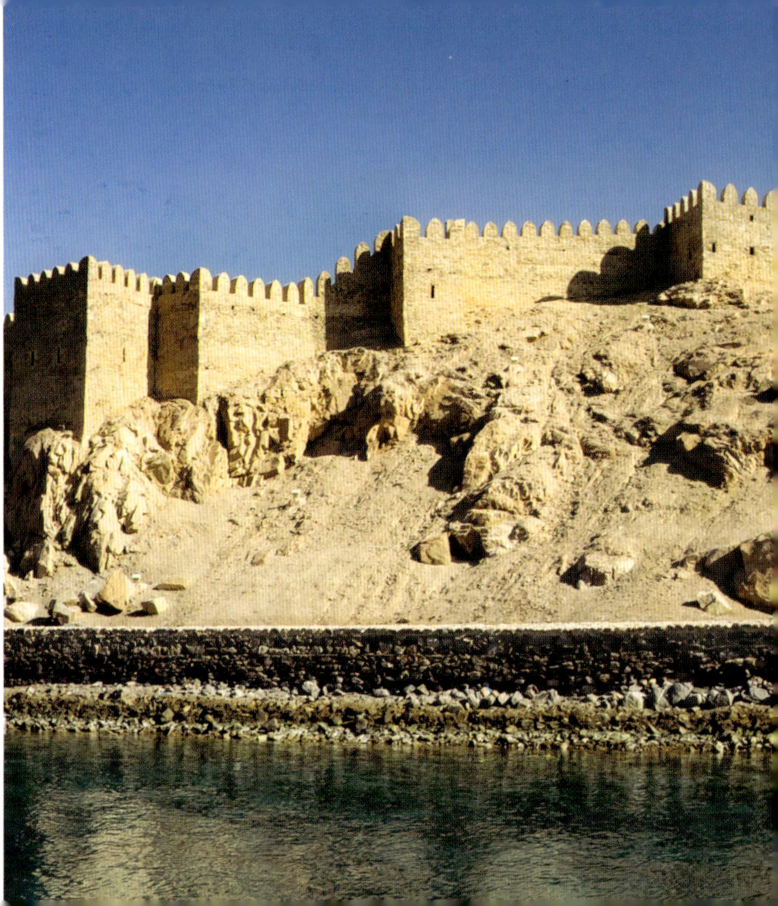

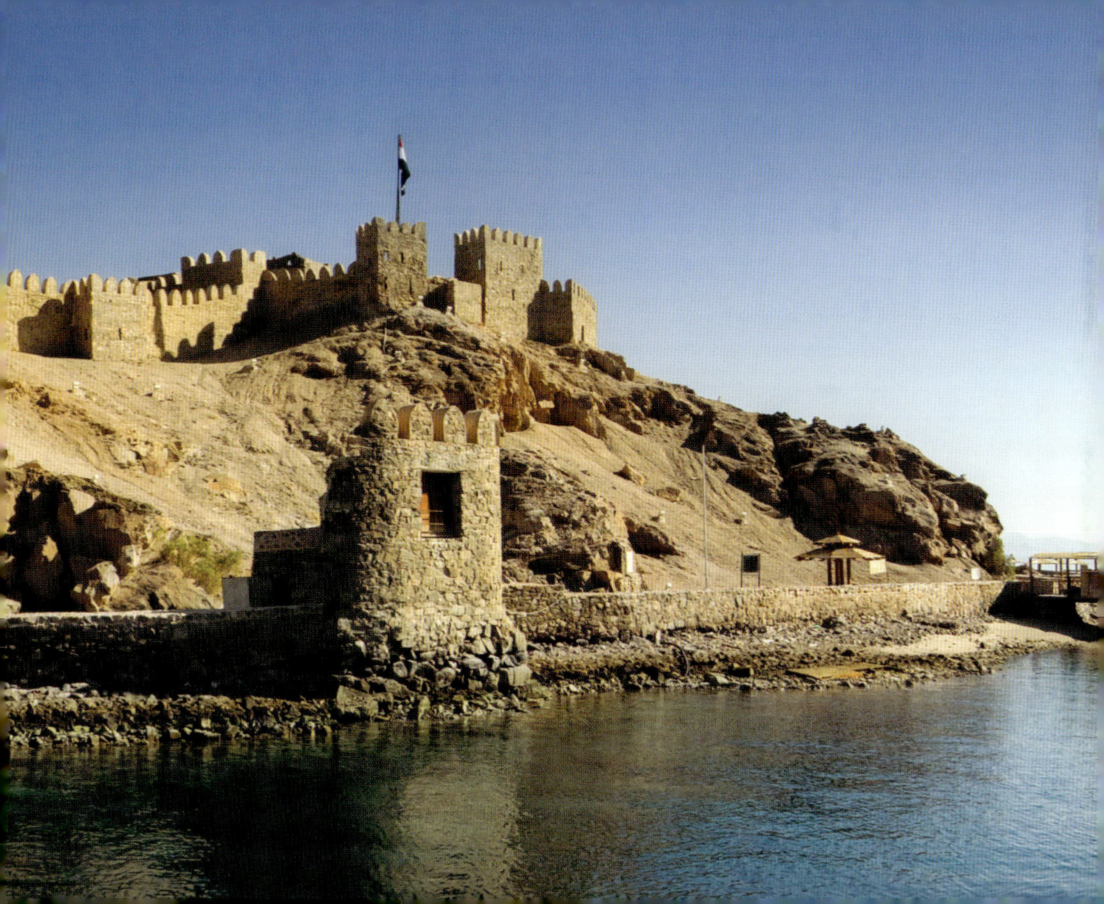

Old Cataract Hotel, Aswan

In many ways the epicentre of Aswan, the Old Cataract is a must-see destination if you are in Upper Egypt. Its history and famed opulence, combined with the grandeur of its architecture and interiors, make a visit essential. Taking tea (or more) on its terrace is to step back in time and share a space enjoyed by, among many others, Winston Churchill, Howard Carter, the Agha Khan and Agatha Christie.

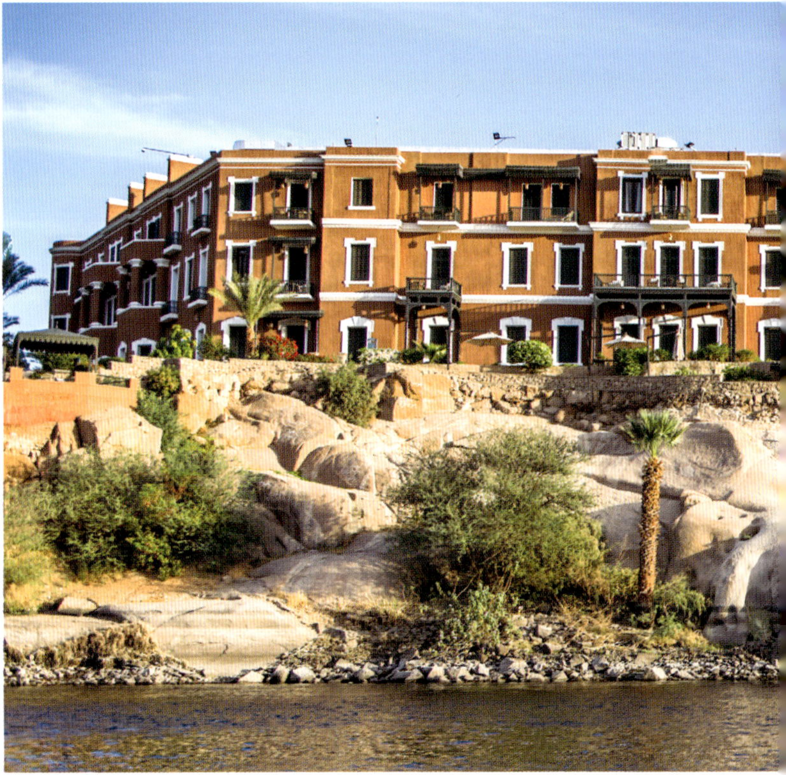

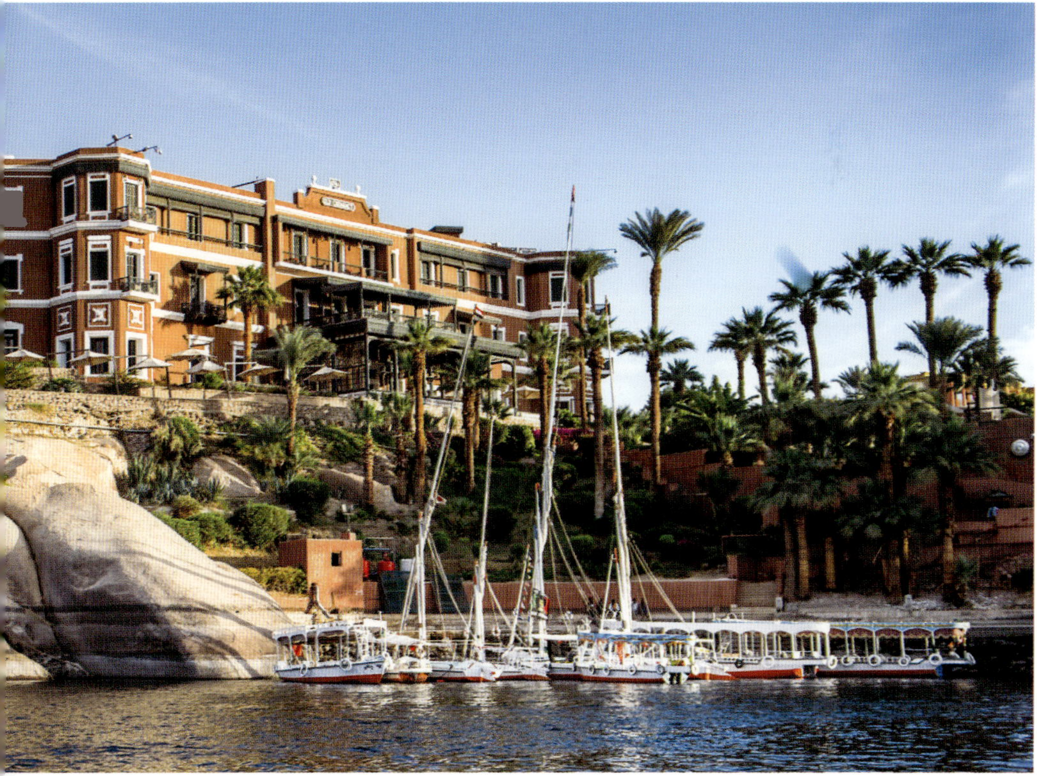

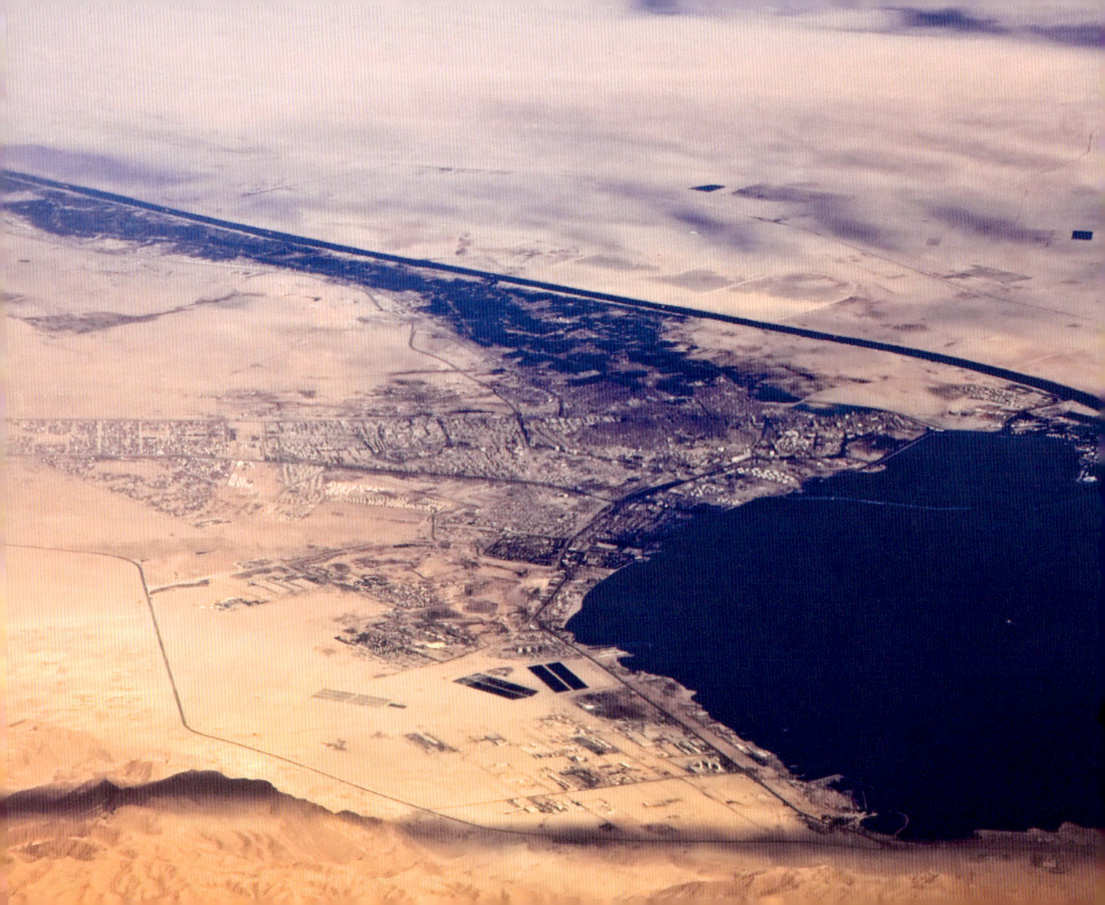

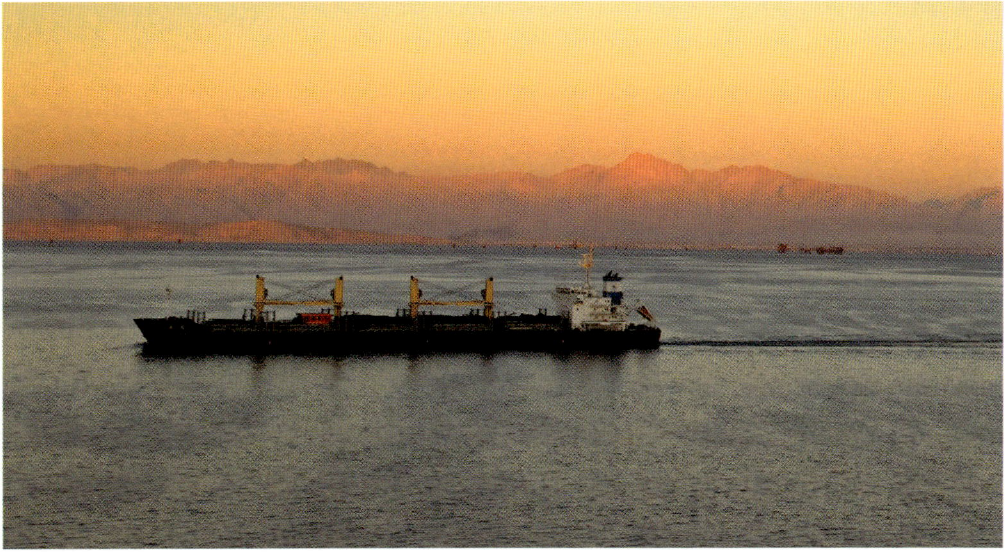

OPPOSITE:

Port Suez and the Suez Canal

The Suez Canal is a vital artery for shipping. Its position connecting the Red Sea to the Mediterranean allows cargo and cruises the chance to avoid the long and expensive sea journey around Africa. Here we see the southern entrance which connects with the Gulf of Suez near Suez Port.

ABOVE:

The Gulf of Suez

This waterway connects the Suez Canal to the Red Sea and passes between the mountains of the Sinai and the desert of mainland Egypt. It is 322km (200 miles) long and marks the boundary between Africa and Asia. As well as its value to shipping, the area is rich in oil and gas.

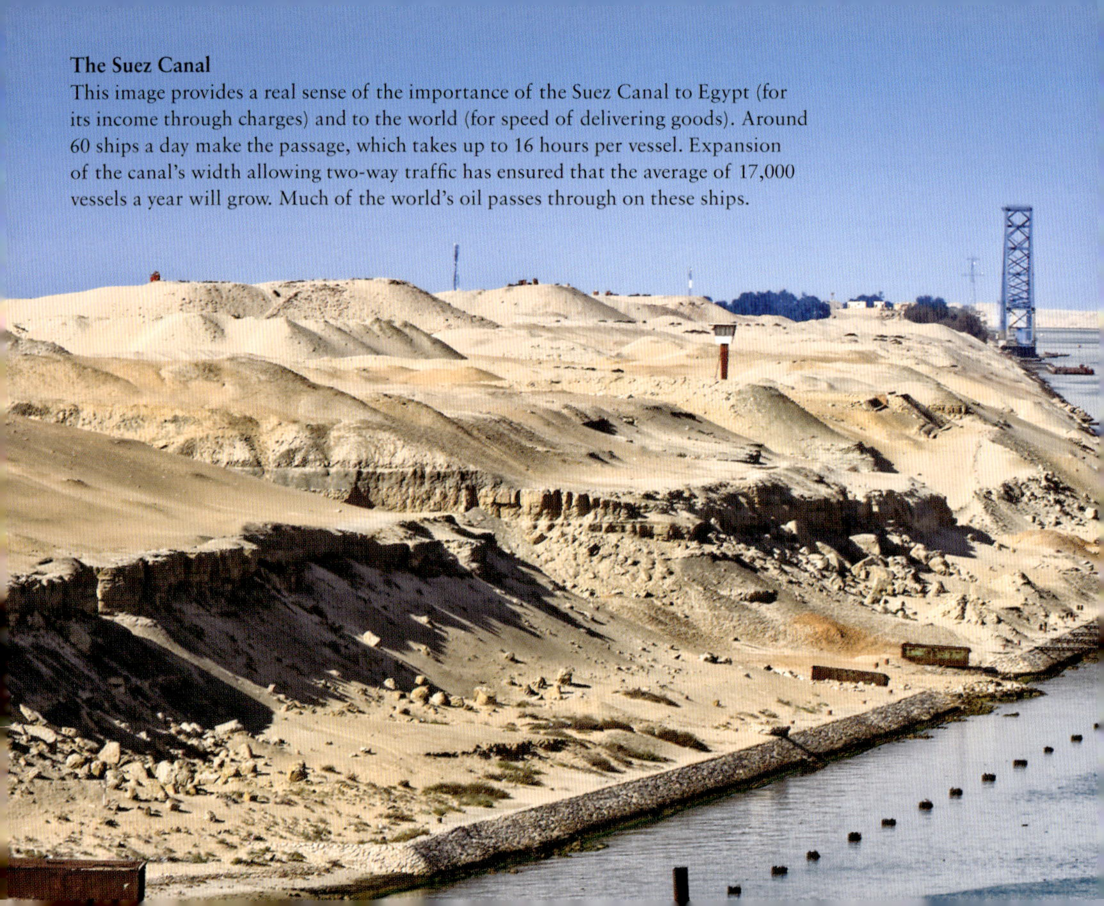

The Suez Canal

This image provides a real sense of the importance of the Suez Canal to Egypt (for its income through charges) and to the world (for speed of delivering goods). Around 60 ships a day make the passage, which takes up to 16 hours per vessel. Expansion of the canal's width allowing two-way traffic has ensured that the average of 17,000 vessels a year will grow. Much of the world's oil passes through on these ships.

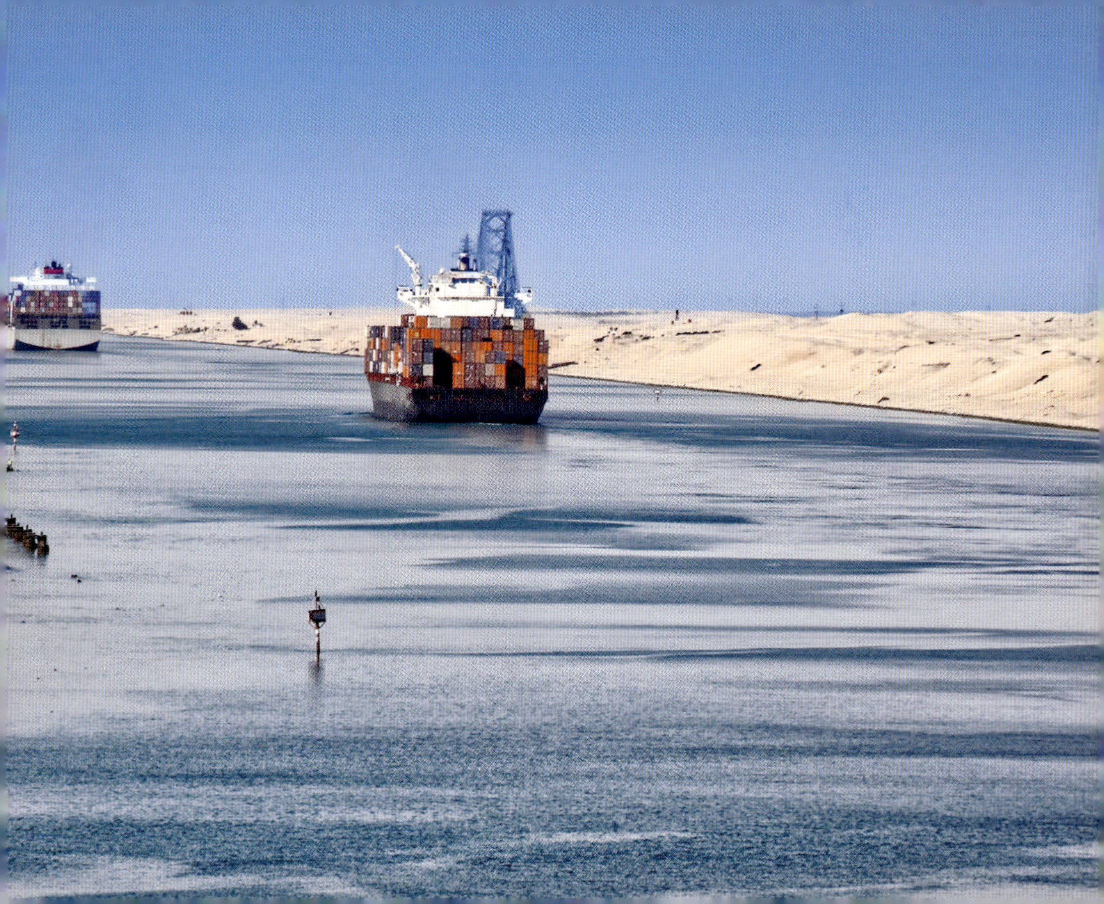

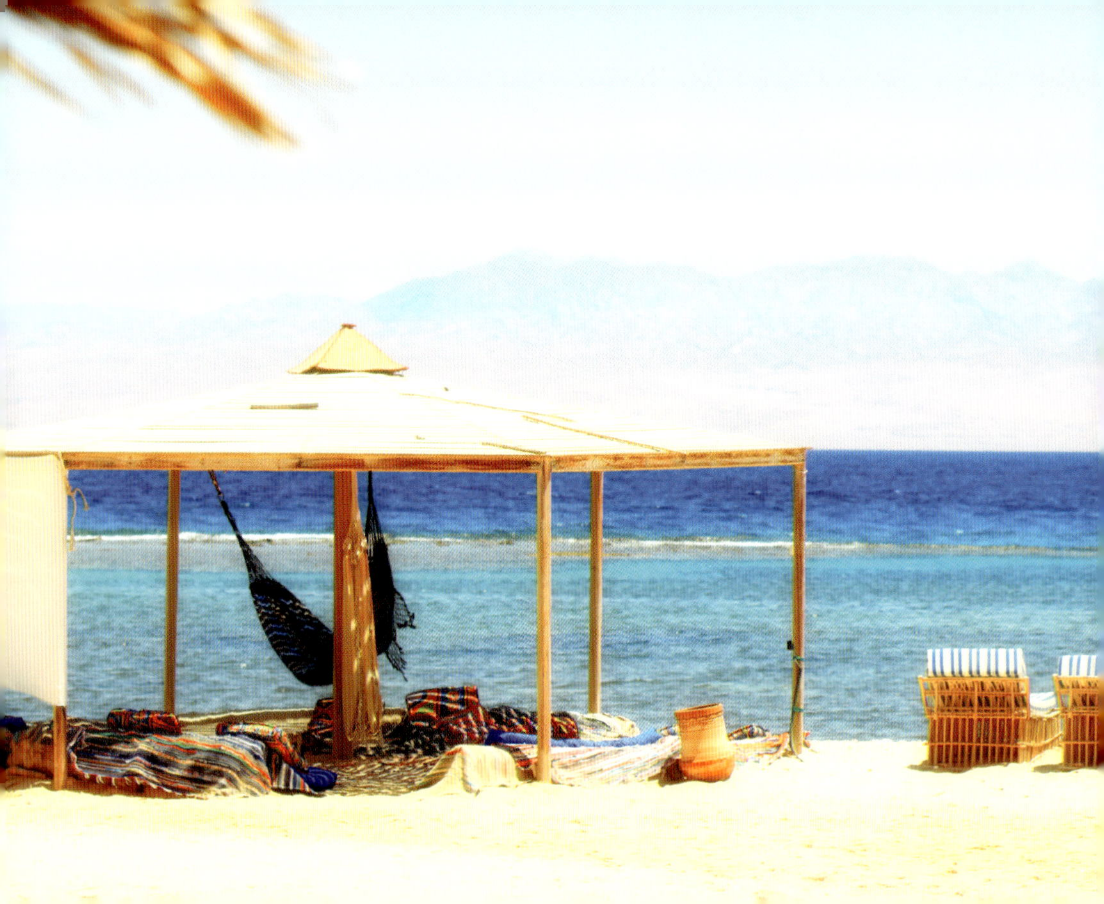

Red Sea Coast

The Red Sea is more than 2250km (1400 miles) long, forming much of Egypt's eastern border. In recent years, this coastline has been developed at breakneck speed with resorts and residential compounds, all overlooking some of the finest beaches and clearest waters imaginable.

The Red Sea is in fact a seawater inlet of the Indian Ocean. It is unclear how its name originated, but one thing is certain – this is one of the bluest seas you will see; a blue that darkens quickly as the sea falls away to an average depth of more than 457m (1500ft).

Along the coast, the modern, party towns such as Hurghada and Sharm el Sheikh contrast with quieter spots like Dahab or Nuweiba in the Sinai. Historic Quseir has been inhabited for more than 5000 years, and was an important port town, providing a link between the Nile Valley and its trade routes north by sea and across to Jeddah and Mecca. It is a sleepy place now as trade has moved away and transport links to Arabia are overland. As for the rest of the world, just look at the horizon, where the ships heading for the Suez Canal are carrying goods to every continent.

OPPOSITE:

Nuweiba, Sinai Coast

Nuweiba is a laid-back town near the Gulf of Aqaba. Its mix of independent hotels, camp-style Bedouin beach huts and diving sites ensure something for every visitor.

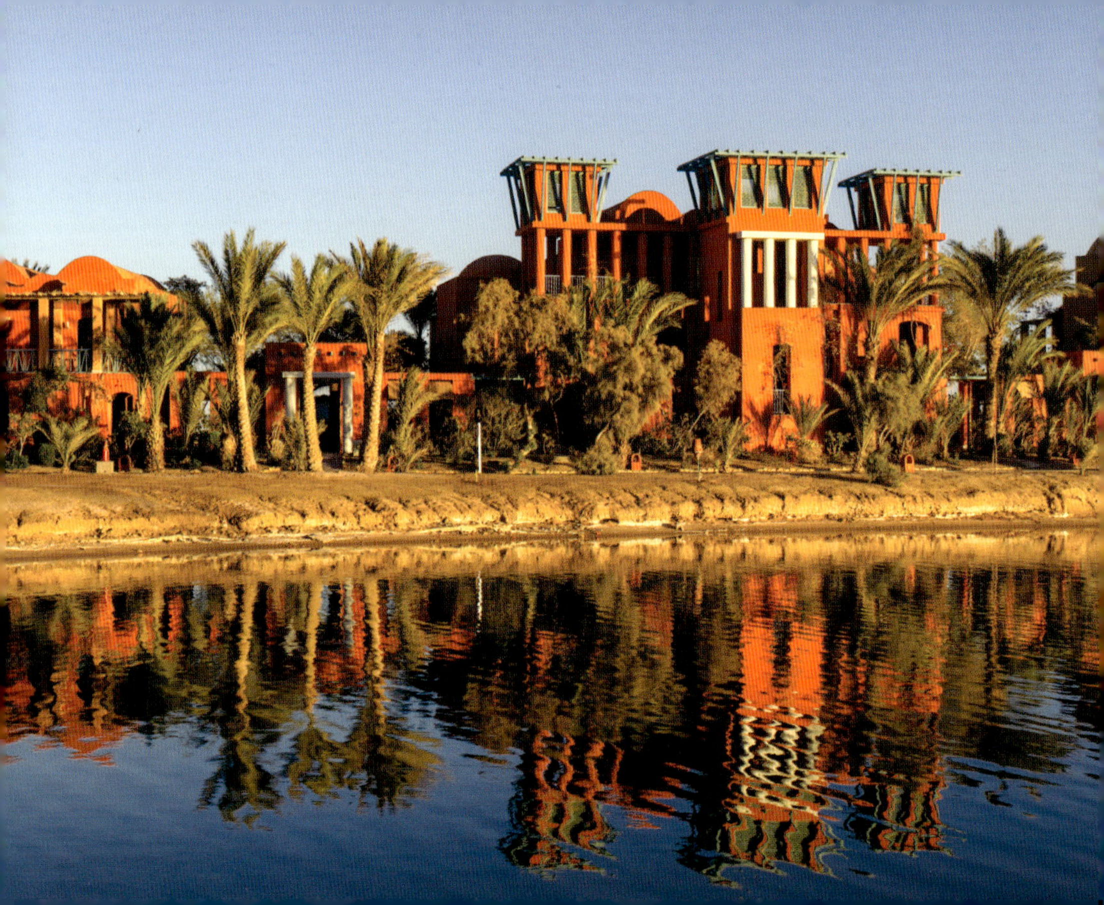

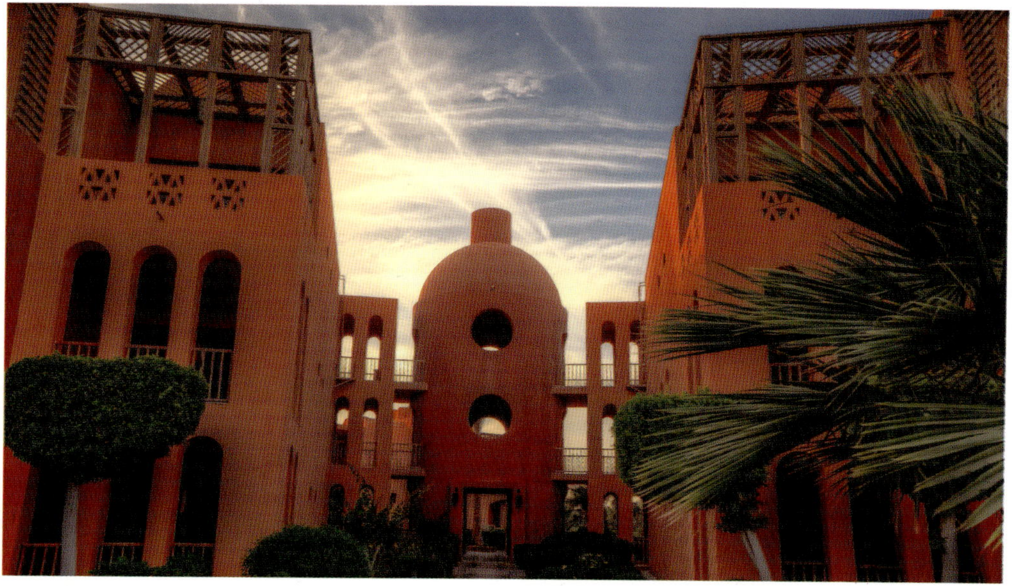

OPPOSITE:

Al-Gouna, Red Sea Coast

Al-Gouna is a relatively new destination on the Red Sea Coast north of Hurghada. Its name means 'The Lagoon'. As one of the most upmarket towns on the Red Sea Riviera, it is often busy and appeals to Egyptians and international tourists alike.

ABOVE:

Al-Gouna, Red Sea Coast

With almost 20 purpose-built hotels sitting on different islands around canals which link them all, al-Gouna is a great place to explore by boat or tuk-tuk (auto rickshaw) – cars are not allowed.

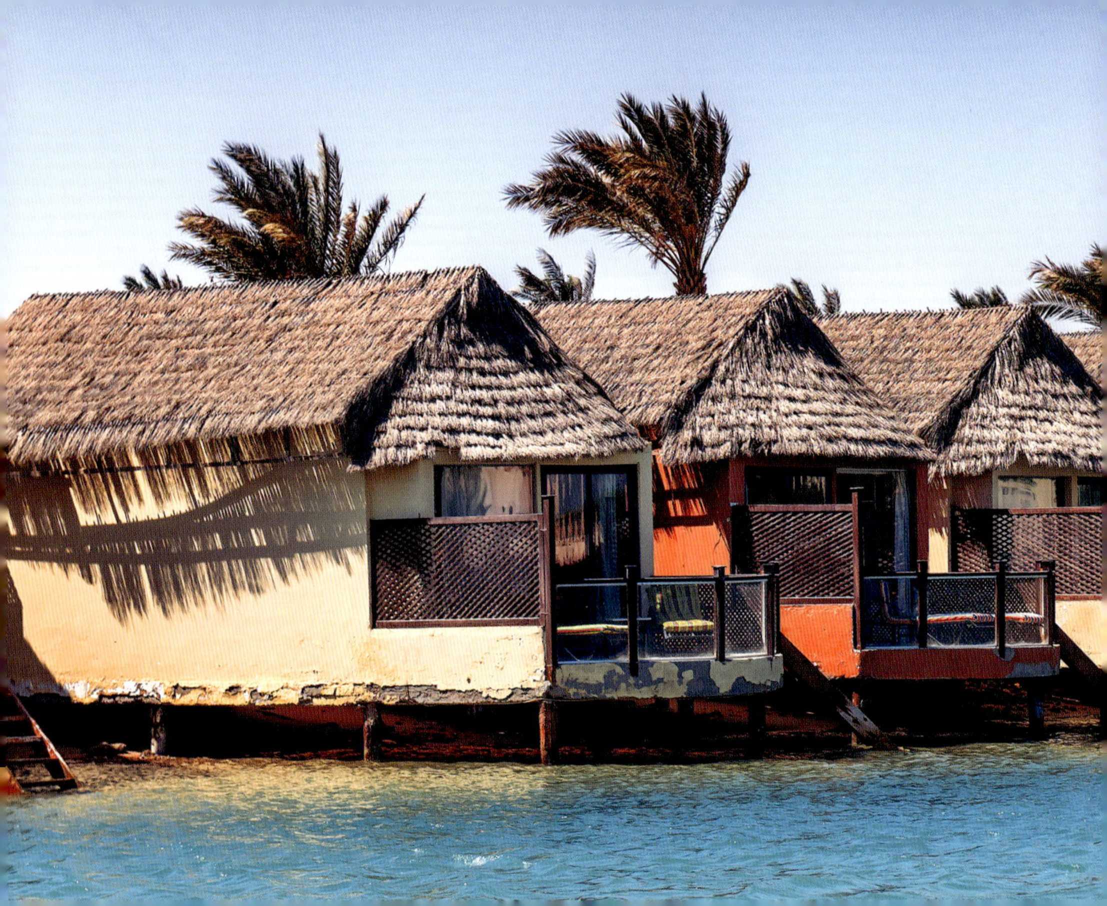

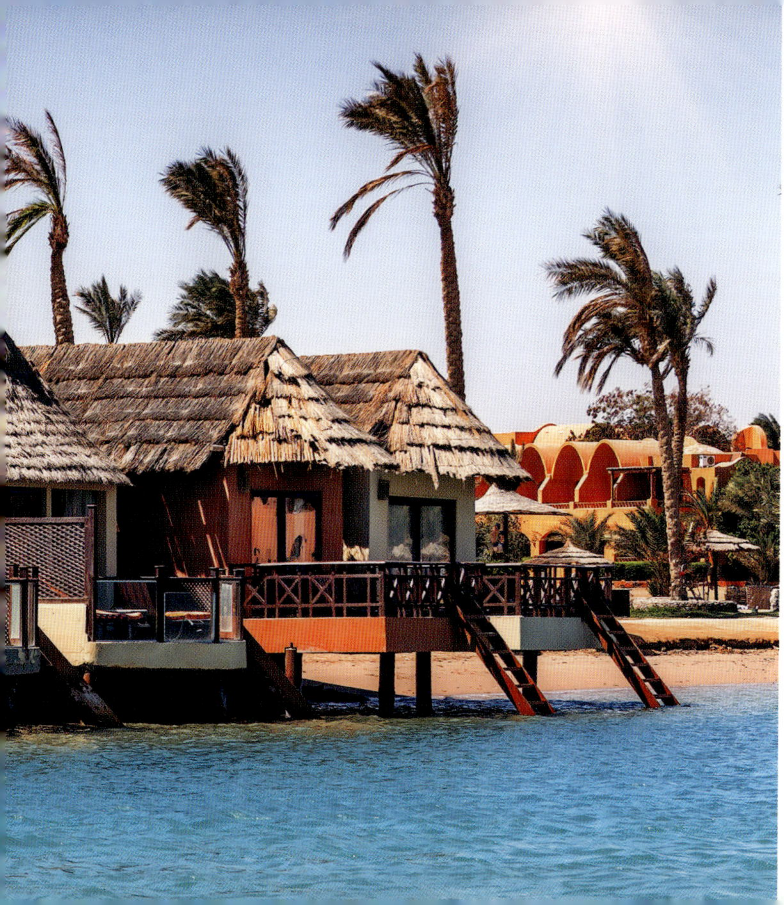

Al-Gouna, Red Sea Coast

With a busy nightlife and some new cultural events such as a film festival, al-Gouna is always lively. However, it remains a place to kick back under the year-round sun. From these beach chalets you can watch the more energetic visitors enjoy the world's premier sites for kite surfing and other watersports. The winds which come across the Red Sea here provide a perfect environment for all types of sailing.

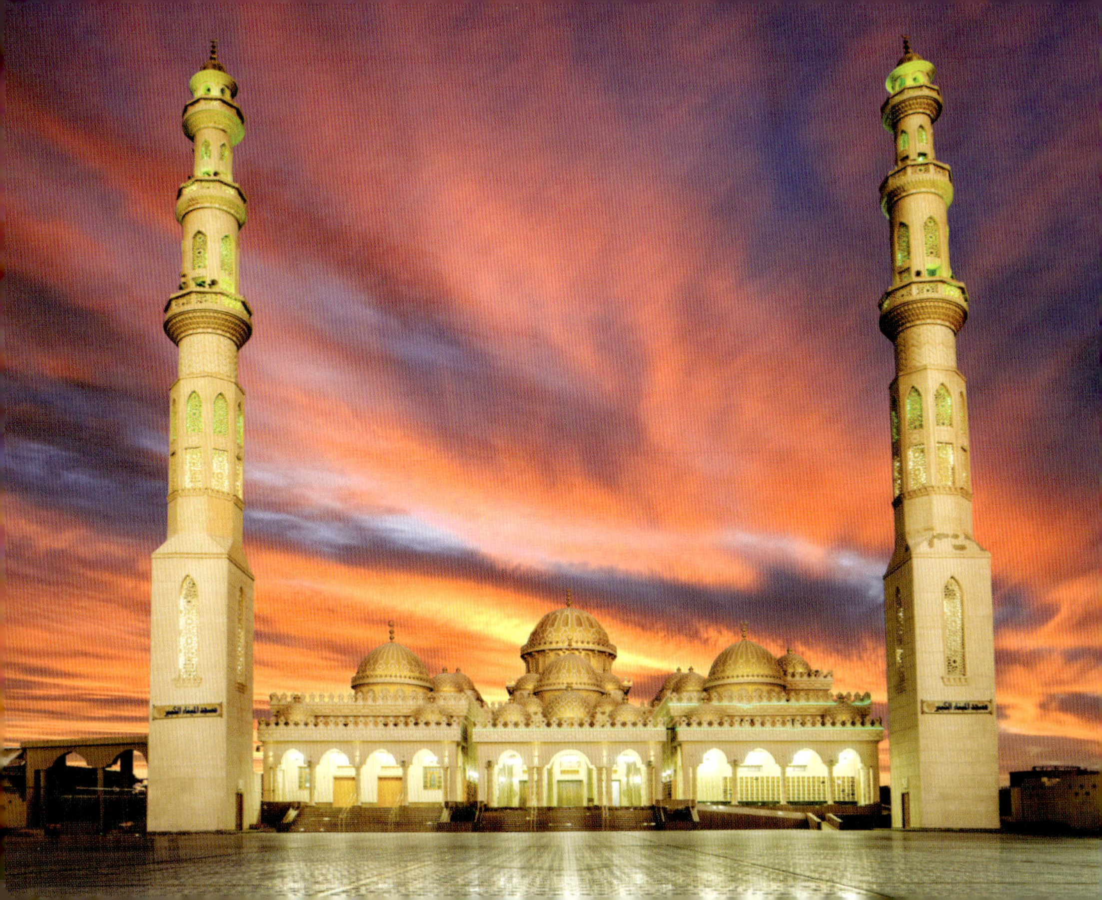

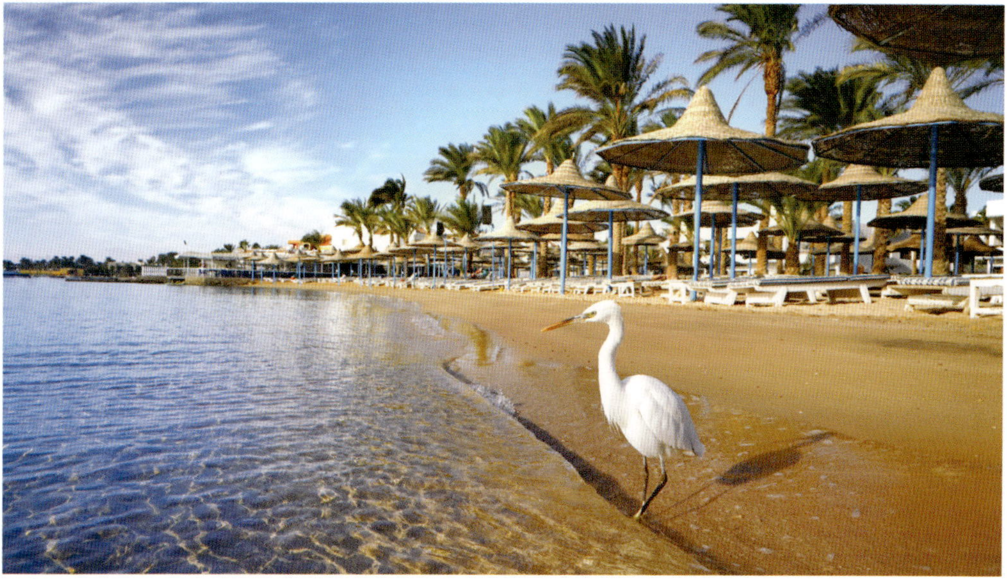

OPPOSITE:

El Mina Mosque, Hurghada

This spectacular mosque is a new addition to the skyline of Hurghada. It opened in 2012 and was created to serve both the local community and to be a destination for tourists to display the best of modern Islamic art and architecture.

ABOVE:

Hurghada Beaches

The coastline around Hurghada is peppered with beach resorts. Hurghada has grown from a small fishing village into the largest resort on the Red Sea. Its warm waters, year-round sunshine and famous nightlife draws visitors from Egypt and abroad.

Marsa Alam, Red Sea Coast

One of the most popular beaches for world travellers in Egypt, Marsa Alam is no longer a secret paradise. With its fine and golden sandy shore touching crystal-clear water and backed by pristine flora, Marsa Alam is the surely the idea of a heavenly beach. This exotic haven is on the southern shores of the Red Sea. Step into the waters and find a tropical aquarium around yourself.

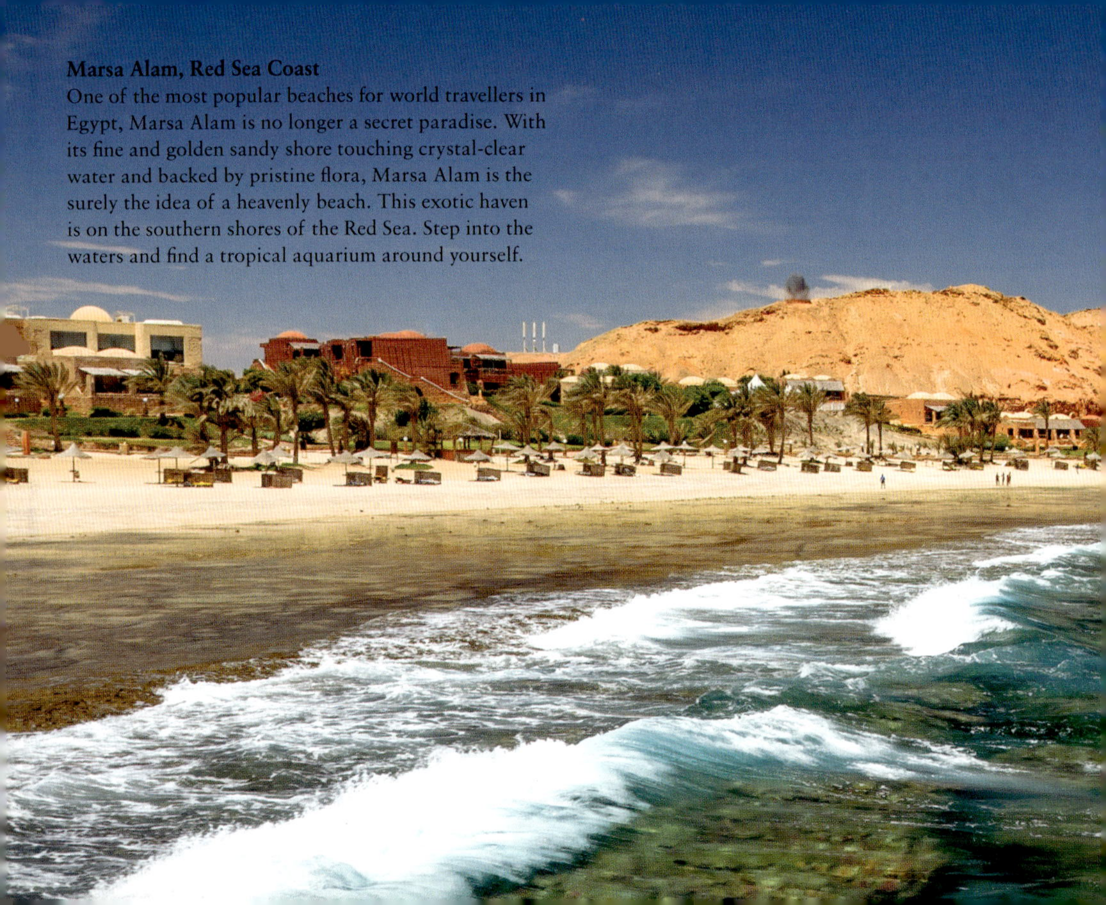

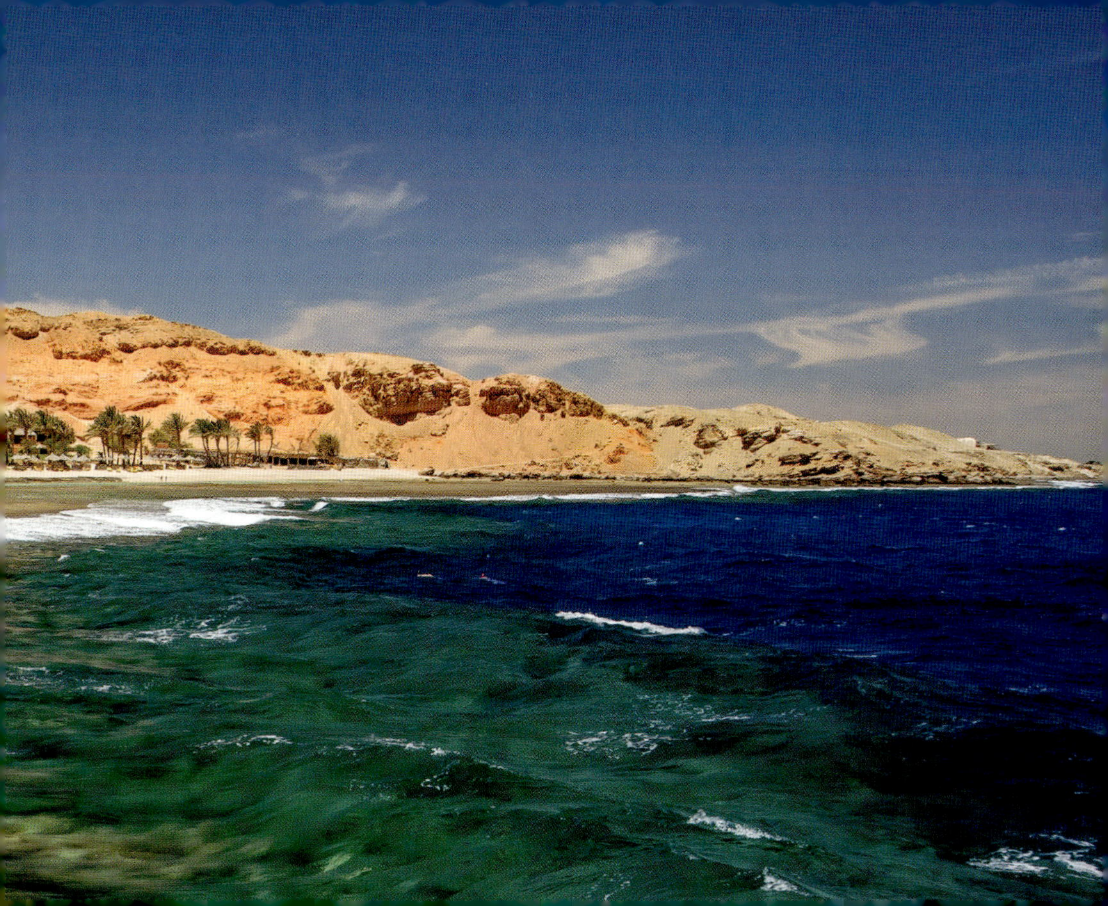

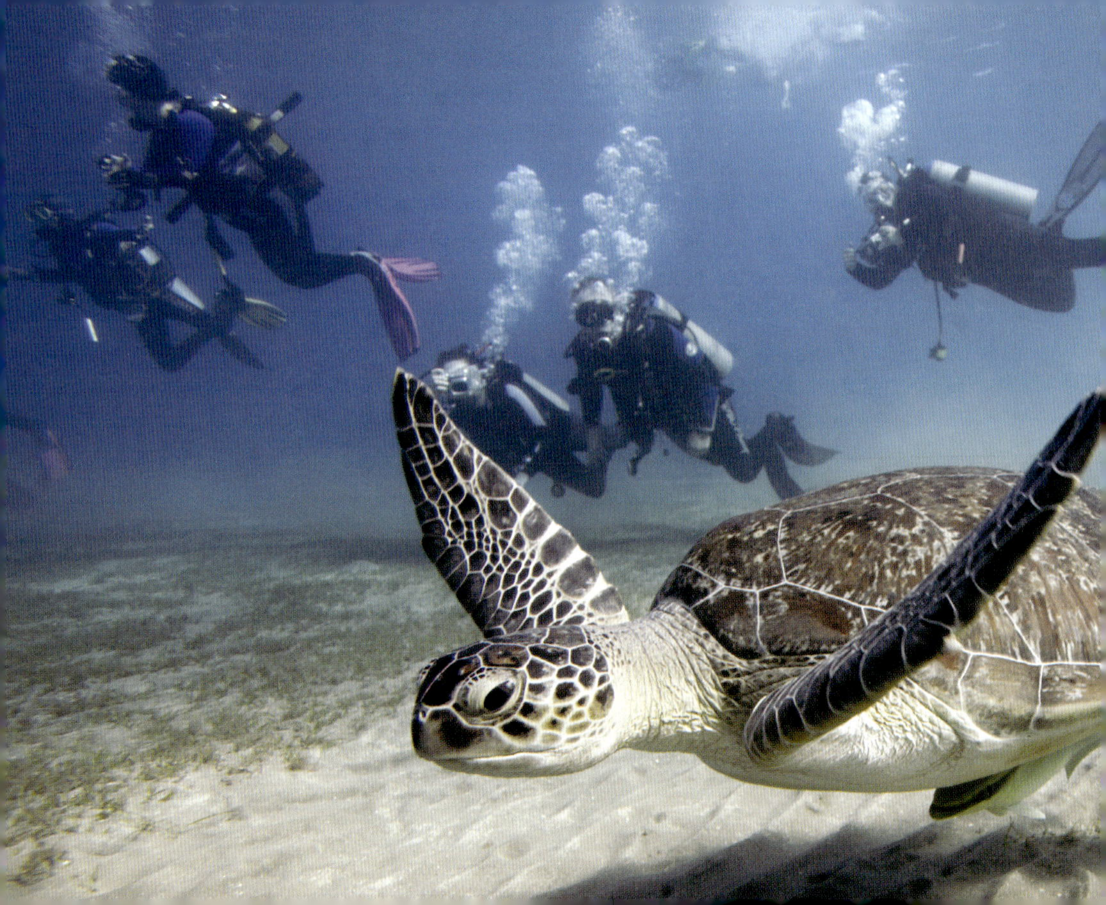

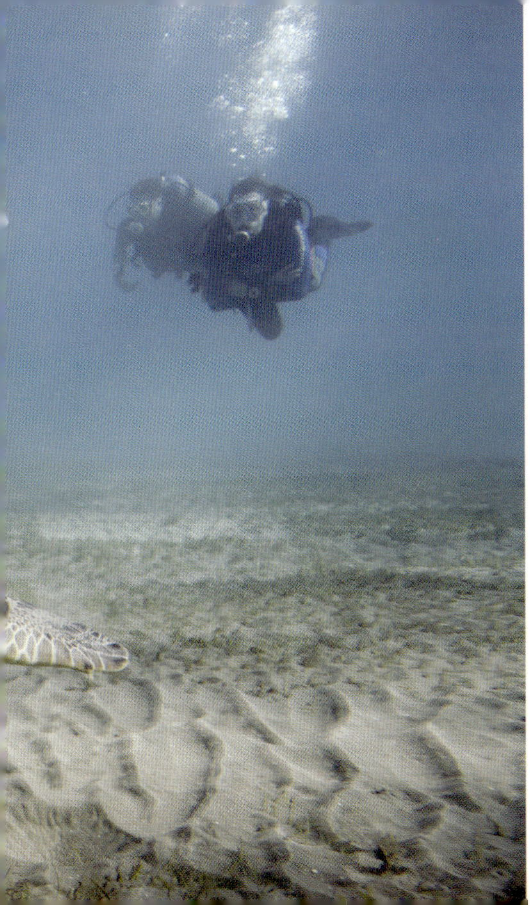

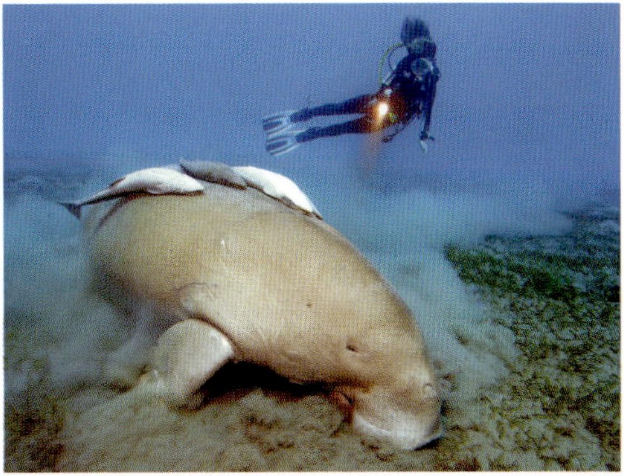

LEFT AND ABOVE:

Marsa Alam, Red Sea Coast

The Red Sea has one of the richest marine ecosystems on Earth, and its waters and coral reefs have attracted divers for many years. The Red Sea is home to five of the seven types of sea turtle and these friendly sea animals are on any diver's list of best things to swim with. Turtles lay their eggs on the many remote beaches along the Red Sea, which stretches beyond Egypt's own borders. You can also expect to see dugongs (above).

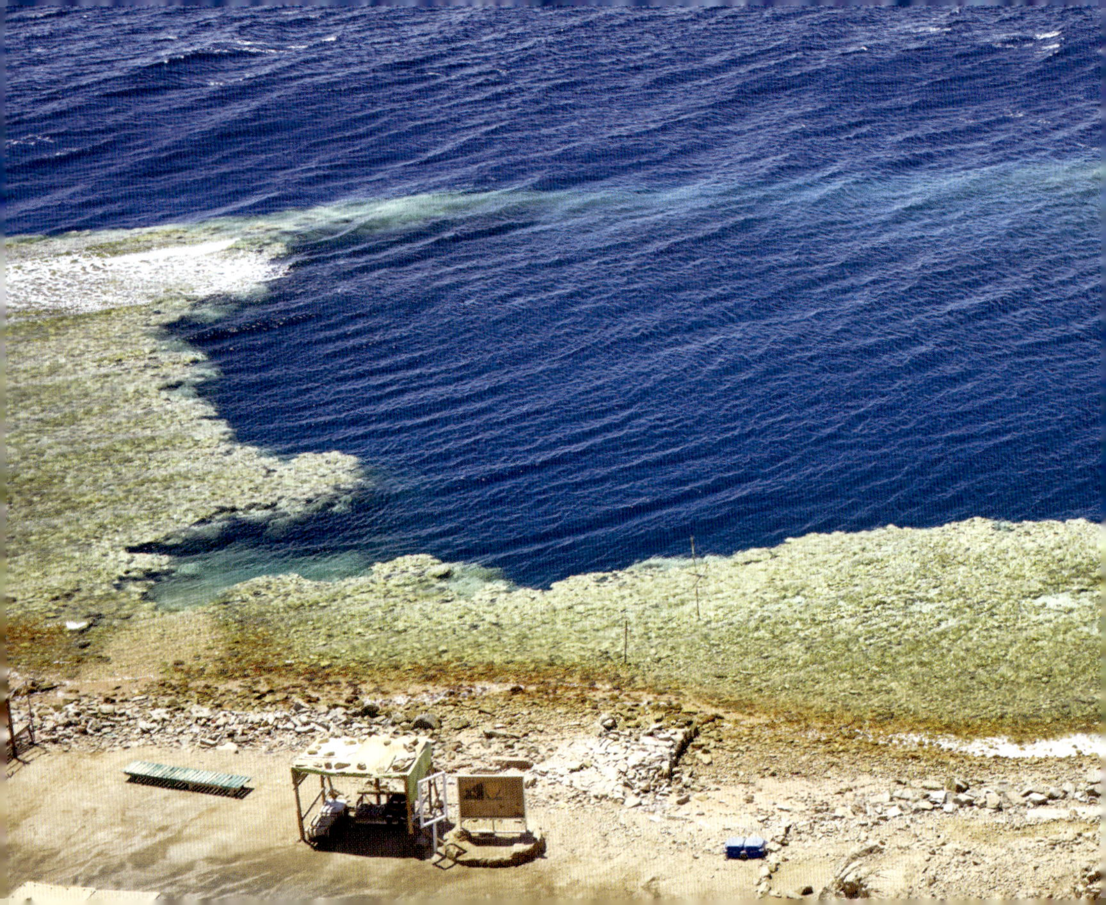

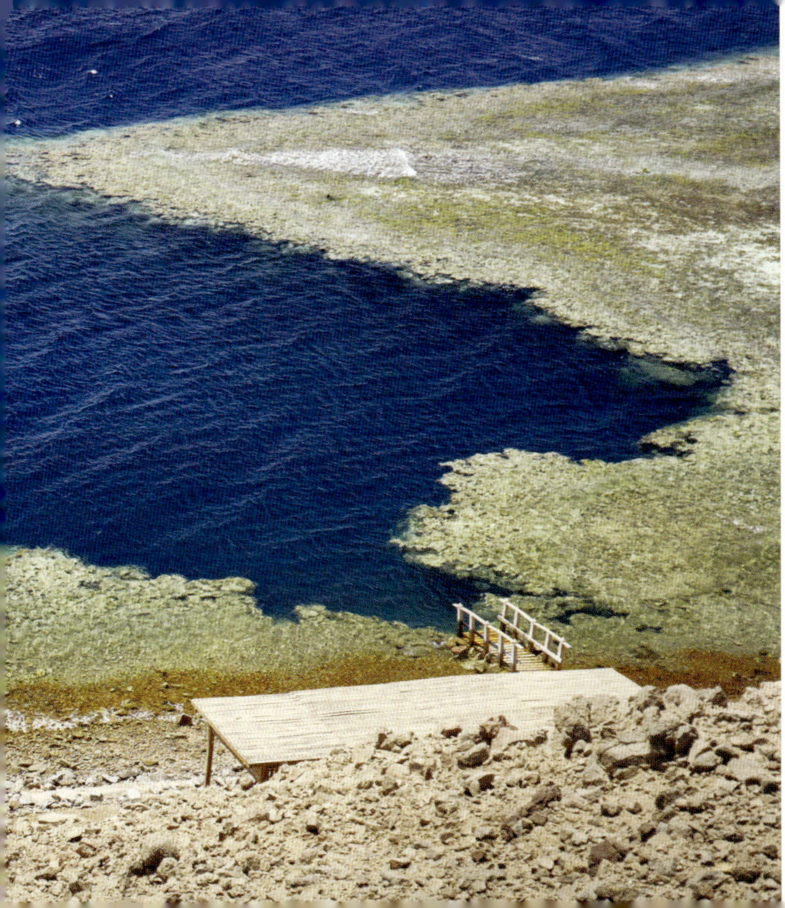

Blue Hole, Dahab
North of Dahab lies one of the most famous and dangerous dive sites on Earth. The Blue Hole provides the ultimate challenge for divers and freedivers. Below the surface lie coral treasures and sea life to a depth of more than 914m (3000ft). This can only be accessed by swimming through a narrow tunnel which has proved fatal to many divers in recent times.

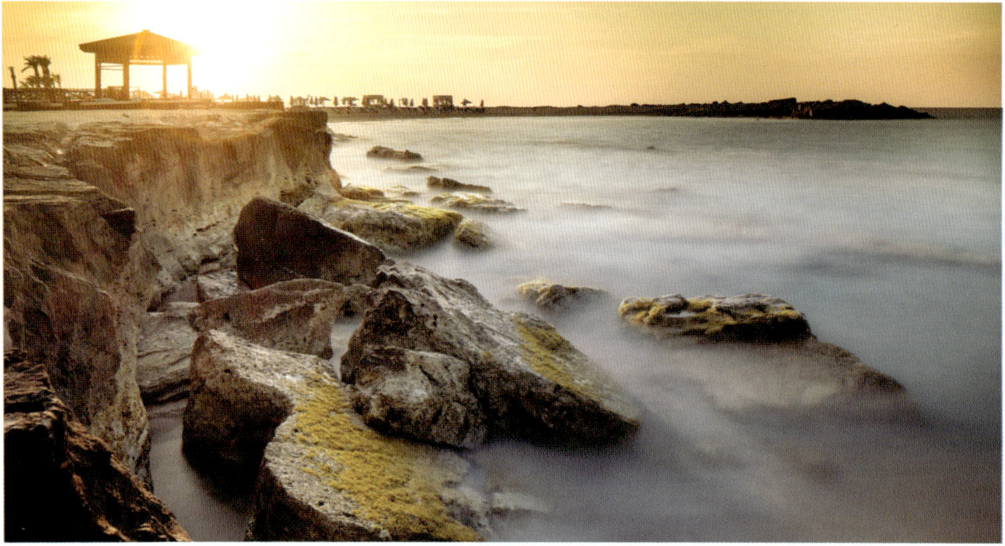

ABOVE:

Marsa Alam, Red Sea Coast

Around Marsa Alam old town are many new resorts and hotels providing a luxurious form of escape in winter, including a championship golf course. For the traveller whose main goal is to enjoy the diving and snorkelling, there are some established beach camps for resting between dives.

OPPOSITE:

Port Ghalib, Red Sea Coast

Close to Marsa Alam's airport is the newly established tourist resort and marina complex of Port Ghalib, a miracle in the desert. The brainchild of a billionaire Kuwaiti business man, Port Ghalib was created from nothing to become one of the New York Times's must-see-destinations worldwide.

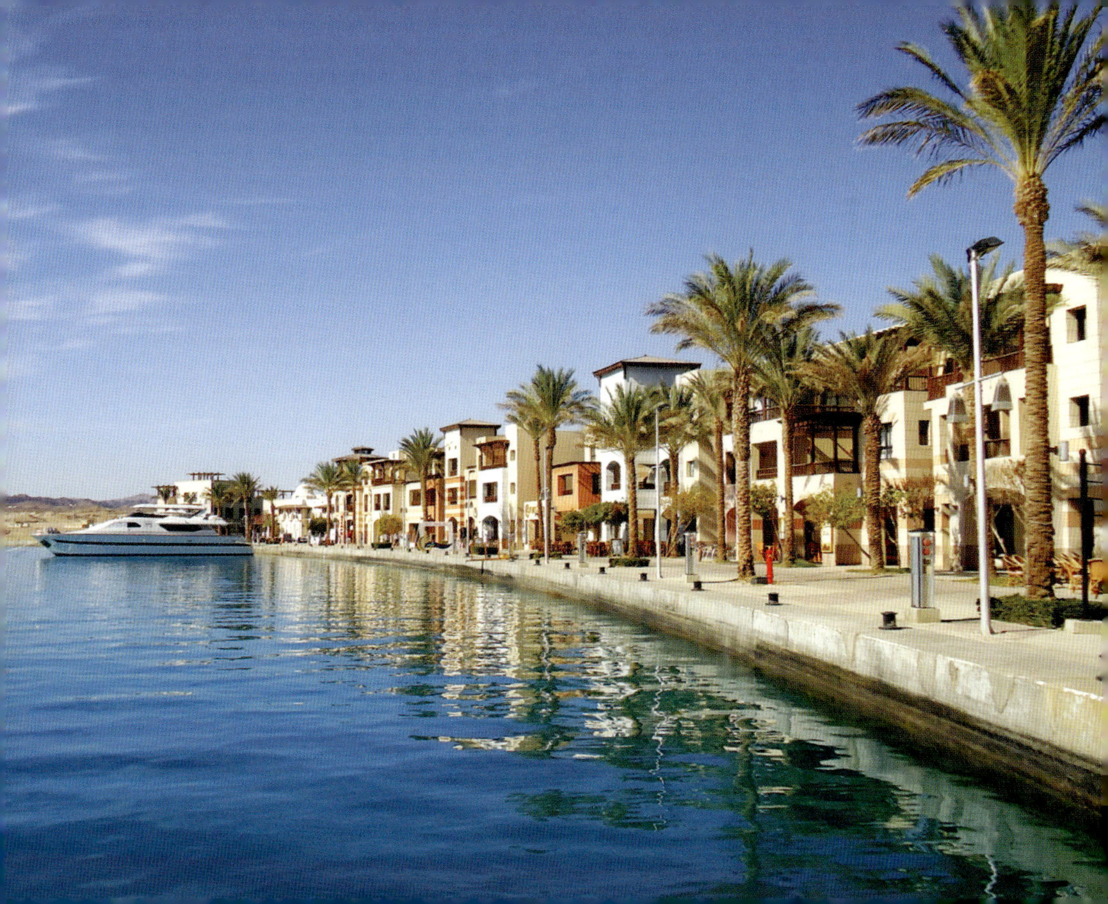

Sharm El Sheikh, Gulf of Aqaba

Sometimes known as the 'City of Peace', Sharm El Sheikh was often of strategic importance in the 20th century. Occupied by Israel in 1956 during the Suez Crisis and again in 1967 during the Six Day War, it was not returned to Egypt until 1982. Now it is a large and popular tourist destination. It provides a useful stopping-off point for visitors intending to explore the Sinai Peninsula.

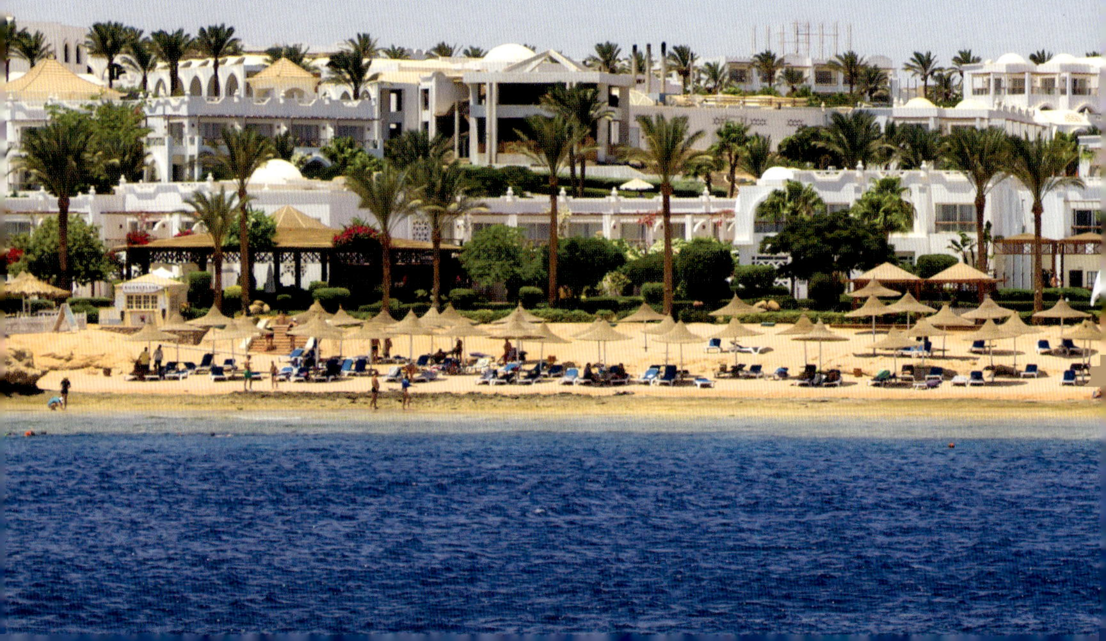

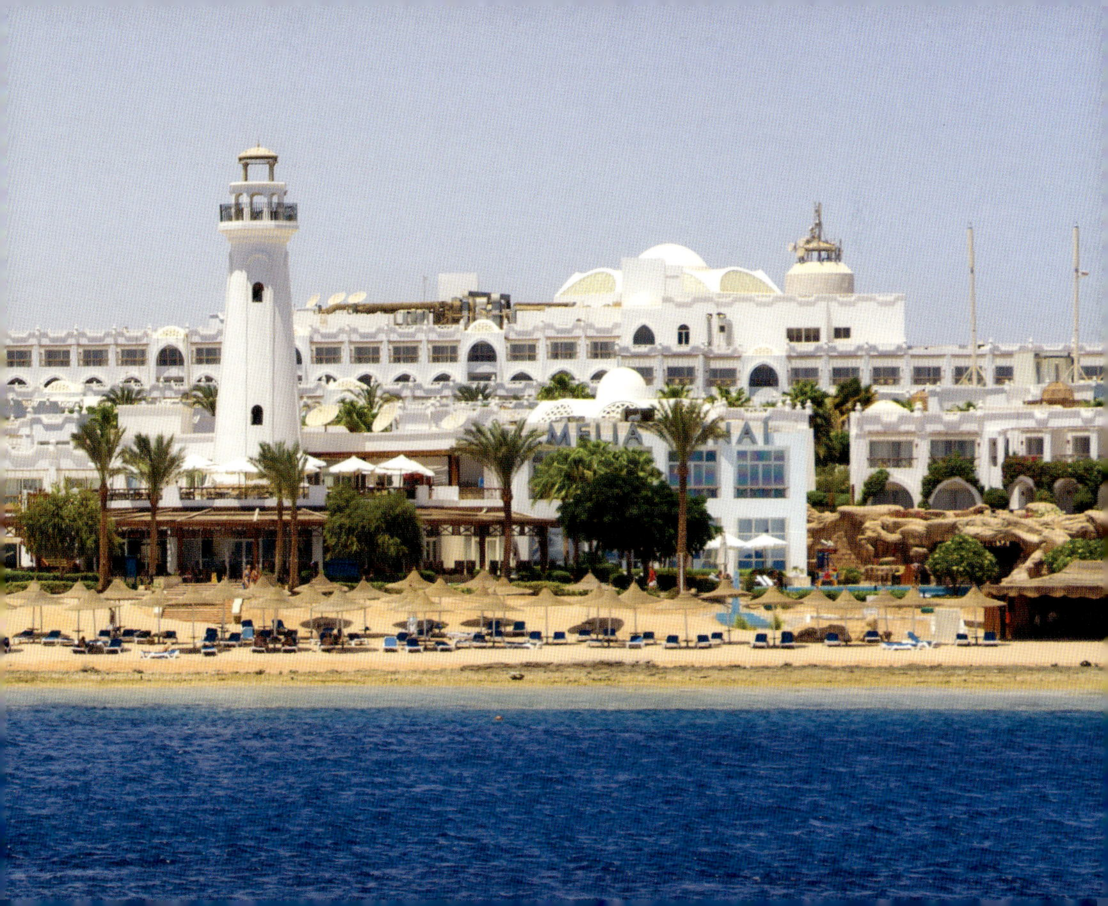

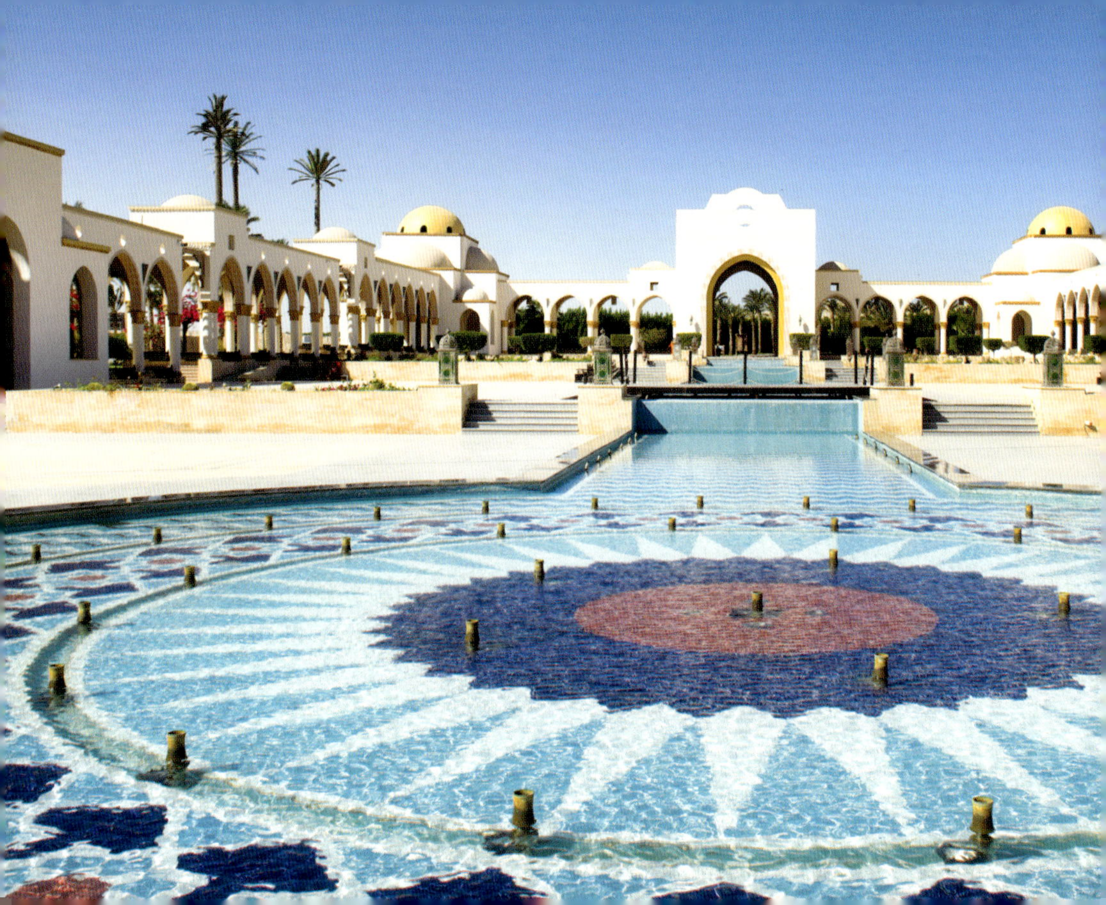

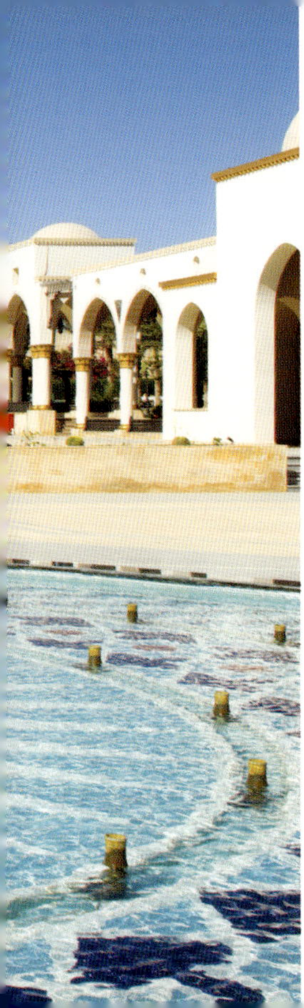

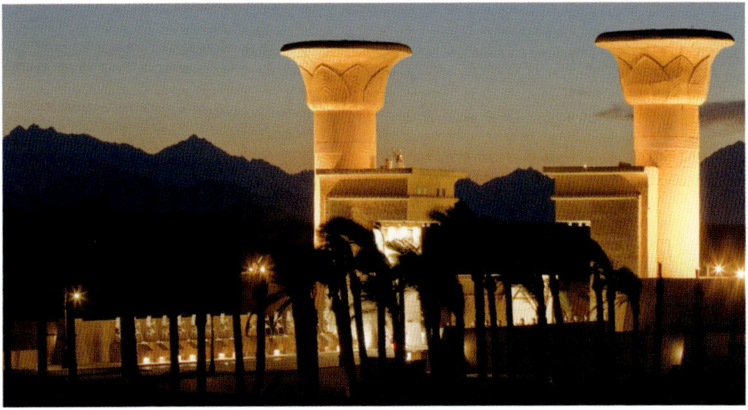

LEFT:

Sahl Hasheesh, Red Sea Coast

A planned community and resort development, Sahl Hasheesh lies 24 km (15 miles) south of Hurghada. The architectural theme relies heavily on the influence of Moorish Spain.

ABOVE:

Sahl Hasheesh, Red Sea Coast

As you approach this new resort from Hurghada, you are left in no doubt that you are in Egypt. The entrance to Sahl Hasheesh is marked by these two enormous columns, as if arriving at the gateway to a pharaonic temple.

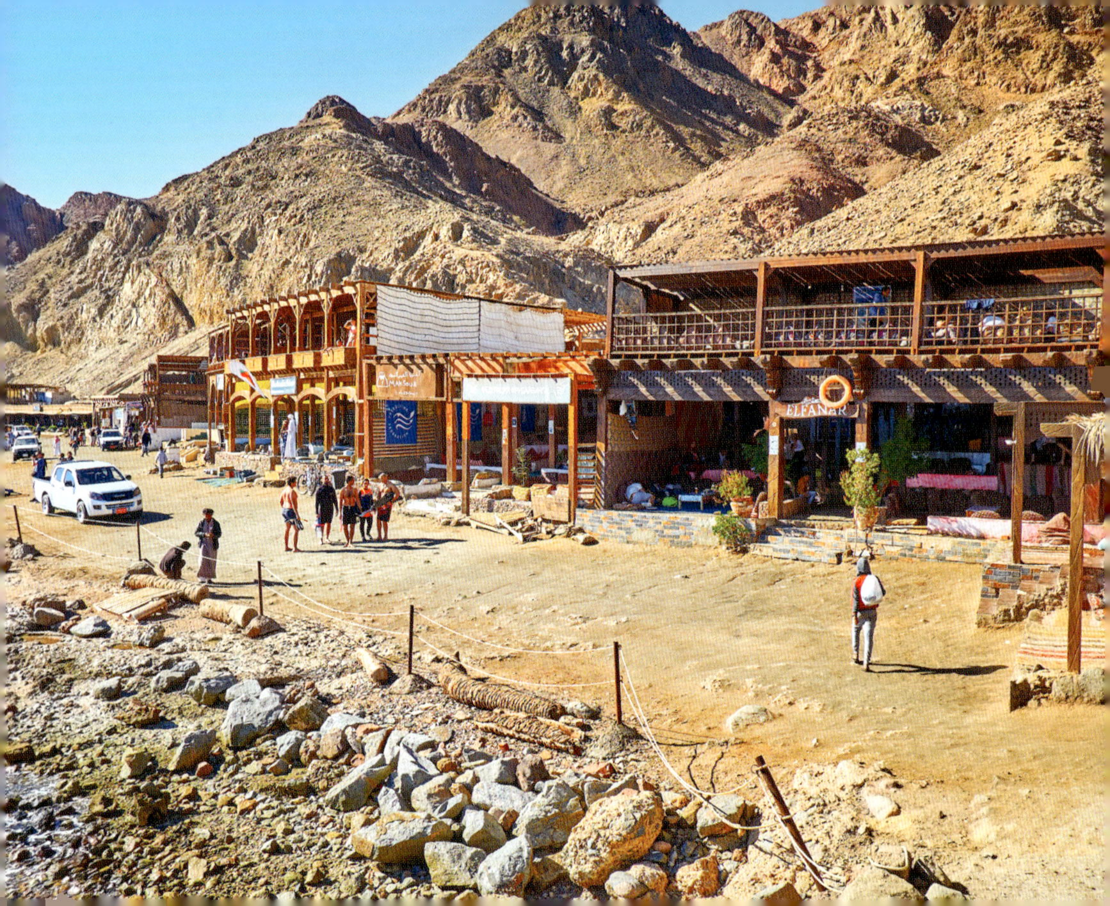
MAKSOUD
ELFANAR

OPPOSITE:

Dahab Village, Sinai

Some 80km (50 miles) north of Sharm El Sheikh is the town of Dahab, for many years an alternative getaway for the younger, independent traveller. Here you can find low price accommodation or you can even sleep on the beach. The waterfront is one line of restaurants, nightclubs and beach huts, all clustered by a sea rich with marine life.

BELOW:

Nuweiba, Sinai Coast

The rich, living coral and constant movement of marine life in the Gulf of Tiran, near Nuweiba, make for some of the best underwater experiences in the world. Here you can swim with, and photograph, schools of brightly coloured fish and the beautiful underwater landscape which blossoms under Egypt's bright sunlight.

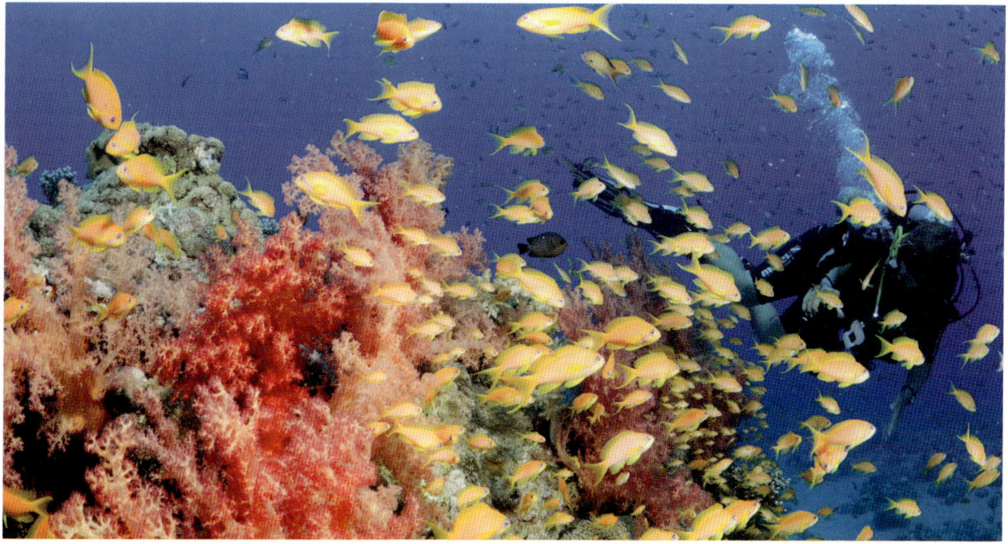

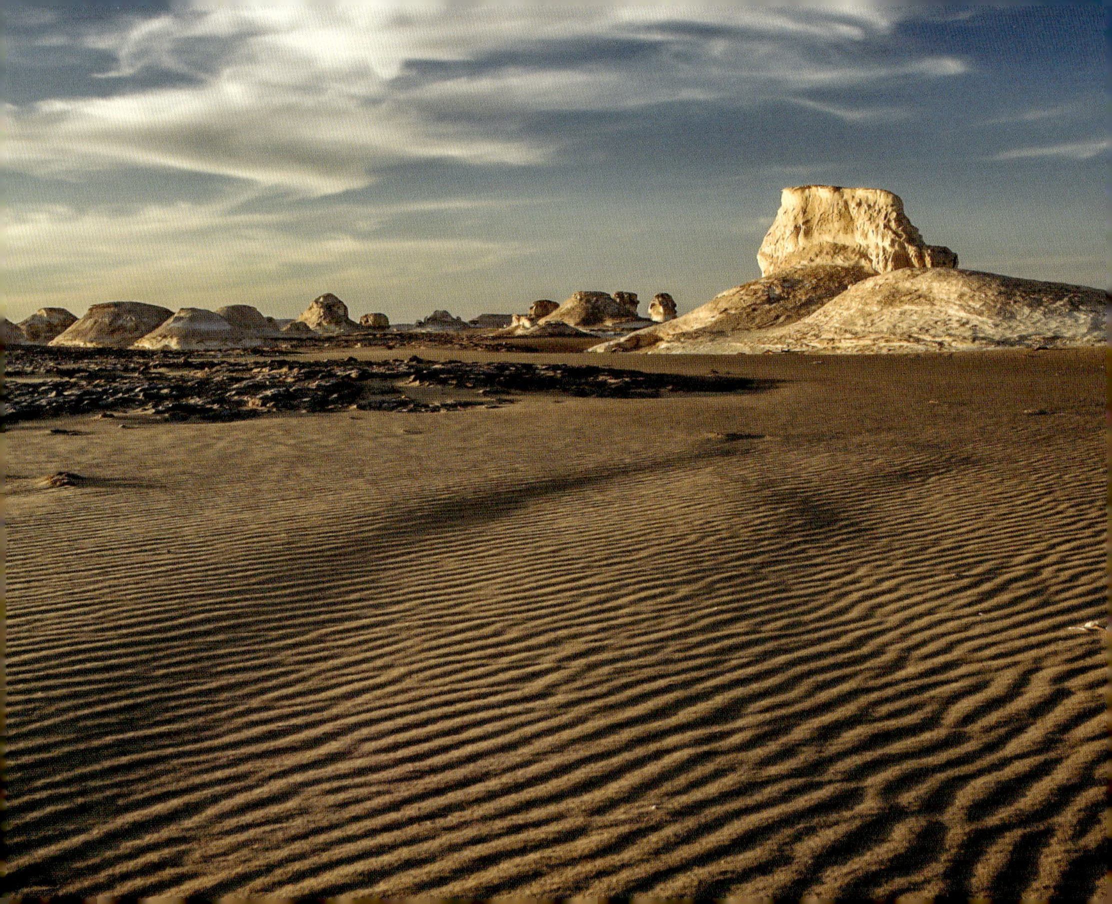

Deserts

Egypt is a desert country, so the urban areas are concentrated close to water, be it fresh or salty. Most visitors see the desert at a distance, perhaps from a Nile cruise boat or from a tour bus. In such cases, the desert may not look inviting, but a hot dusty and monotonous place to avoid. However, the deserts of Egypt are not all the same. Travelling into them and camping out under desert skies provides an unforgettable experience.

In this section you'll get a flavour of the diversity of the deserts, from the surreal rock formations and vivid colours of the White Desert, to the Oasis of Siwa and its pristine, high sand dunes and hot springs. Yet another challenge is found in the mountainous Sinai where the flora and fauna – desert foxes, gazelles, chameleons and birds of prey, along with people – prove that life can thrive in such harsh climates. Also, evidence of ancient Egyptian, Coptic and Roman era life, as well as many of the region's later invaders, found far from the Nile Valley helps us imagine the routes once traversed across these beautiful desolate expanses.

OPPOSITE:

Farafra, Western Desert

Farafra is the gateway to the White Desert. Its eerie white rock formations and sands are a unique mix of colours and the desert is a wonderful place to camp.

BELOW:

Lake Qarun, Fayoum Oasis, near Cairo

The Fayoum is an area, rather than an oasis, settled in a basin which hosts some of Egypt's most fertile land. Lake Qarun is its largest obvious feature, reaching more than 48km (30 miles) in length. The region is fed by Nile waters, rather than springs, and its towns and villages are now home to some three million Egyptians.

RIGHT:

Wadi al-Rayyan, Fayoum Oasis

This valley area has been filled with waters drained from the Fayoum to create two lakes around which sits the Wadi al-Rayyan nature protectorate, an area rich in animal and bird life which attracts visitors on safari. Dune driving, camping, swimming and even hang-gliding are possible here.

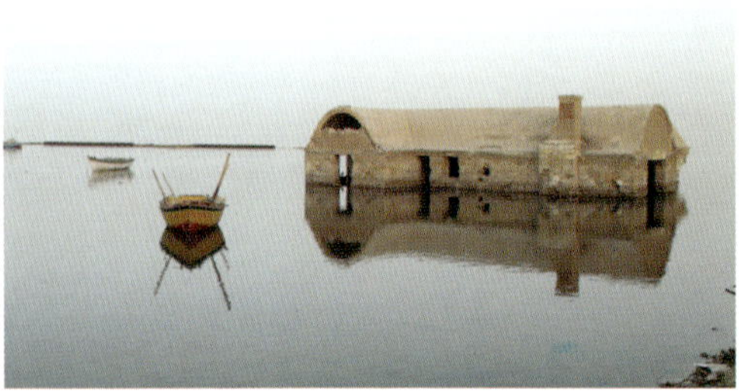

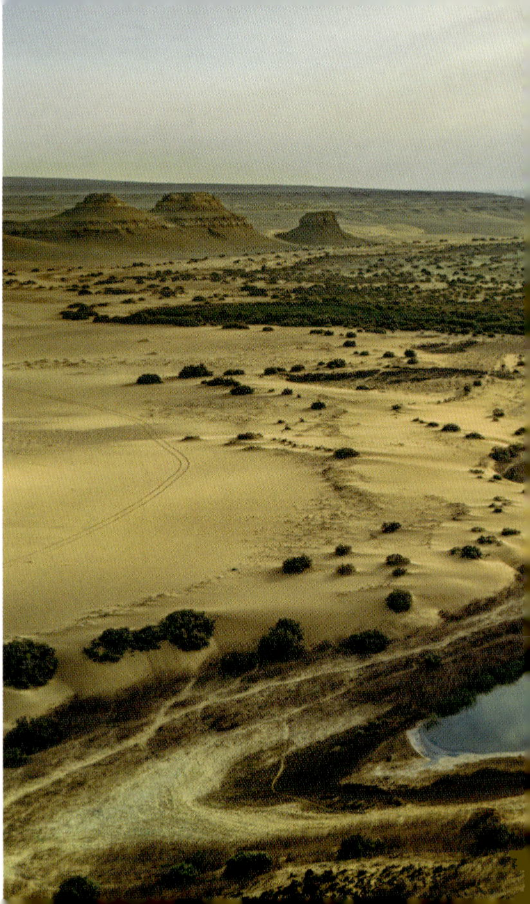

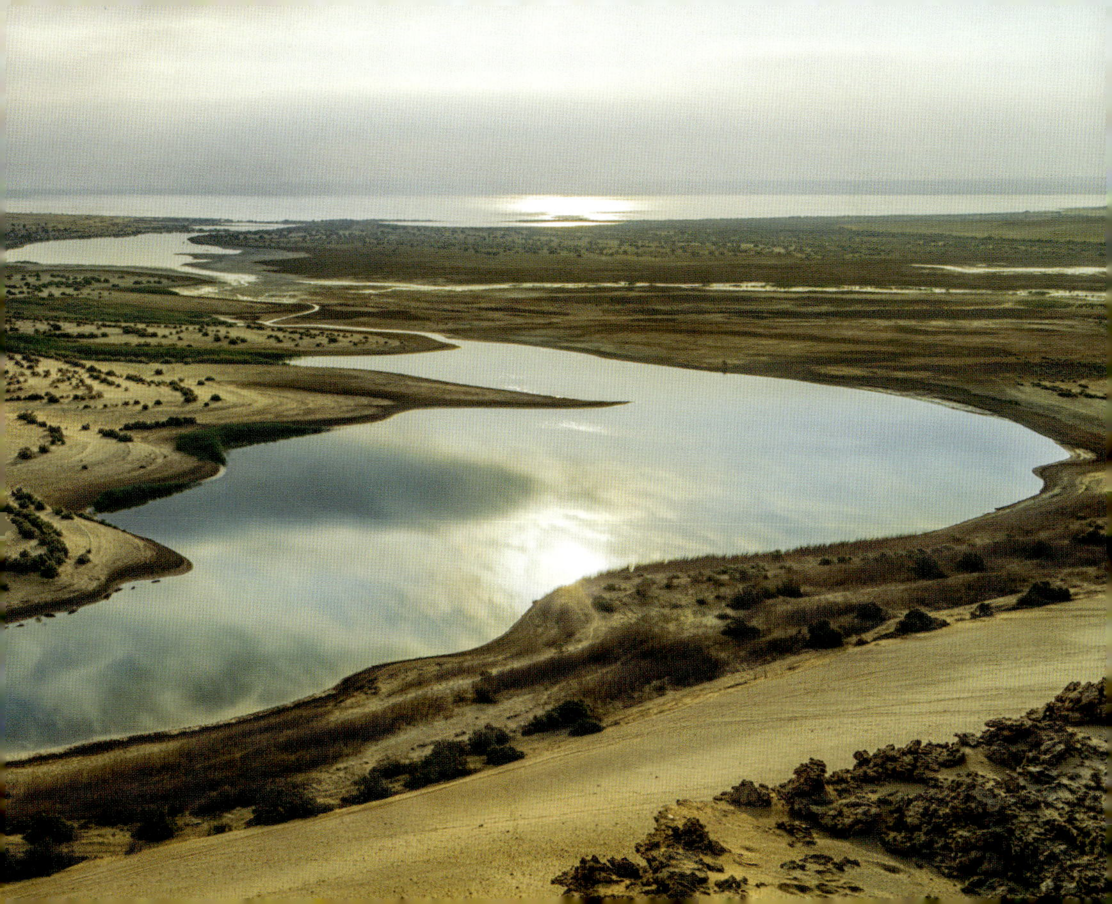

Wadi al-Rayyan, Fayoum Oasis

The lakes and inlets which make up Wadi al -Rayyan are surrounded by deserts and mountains. This is a fascinating region for those interested in geology and prehistory, as the area is rich in marine fossils. Sport loving visitors can enjoy sandboarding down soft dunes into the clear waters shown here.

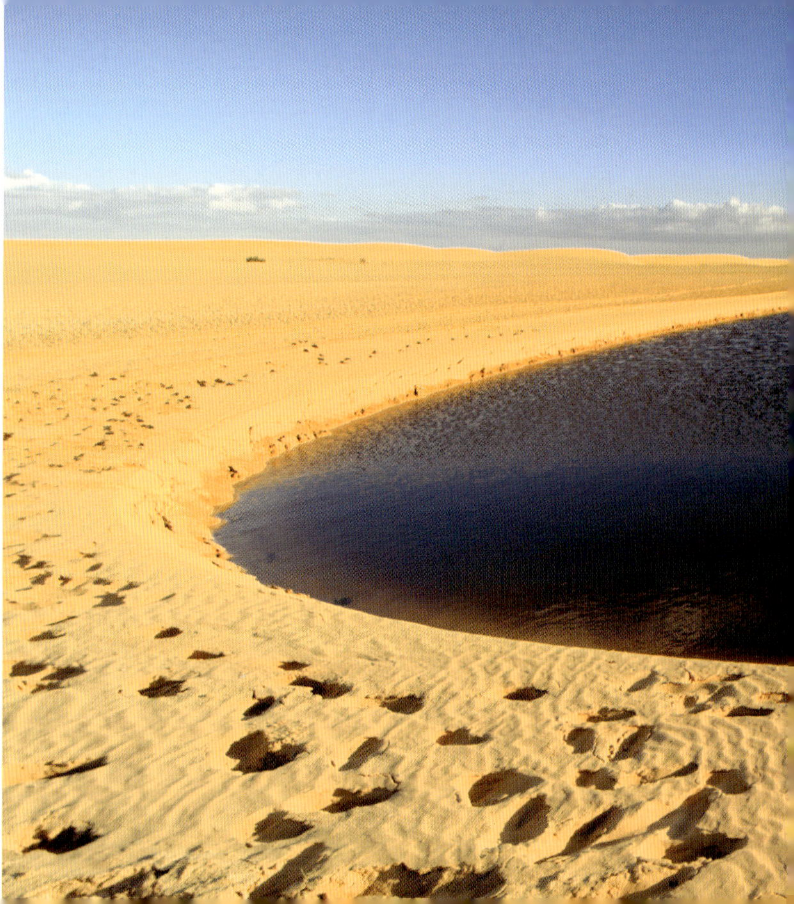

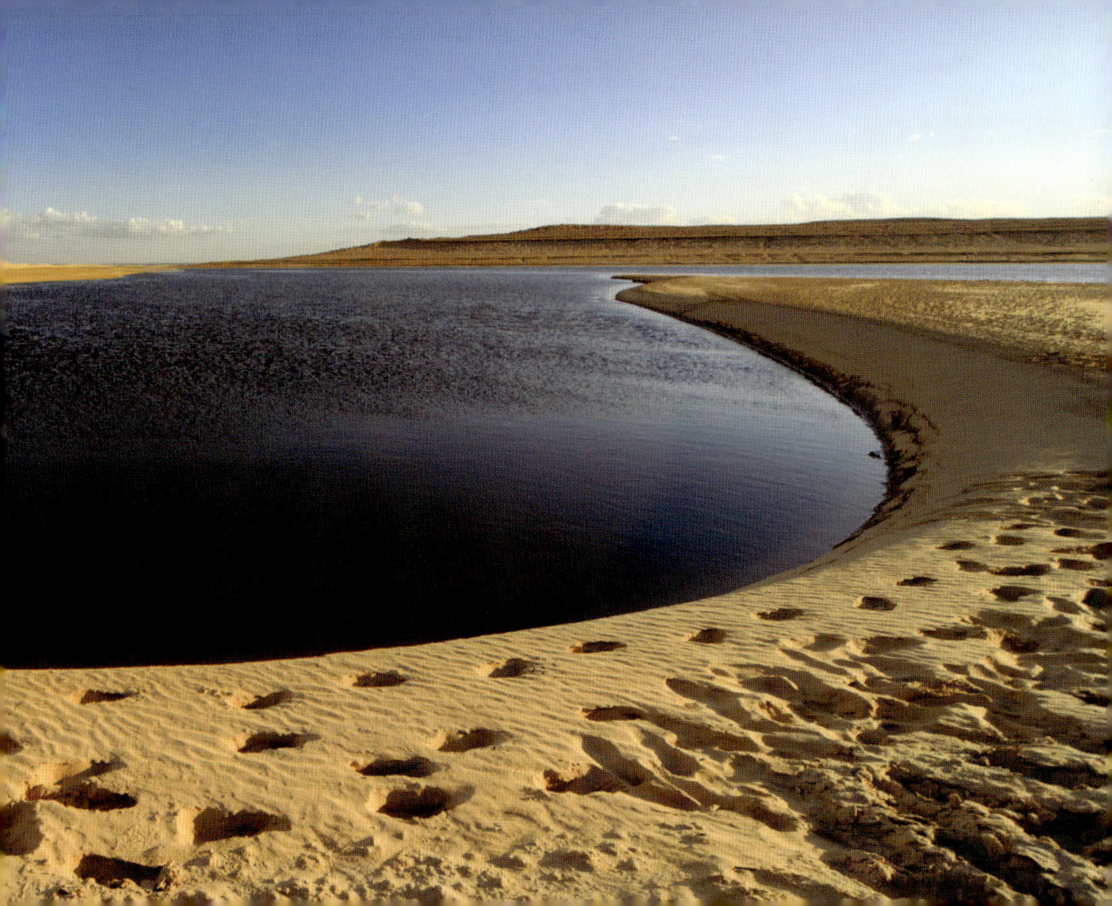

BOTH PHOTOGRAPHS:

Monastery of St. Simeon, Aswan

This fortress-like early Christian monastery sits across the Nile high on the west bank near Aswan. Within its large enclosure lived a community of 300 monks who welcomed the hundreds of pilgrims passing through. The complex was large enough to feed and house them all. These pilgrims would travel south to attempt the conversion of Nubians to Christianity.

St. Simeon is the oldest such site in Egypt. First built in the 7th century, it was reconstructed in the 11th century, although destroyed by Saladin's army in 1173. Within it remain some very early wall paintings, including depictions of the Virgin.

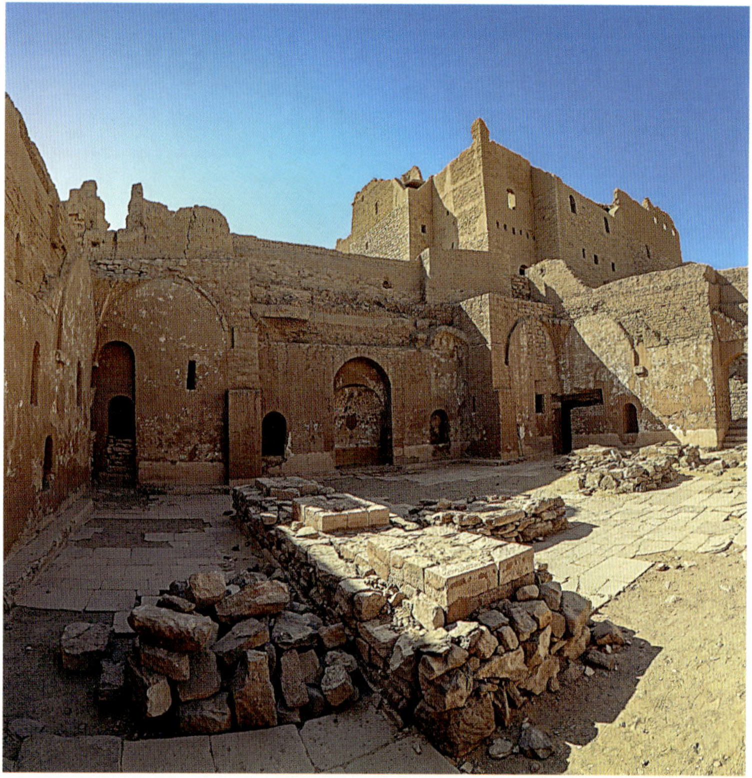

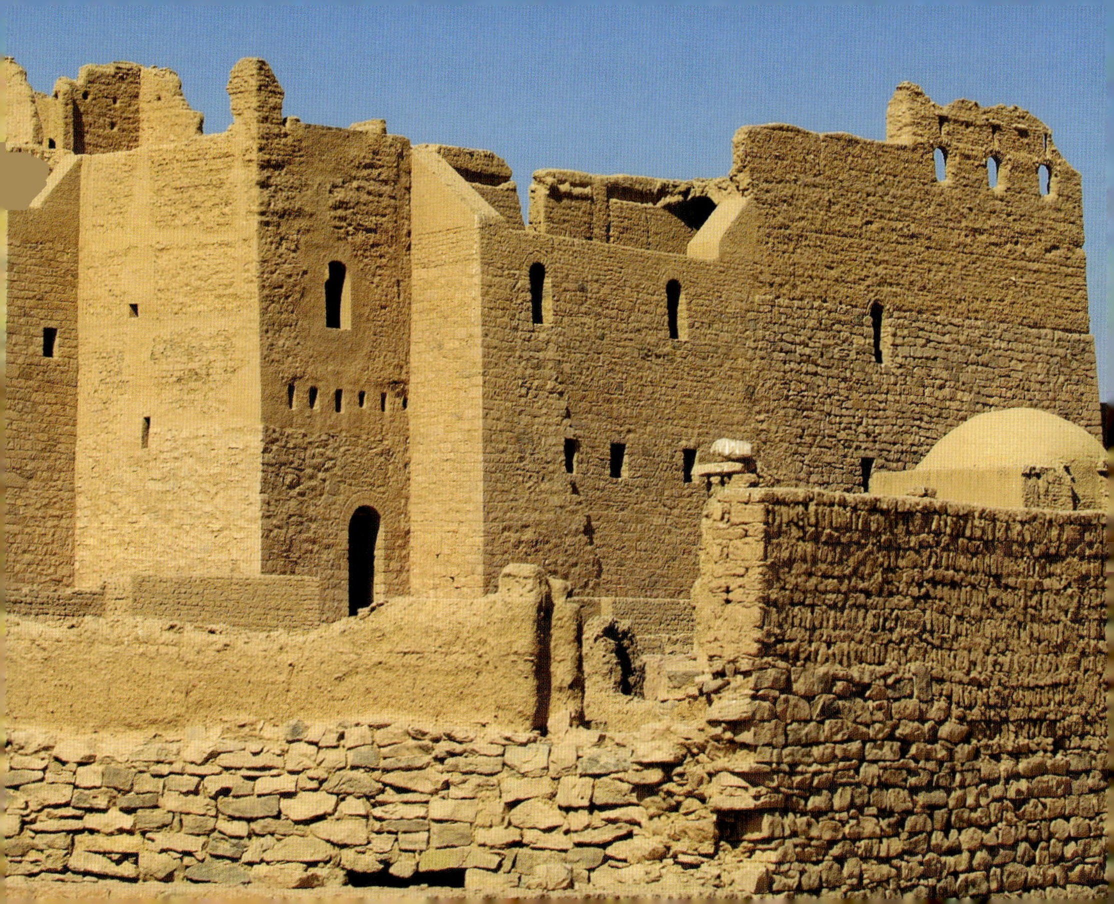

BELOW:

Bahariya Oasis, Western Desert

Bahariya is an oasis some 400km (250 miles) south east of Cairo and its main town, Bawiti is shown below. It is possible to bathe in the many natural springs in the area.

RIGHT:

Gebel El Dist, Bahariya Oasis

Gebel El Dist mountain has a distinctive pyramid shape and its size makes it visible for miles around. This area is rich in fossils and dinosaur bones were found here a century ago.

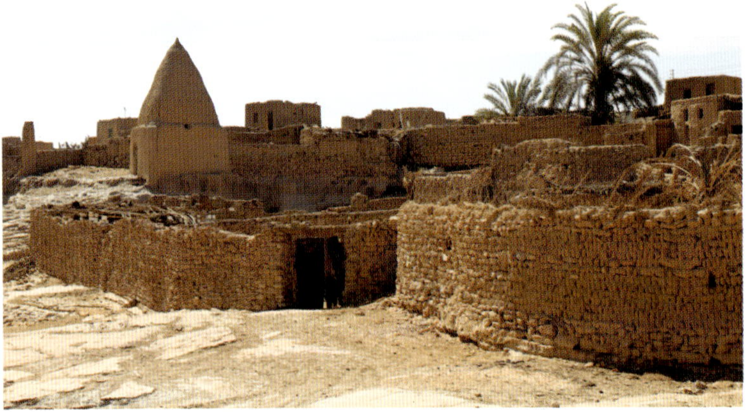

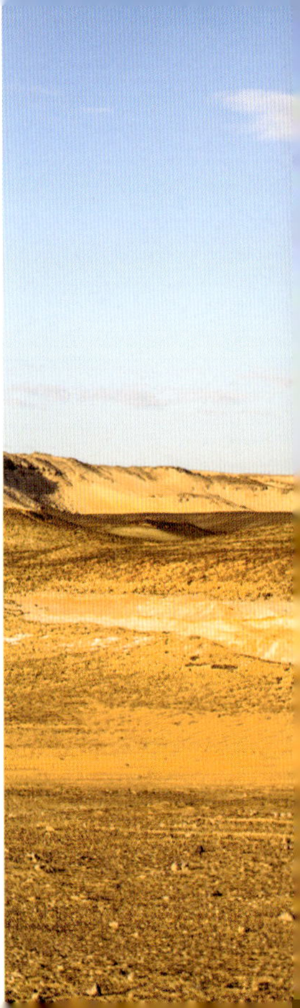

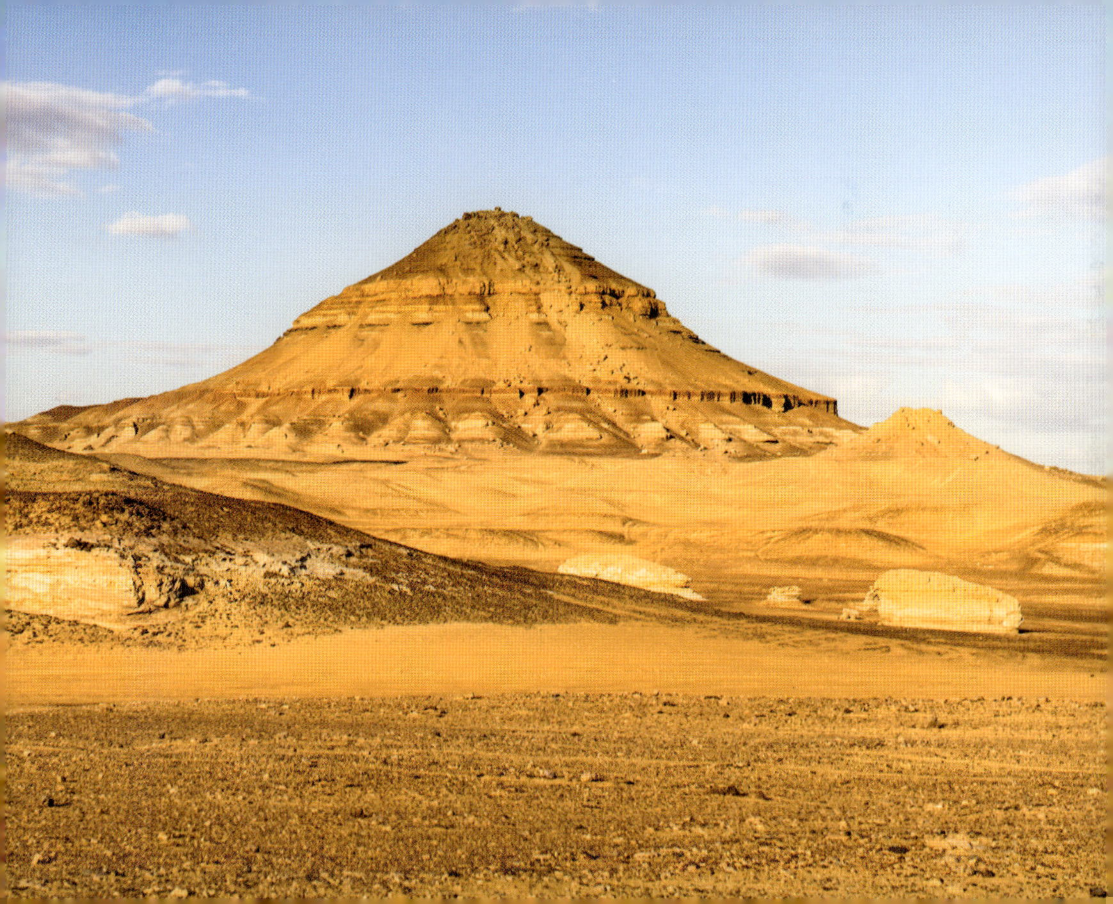

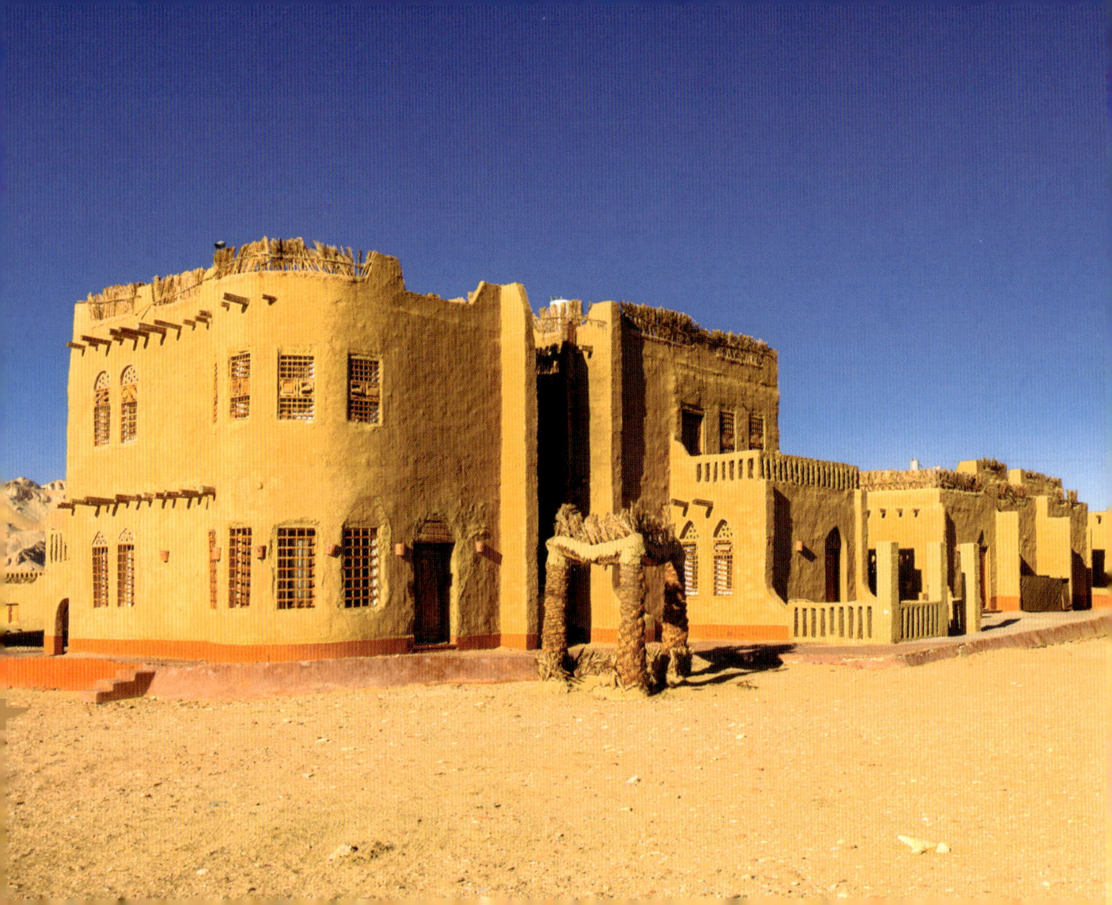

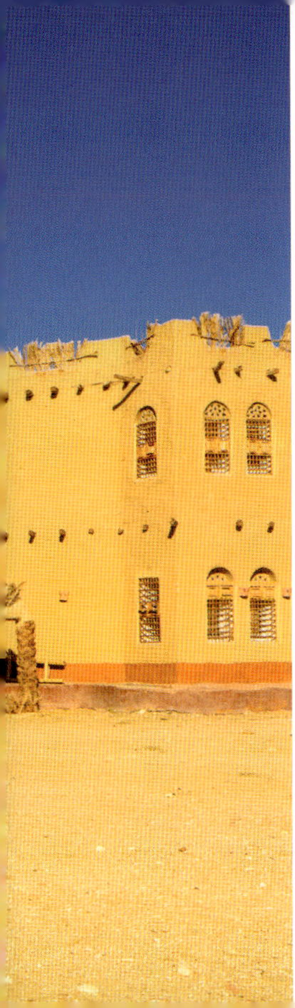

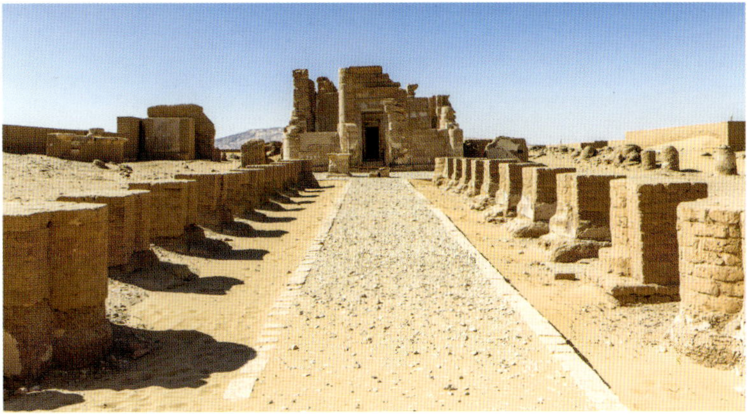

LEFT:

Al-Qasr, Western Desert

This fascinating medieval town and its sights are part of the area known as Dakhla Oasis, which is a particularly beautiful valley area rich in agricultural land, springs and date palms. A walk around the narrow, winding streets of Al-Qasr are a trip back in time.

ABOVE:

Deir el-Hagar, Dakhla Oasis

Close to Al Qasr are older sites of interest, including a Roman cemetery. Also close by is Deir el-Hagar, a temple built in the era of the Roman Emperor Nero in the 1st century CE and dedicated to three Theban deities – Mut, Amun and Khonsu.

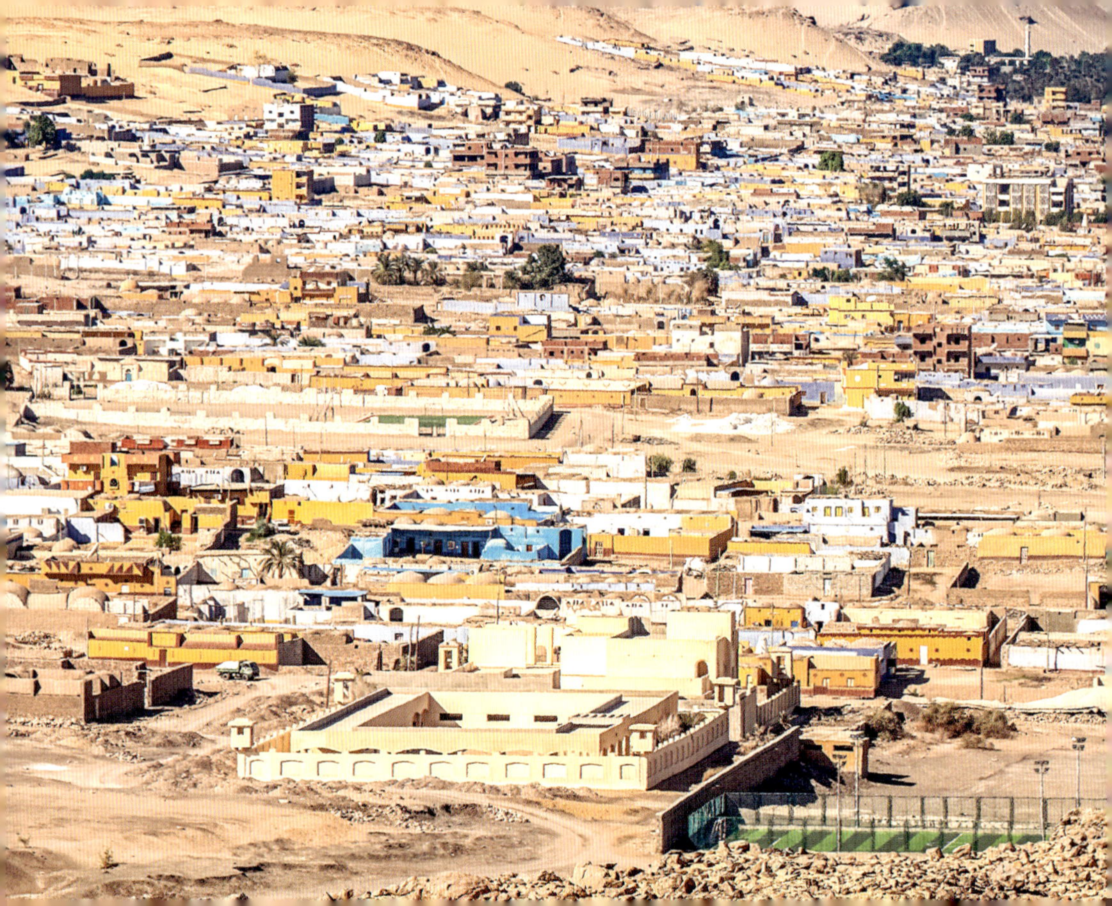

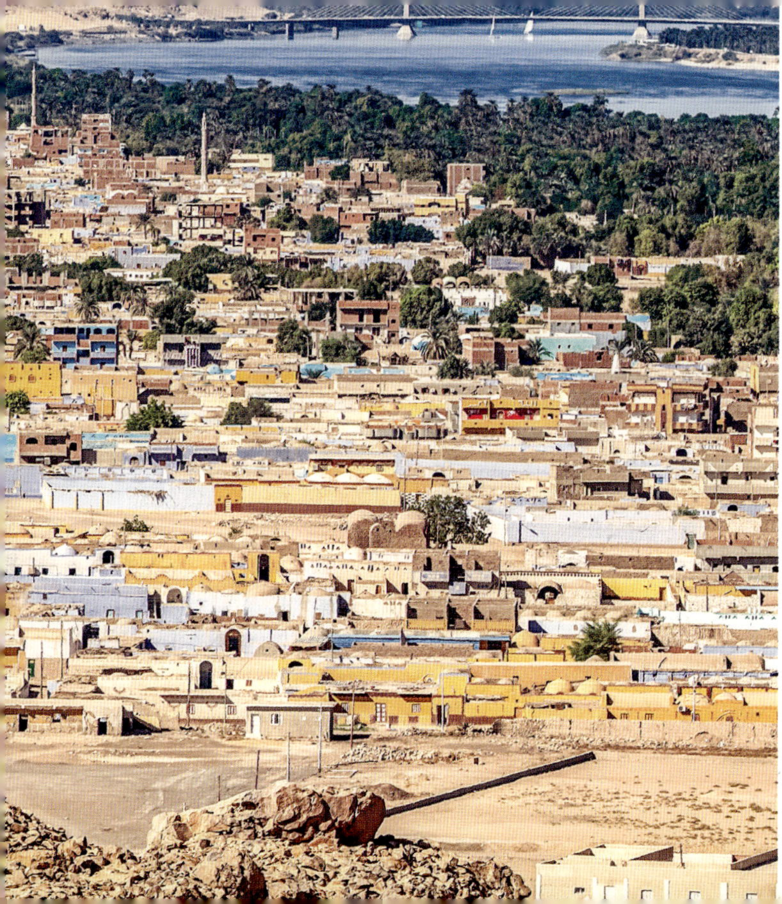

Nubian Town, Aswan
The building of Aswan Bridge added a vital connection for business and development in Upper Egypt. Aswan's growing population and Egypt's future plans for Nubia have seen major new investment in the region. Plans include a drive towards more schools, universities and technology companies as a way to build a workforce for the future.

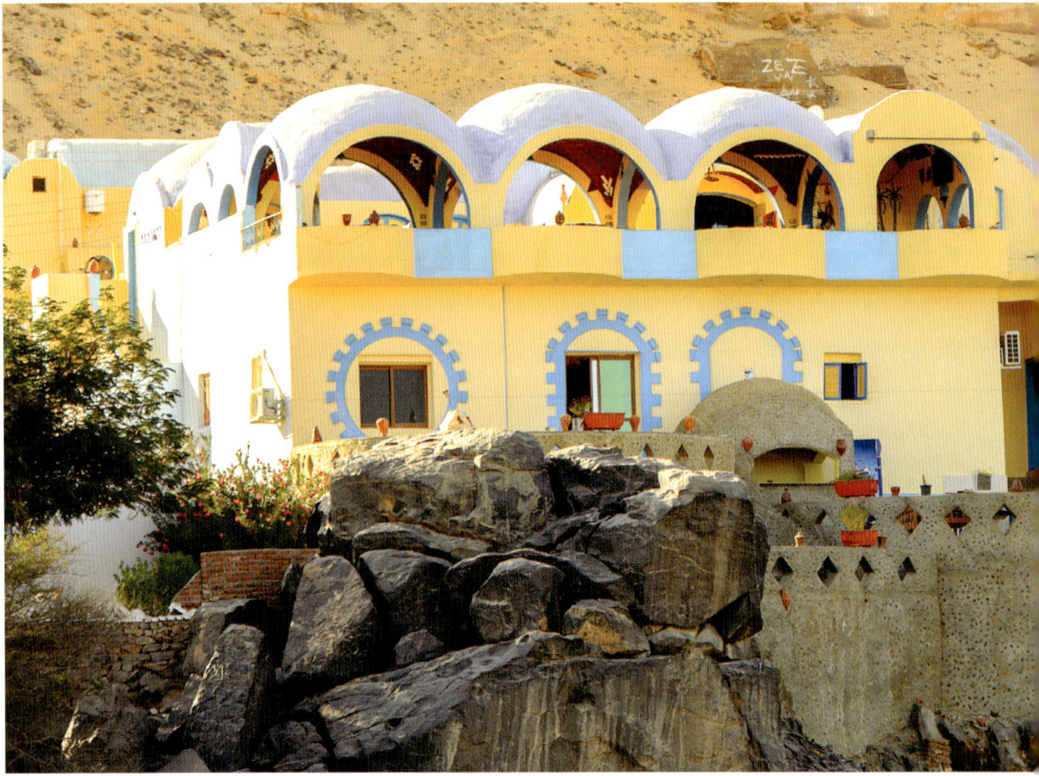

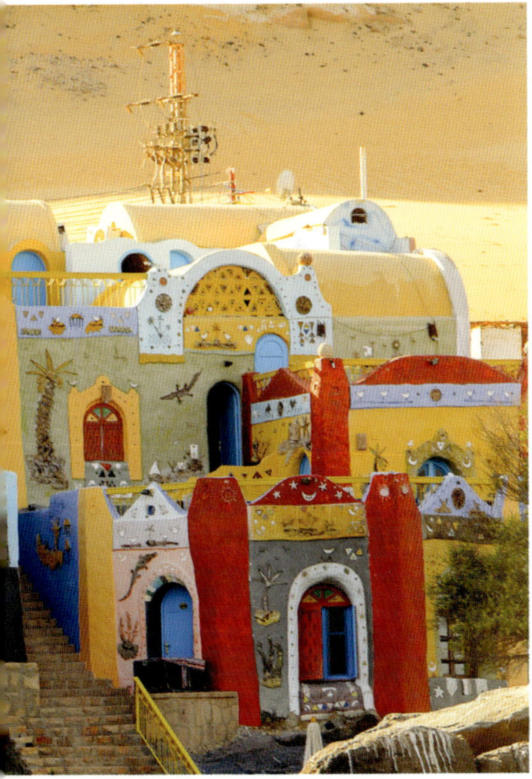

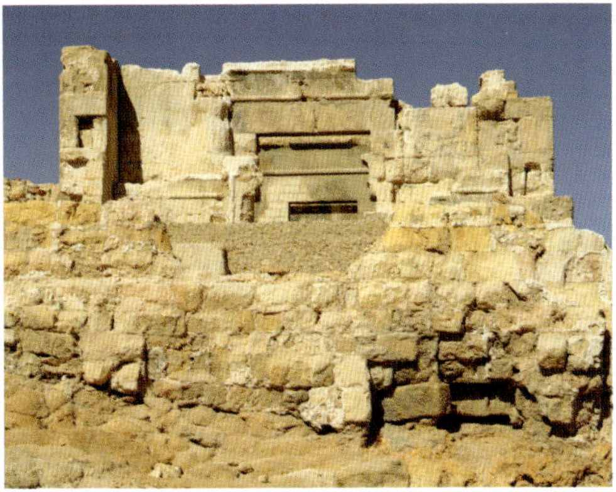

LEFT:

Nubian Village, Aswan

The visitor to Aswan will see the more traditional side of Nubian life. Several Nubian villages are accessible by boat from Aswan and their colourful painted houses and friendly people make you a welcome guest. Sit by the Nile and drink tea, do some shopping or enjoy a desert camel ride.

ABOVE:

Temple of the Oracle, Siwa Oasis, Western Desert

The Temple of the Oracle was built more than 2,500 years ago. One of the major cult sites of the ancient world, the Oracle is believed to have been visited by Alexander the Great in 332 BC.

Red Sea Coast Mountains

As you travel by the Red Sea and through the Sinai desert you will encounter miles and miles of deep red and orange mountains leading to the water's edge or astride deep valleys. This spectacular and inhospitable landscape has been the home of bedouins and a place of religious retreat for centuries. Today you may take walking tours, or trek through them on camel or horse to remote camps in national parks.

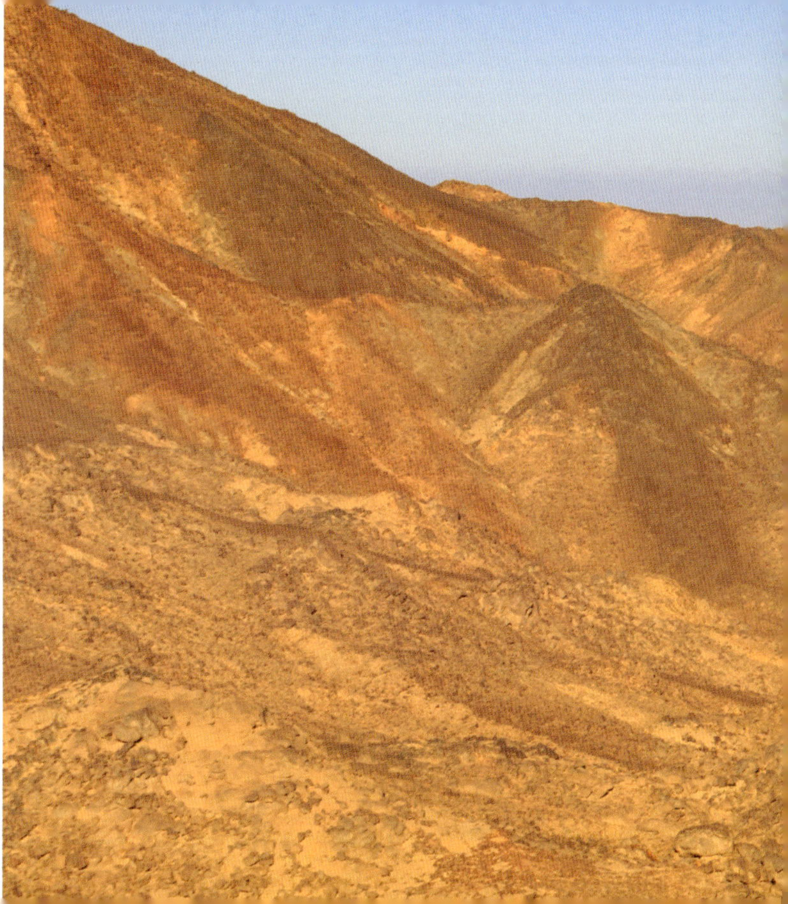

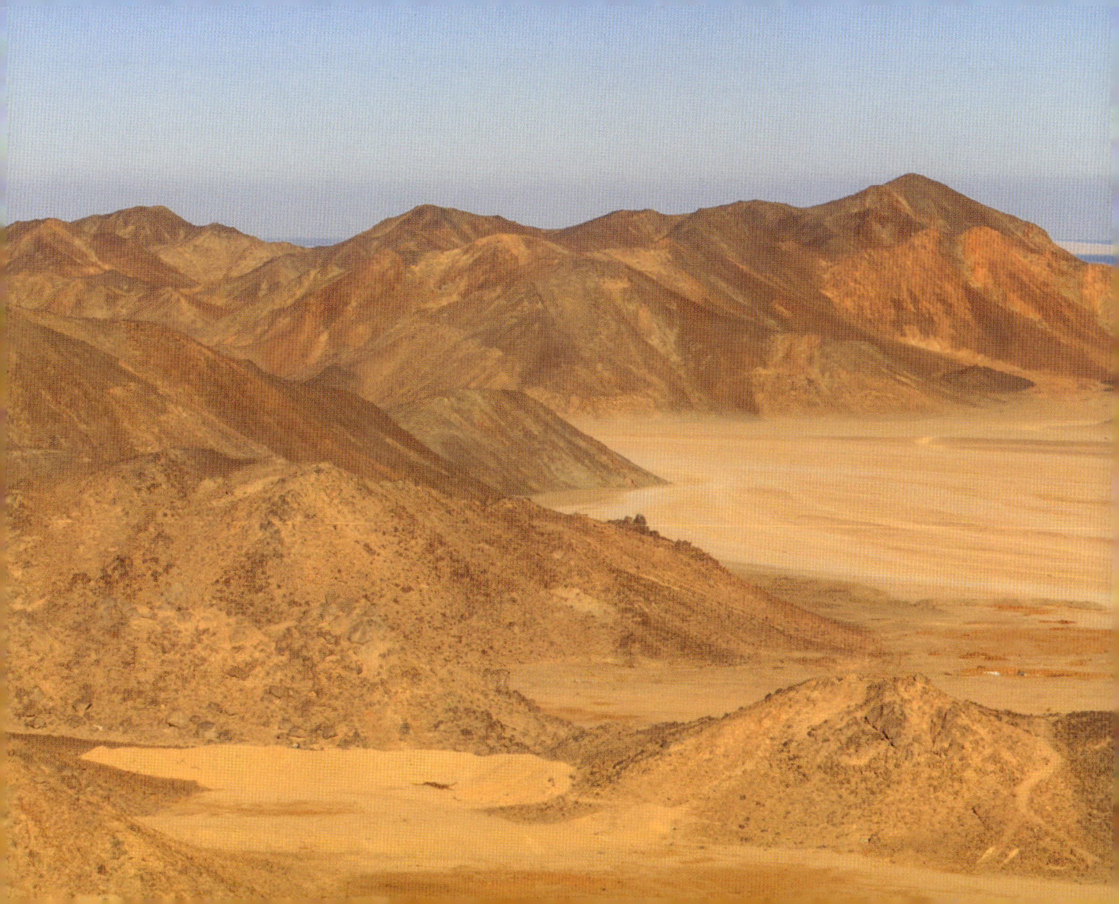

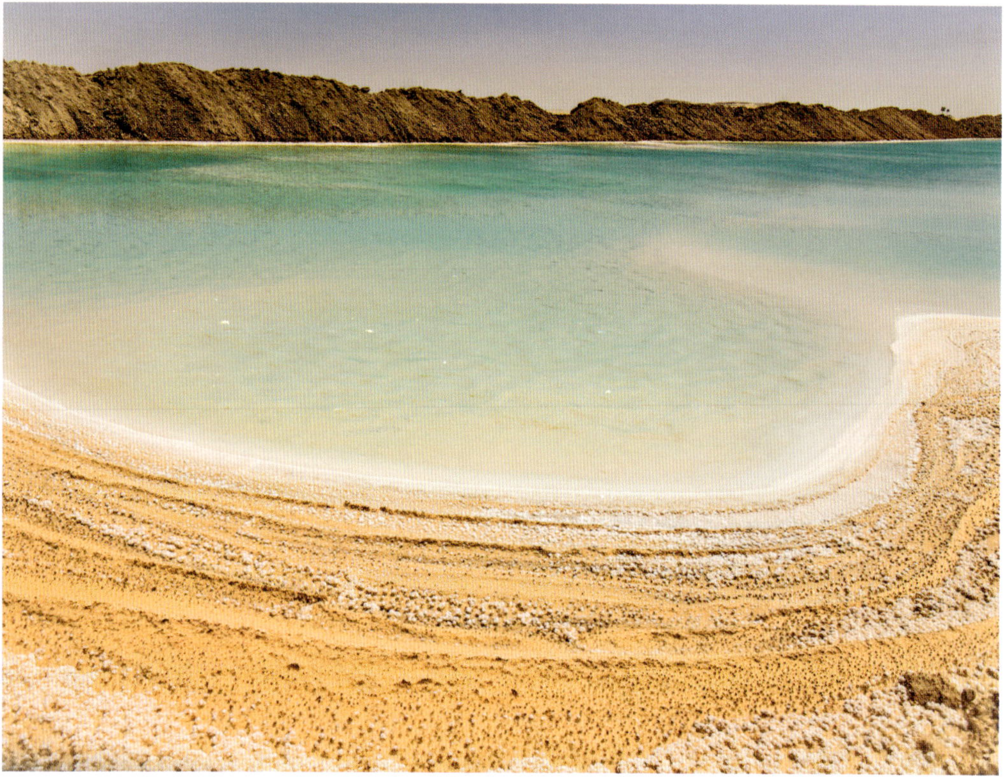

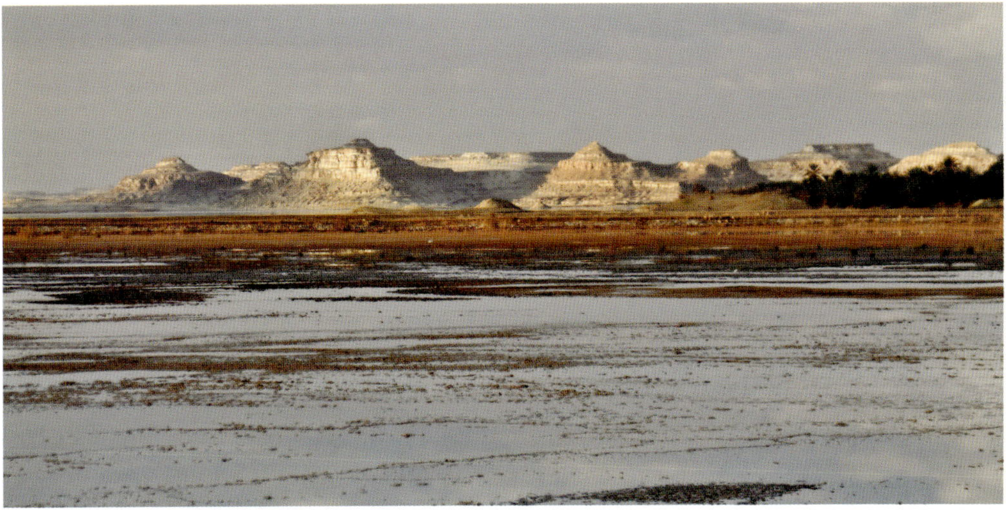

OPPOSITE:

Siwa Salt Lake, Siwa Oasis

The area around the distant oasis of Siwa, which lies close to the Libyan border, has a rich layer of salt created by the evaporation of salt water thousands of years ago. There are lakes today which are rich in salt and visitors to the area use these for swimming, relaxation and to enjoy the healing benefits of their warm waters.

ABOVE:

Siwa Salt Lake, Siwa Oasis

An early morning drive out of the town in Siwa Oasis takes you to a landscape unlike any other. The ground below your feet can be sand, salt or rock, and together they have created a world almost like another planet. When set against the vivid blue of Siwa's skies or reflected in the shallow shimmering lake, you know you are in a unique setting.

The Shali, Siwa Oasis

The heart of Siwa town is dominated by the quite spectacular shape of the Shali, which fills the skyline with a shape very different from most buildings of the past. This area was the original fortress of the oasis and what you see are the remains of a 13th century bastion. These unplanned, uneven mud-brick rooms and homes were up to five storeys high and housed thousands of Siwans. They were a remote group of oasis dwellers with their own language and distinct customs and traditions, many of which live on today in what is a distinctly conservative area.

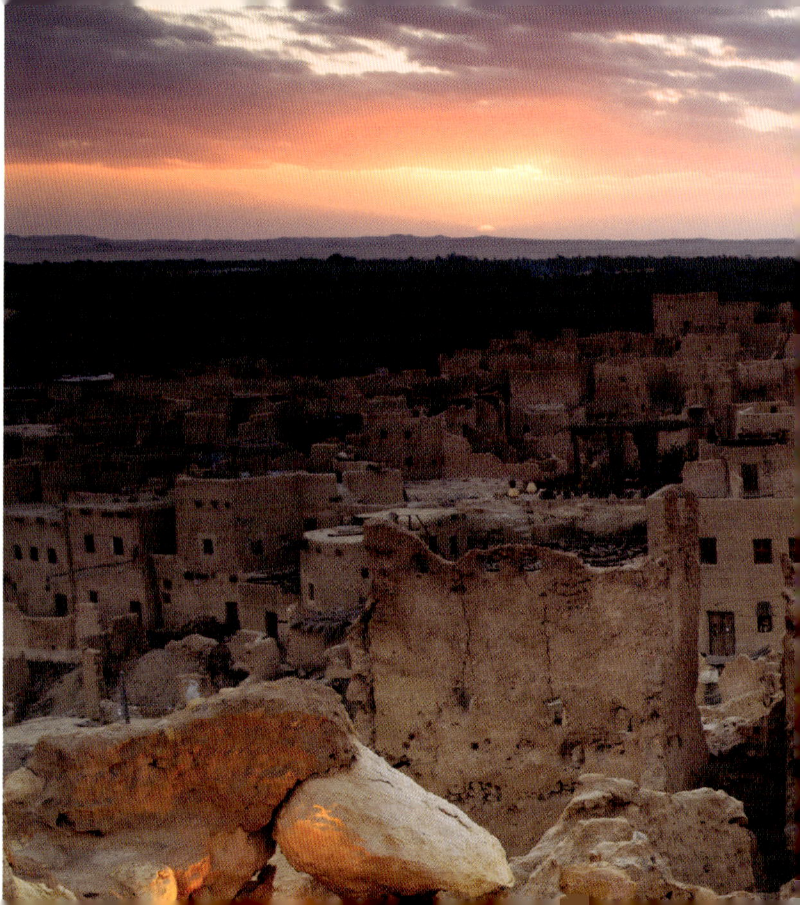

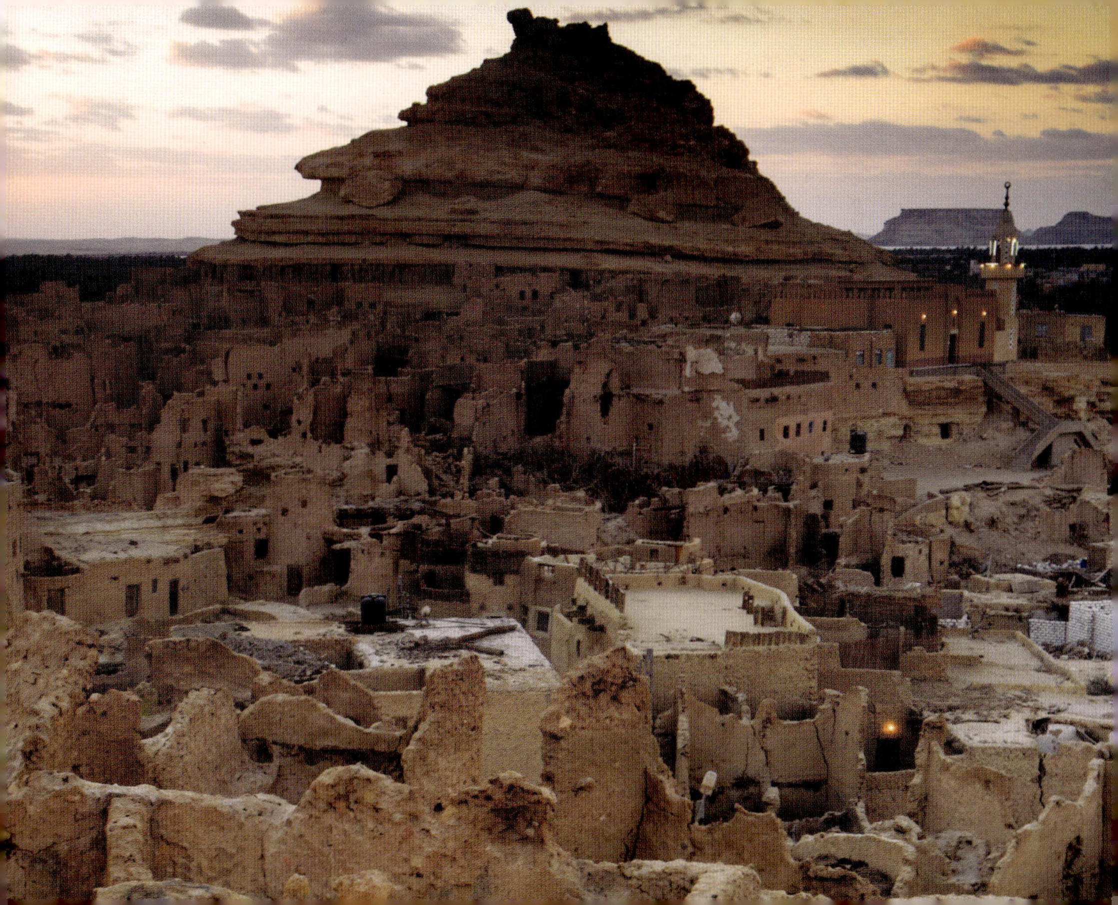

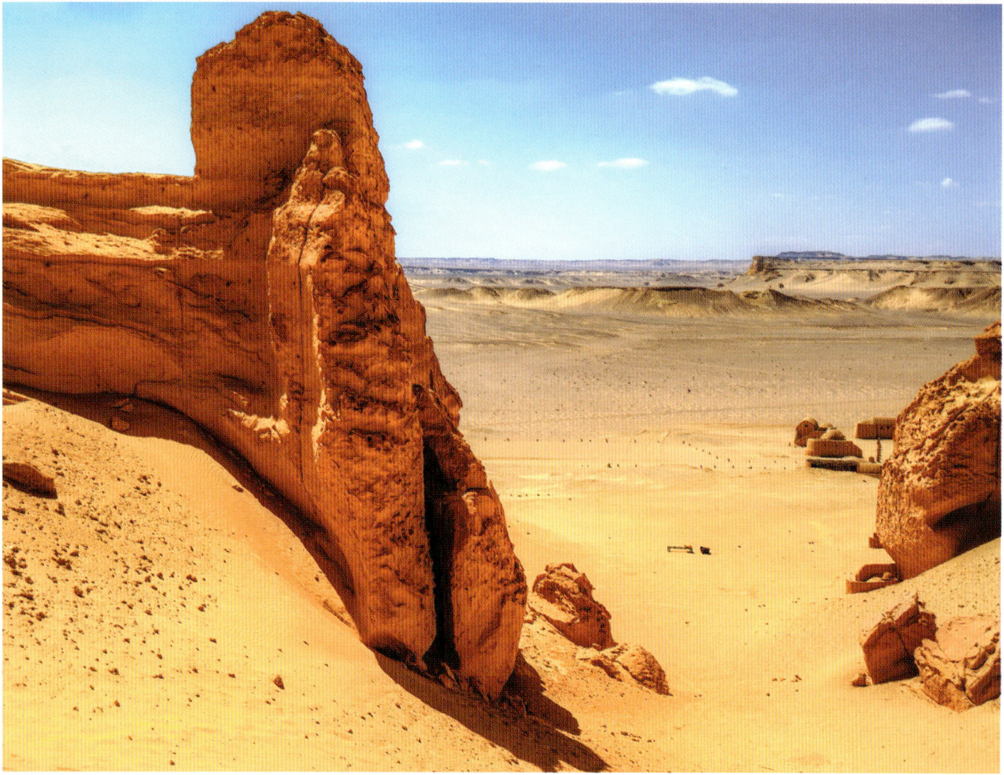

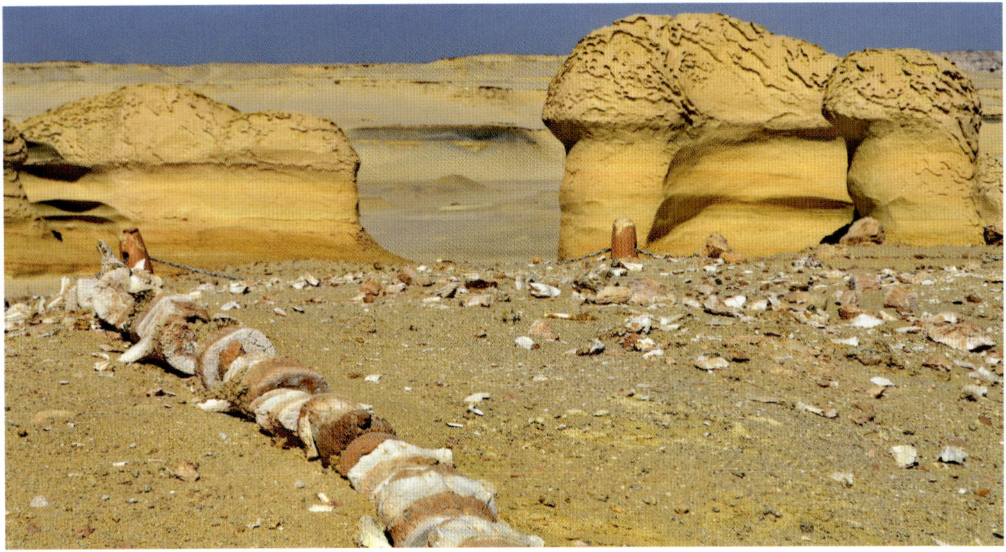

OPPOSITE:

Valley of the Whales, Fayoum

An hour's drive from Fayoum lies the world's most important site for the study of whale fossils. Wadi al Hitan means 'Valley of the Whales'. The area is a UNESCO World Heritage Site and has been carefully maintained and organized to give visitors a special experience of the past.

ABOVE:

Valley of the Whales, Fayoum

The remains of the whales found here are shown along a marked path with information points. These fossils showed a species of whale which still had the remains of hind legs, marking them as a transition point from land animals to marine mammals when this area was part of a vast ocean.

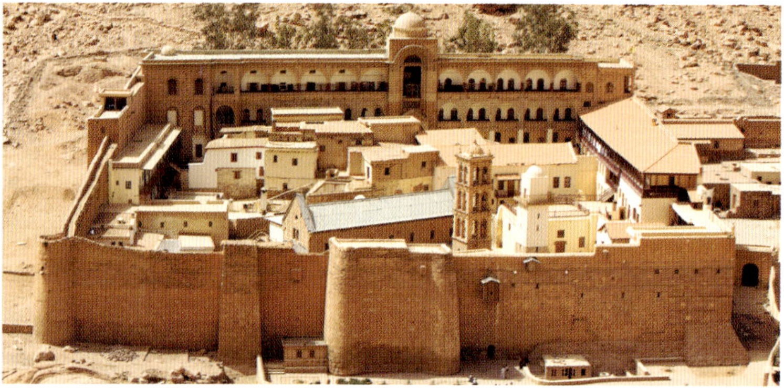

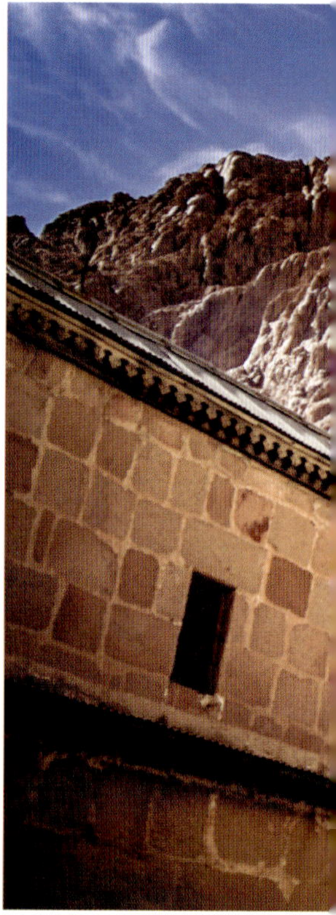

ABOVE:

St. Catherine's Monastery, Sinai

St. Catherine's Monastery is a highlight for tourists to Egypt, but also for the many pilgrims who visit each year from all over the world. The monastery is a Greek Orthodox site founded in 530 CE by the Emperor Justinian and has been in use ever since, protecting the treasures of its magnificent library and providing shelter for the monks who live within. It is a perfect example of a building built on faith, hardship and devotion to duty.

RIGHT:

St. Catherine's Monastery, Sinai

From within the monastery one can see mountains all around, but St. Catherine's lies at the bottom of Jabal Moussa (Mount Sinai) for a reason, and climbing the mountain is one of the principle reasons visitors flock to this remote place. It was on Mount Sinai that Moses is said to have received the Ten Commandments and pilgrims climb or take camels to visit this spot.

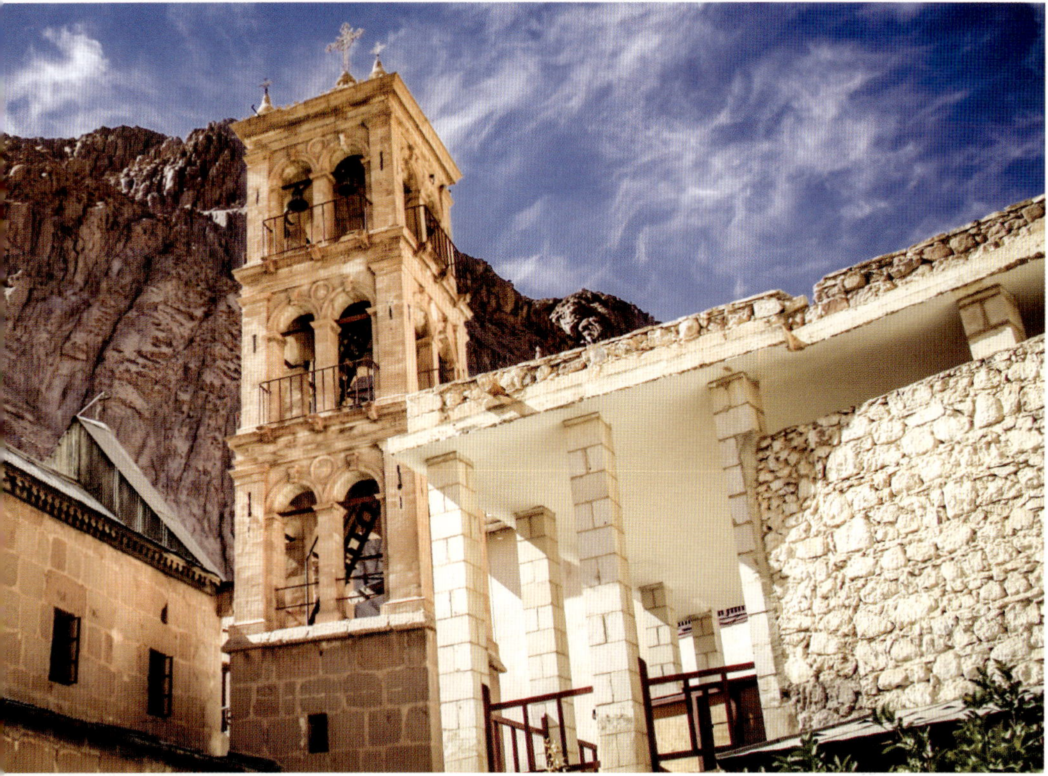

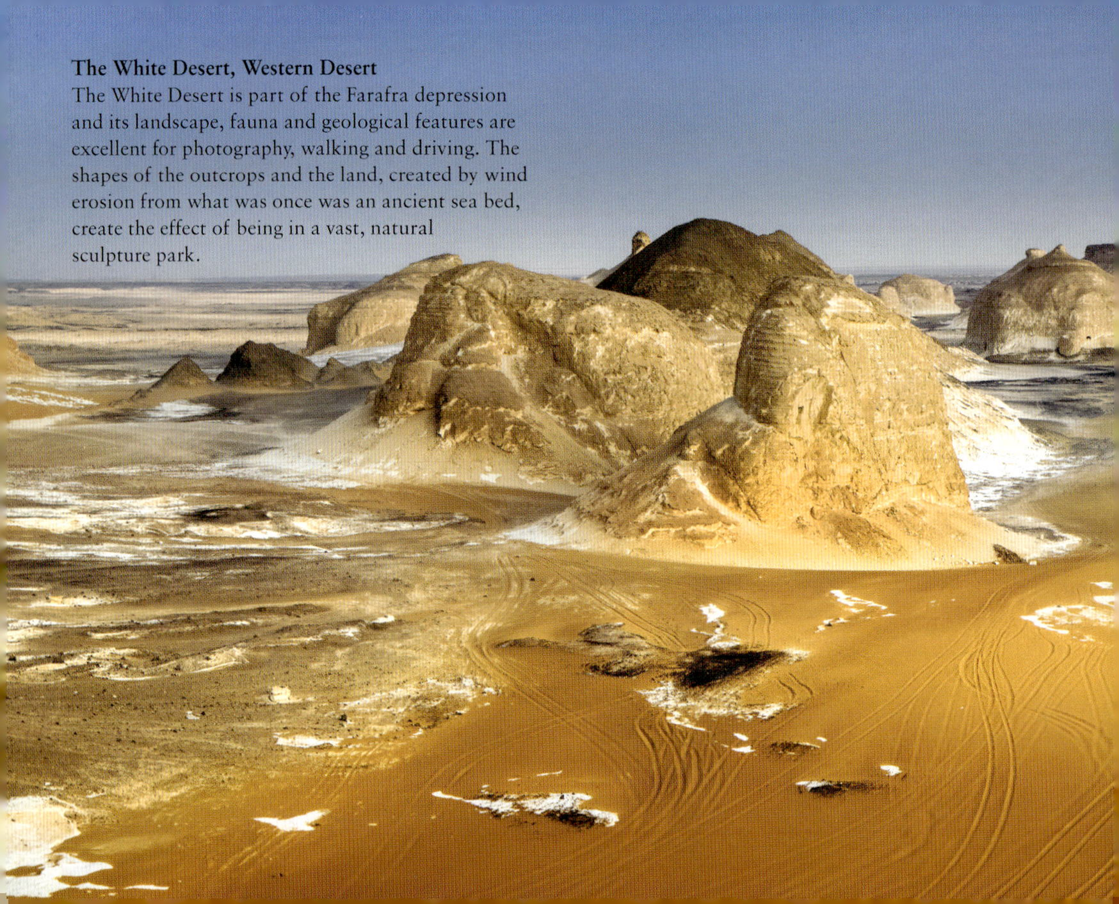

The White Desert, Western Desert
The White Desert is part of the Farafra depression and its landscape, fauna and geological features are excellent for photography, walking and driving. The shapes of the outcrops and the land, created by wind erosion from what was once was an ancient sea bed, create the effect of being in a vast, natural sculpture park.

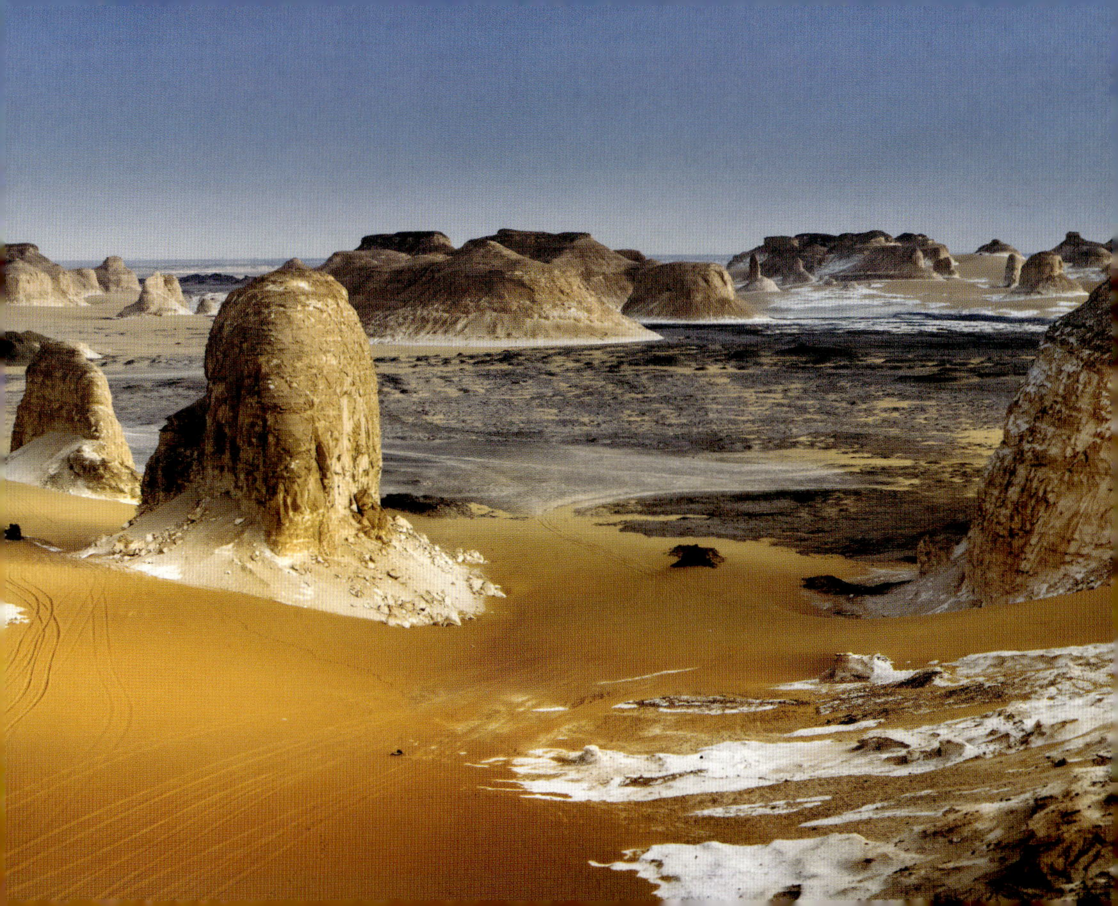

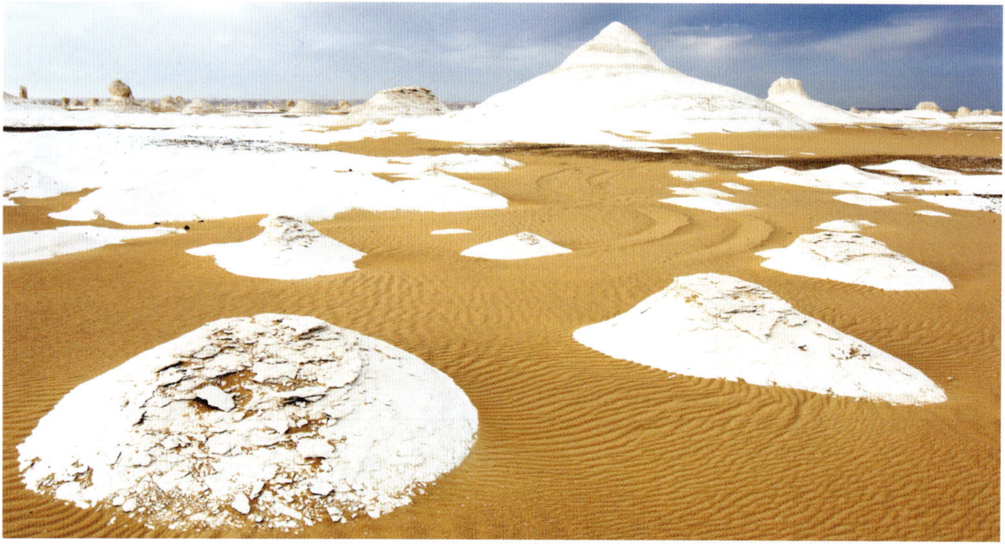

ABOVE:

The White Desert, Western Desert

The area's striking white rocks give the desert its name. Chalk rock formations stand tall, but there is also limestone as well as minerals such as quartz, crystal and pyrite. This large desert depression was part of an ocean millions of years ago, and the ground today still has many fossils of sea creatures buried in its rocks.

OPPOSITE:

The White Desert, Western Desert

This famous and oddly shaped outcrop is possibly the most popular of all for photography. It is a puzzle as to how its seemingly impossible outline came to be. Its distinctive shape and size mean this strange natural feature is also used as a navigation and meeting point by travellers.

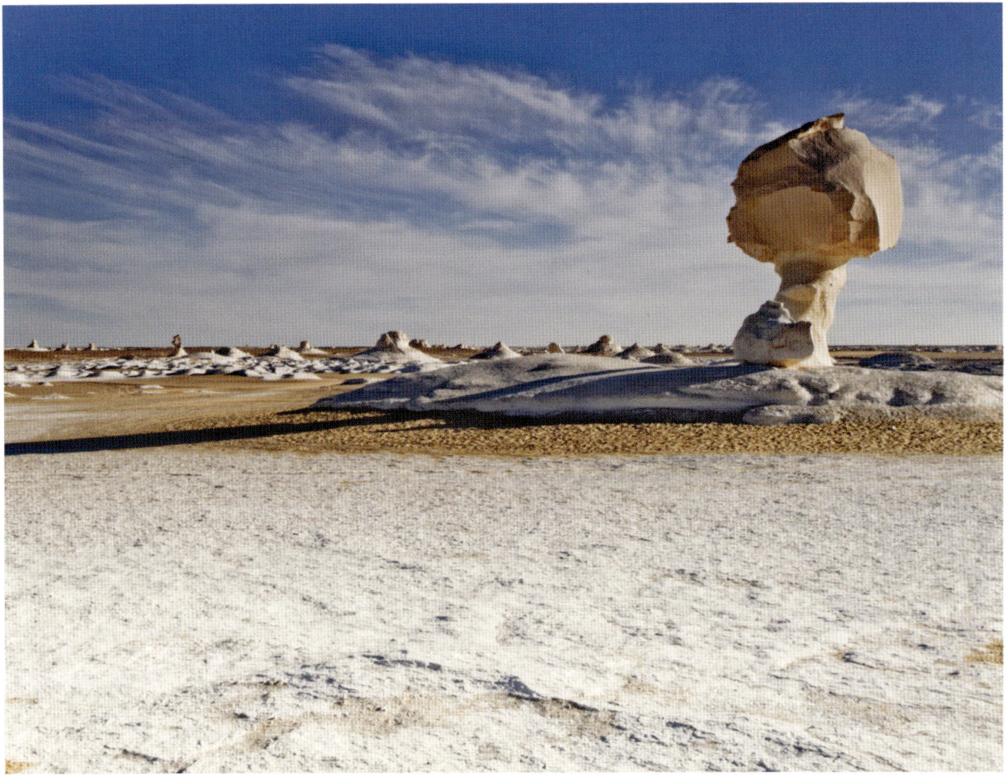

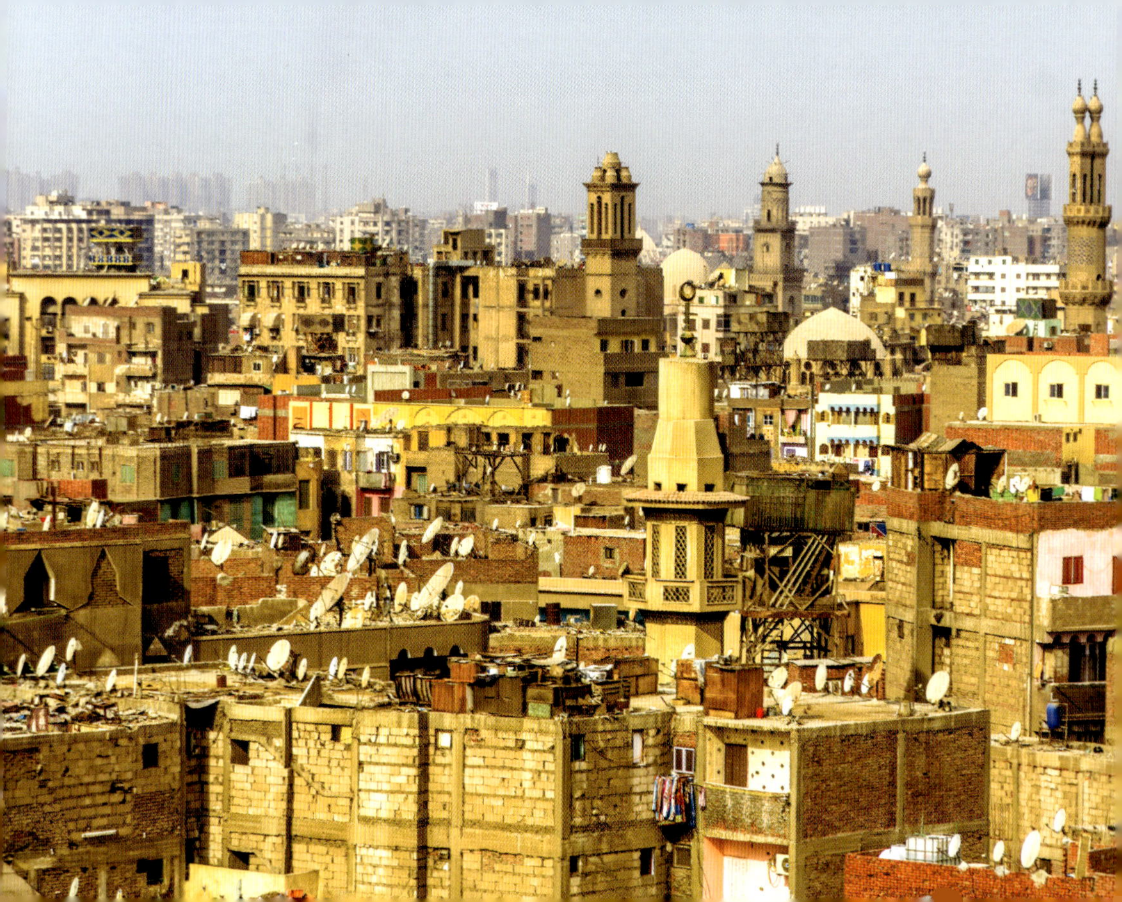

City Life

In a country where the population grows so quickly, putting urban areas under pressure, your first impression of Cairo is likely to be shock at the noise and chaos which surrounds you. Look beneath this crazy surface, however, and you will find a city unlike any other. This is a place where people may look at you as you pass by, but will then offer you the chance to sit with them and break bread, or take coffee, even if they cannot speak your language. The word 'welcome' is something that is known to all, and used with genuine feeling.

So take a deep breath and jump into Cairo, Alexandria, or any other large city and see what happens next. On any day there are many events taking place in Cairo and you will be welcome anywhere. The city centre comes alive by night, and there are hundreds of places to eat and drink, to shop and sit, or take a boat to see the city from the Nile.

In the heat of summer, night becomes day as Egyptians escape the punishing sun and come out after dark. If you can adapt to Egypt's summertime hours, you will truly enjoy its city life.

OPPOSITE:

Islamic Cairo Skyline, Cairo

The area known as Islamic Cairo is named after its historically rich Muslim heritage. Today it is a densely populated area. The skyline here is a mix of minarets, satellite dishes, pigeon lofts and washing lines.

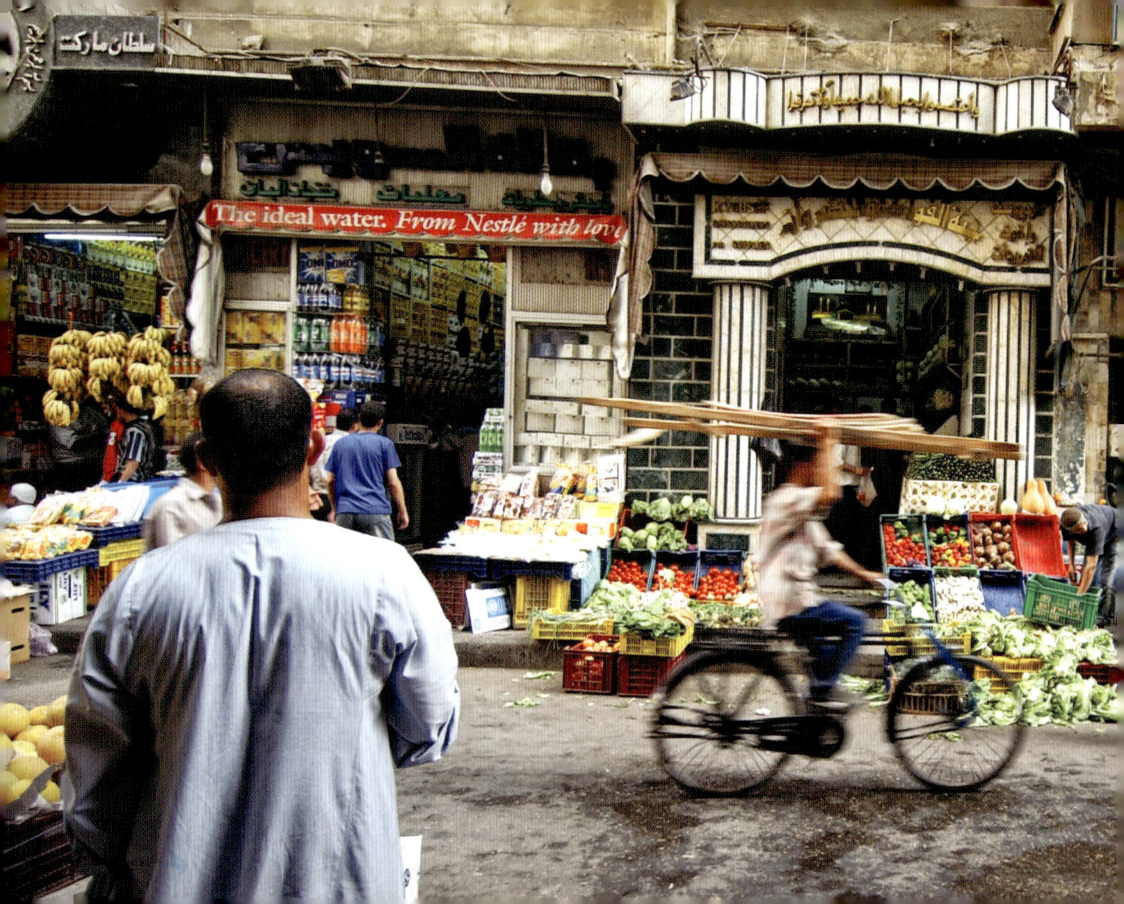
سلطان ماركت
The ideal water. From Nestlé with love

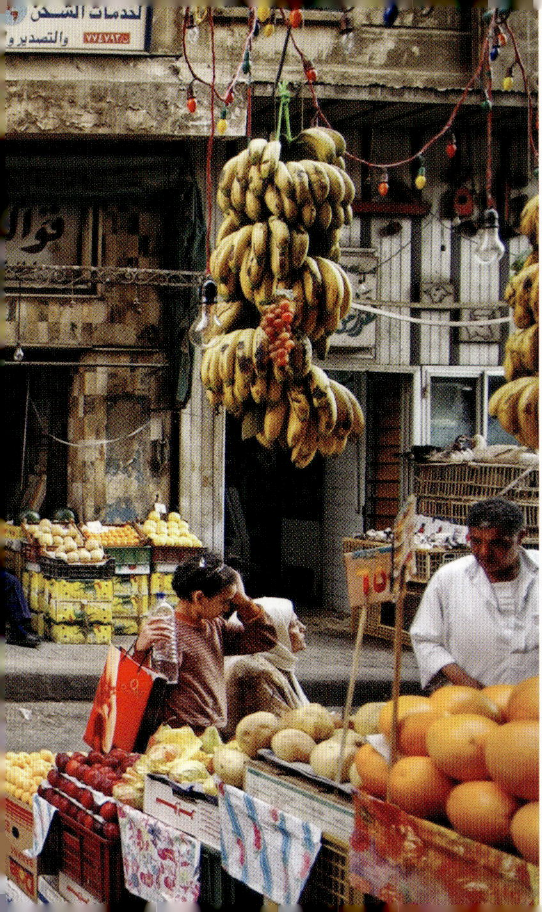

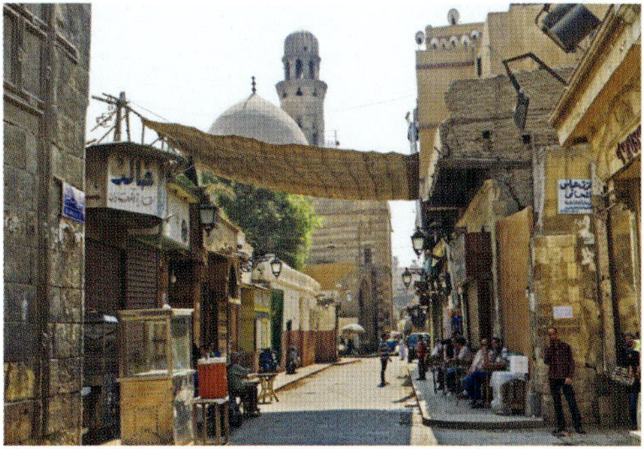

LEFT:

Traditional Cairo Streetlife

In many older parts of the city, little has changed. Street markets and the daily business of supplying customers remain a local tradition. In the more modern suburbs, supermarkets have become common.

ABOVE:

Traditional Cairo Streetlife

After a morning's walk around these historic Cairo backstreets, Egypt's hot sun may be overhead. Wherever you wander, you will be close to a coffee shop where you can indulge in Egypt's special variety of Turkish coffee, tea and shisha.

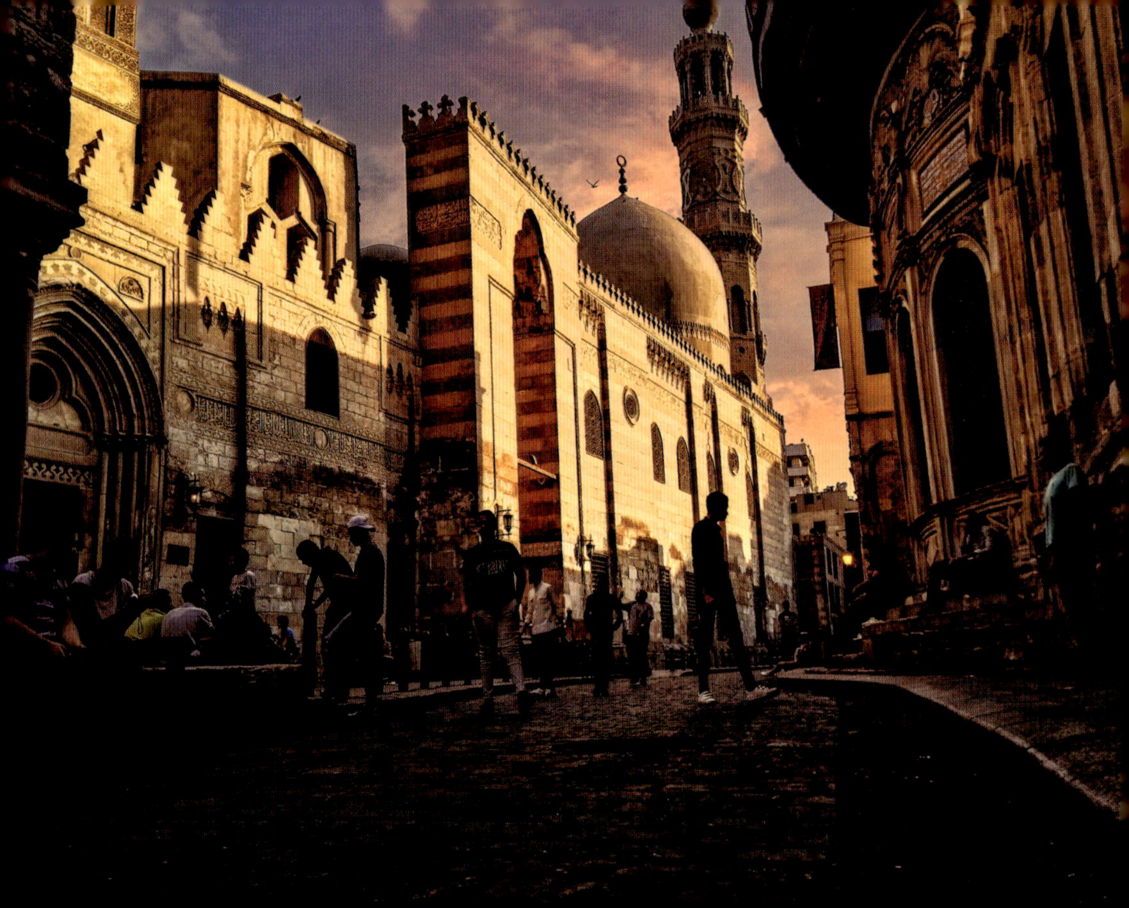

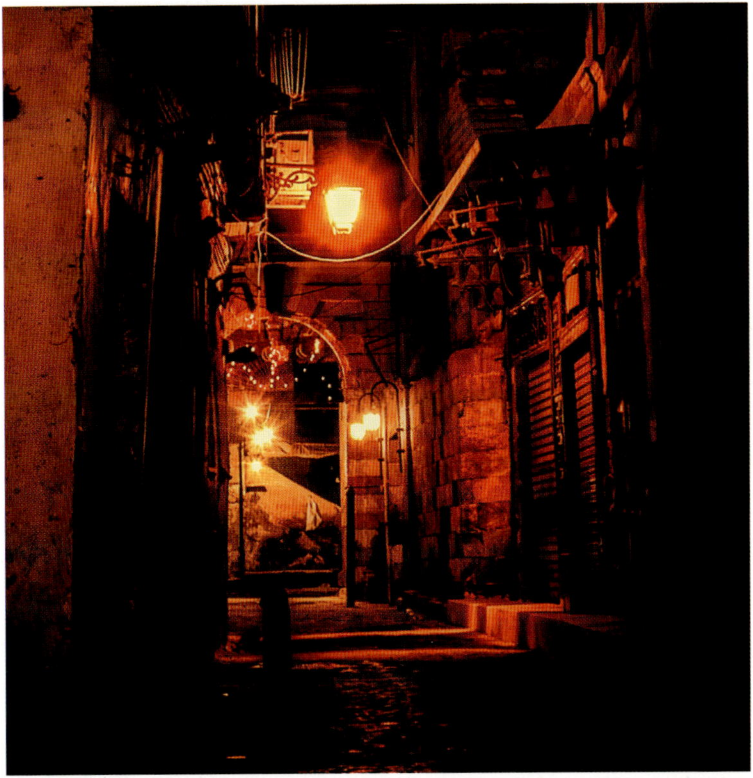

LEFT:

Muizz Street, Islamic Cairo

At night, the backstreets of Islamic Cairo evoke scenes from the works of the Egyptian writer, Naguib Mahfouz, who made this area famous in a series of novels. His most popular work is *The Cairo Trilogy*, a saga set in this area in the period following World War I.

OPPOSITE:

Muizz Street, Islamic Cairo

Muizz Street is a traffic-free zone, which makes it an atmospheric reminder of times past. Cairenes, young and old, love to wander its streets. They meet together and enjoy the many different Islamic monuments which make up this preserved area.

Al-Azhar Park, Cairo

In 1984, the Agha Khan IV visited Cairo and decided to help the city after seeing an area filled with mountains of waste. He gifted 30 million dollars to clear land which had been a rubbish tip for 400 years, and create a vast garden and urban park for Cairenes to escape the crowded streets which surrounded the area. In 2005, this beautiful space opened to the public and to worldwide acclaim. Today, Al-Azhar Park provides a vital space for local people to enjoy at the weekend and on public holidays.

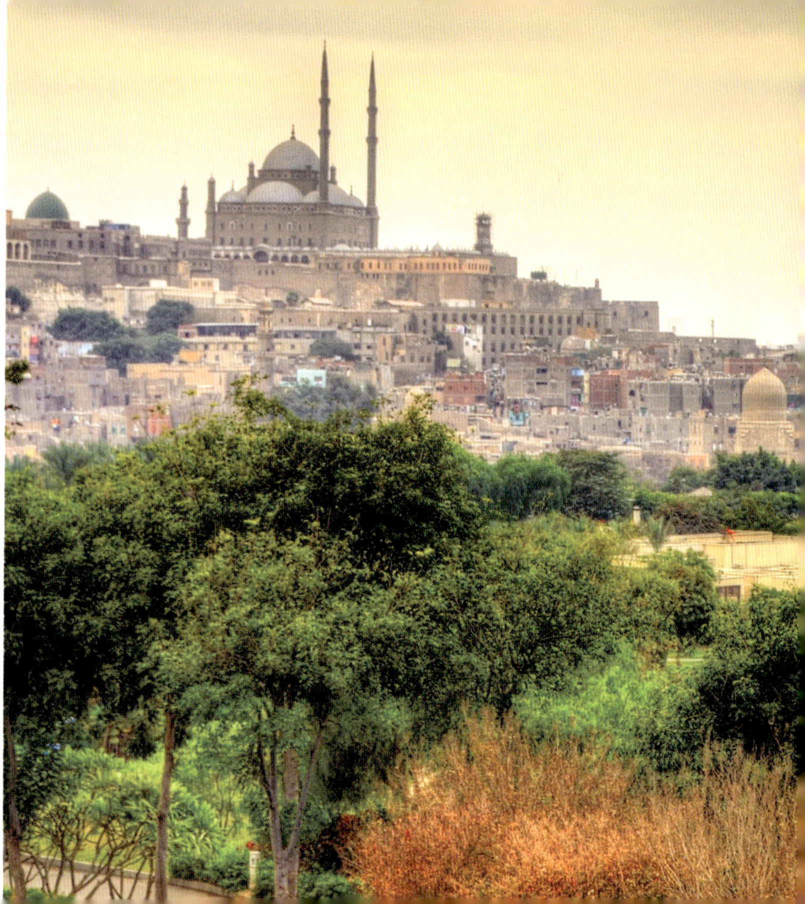

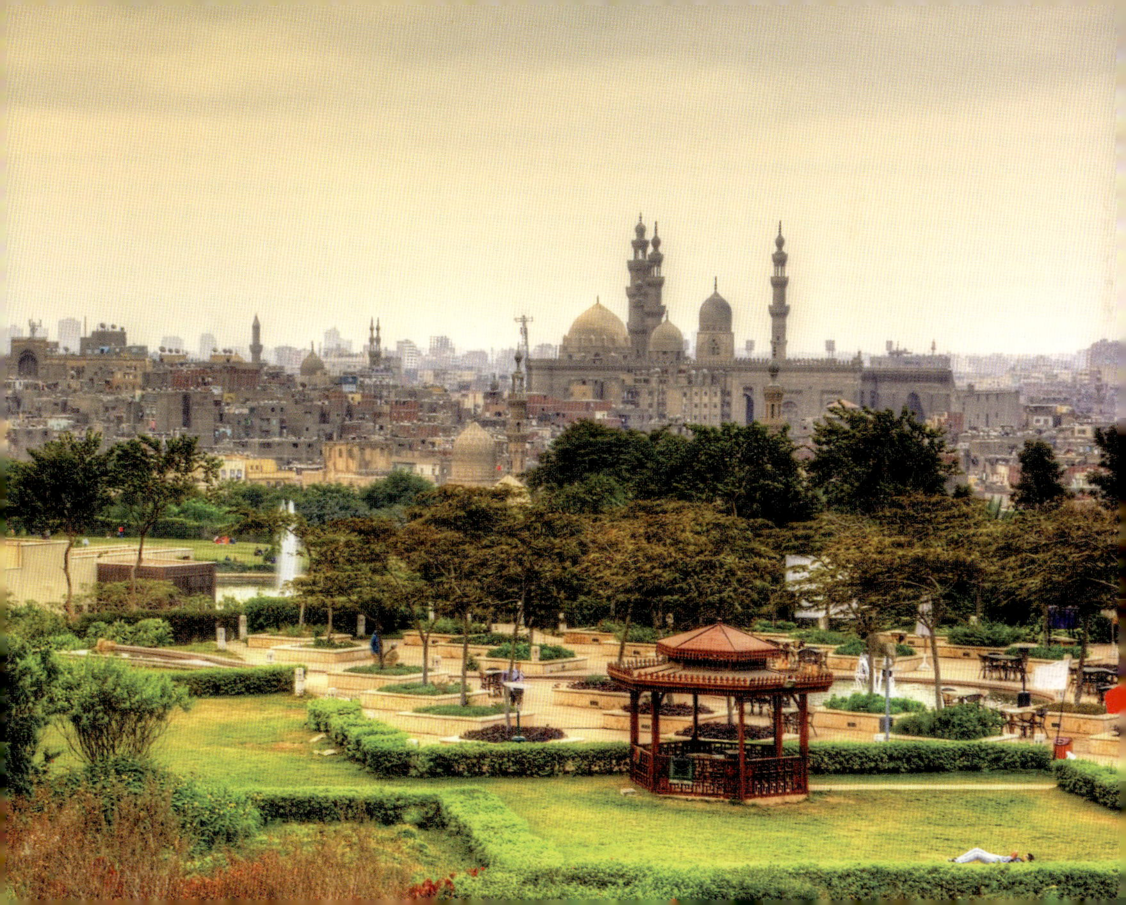

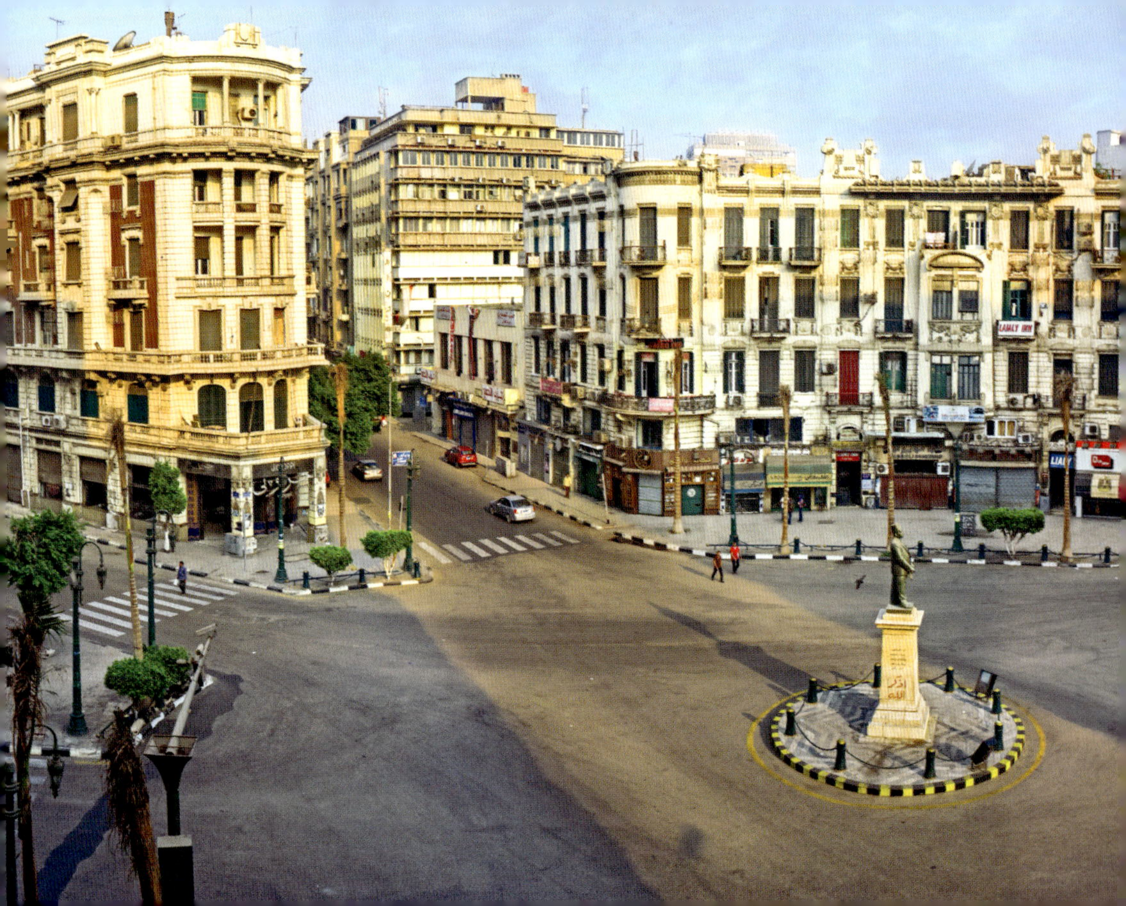

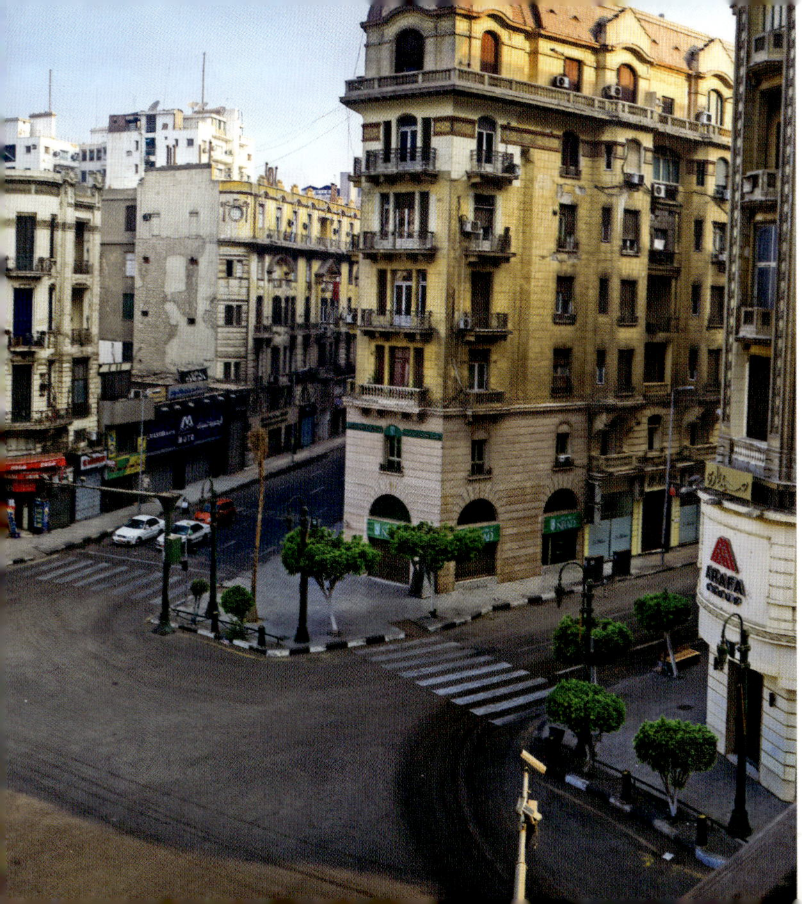

Talaat Harb Street, Cairo

This busy intersection connects Tahrir Square to an area filled with French neoclassical style architecture. It was the dream of Khedive Ismail to build an equivalent of Paris on the Nile. These 19th century buildings still carry the graceful lines of Egypt's Belle Epoque era. Long neglected, this vibrant area has been given a facelift which has restored Downtown Cairo to its former glory, and increasingly attracts walking tours exploring its rich modern history.

The Street of the Tentmakers, Cairo
A covered street situated just outside the medieval city walls. It is a street full of individual artisan stores whose families have been creating intricate hand-crafted tapestries for centuries. Today, shoppers can find printed cloth, cushions and weavings for the tourist market but the tradition of making items to order continues. Historically, it was within this street that craftsmen would create the special tapestry sent each year to cover the Kaaba stone used for the annual Hajj at Mecca, which would be transported from Cairo.

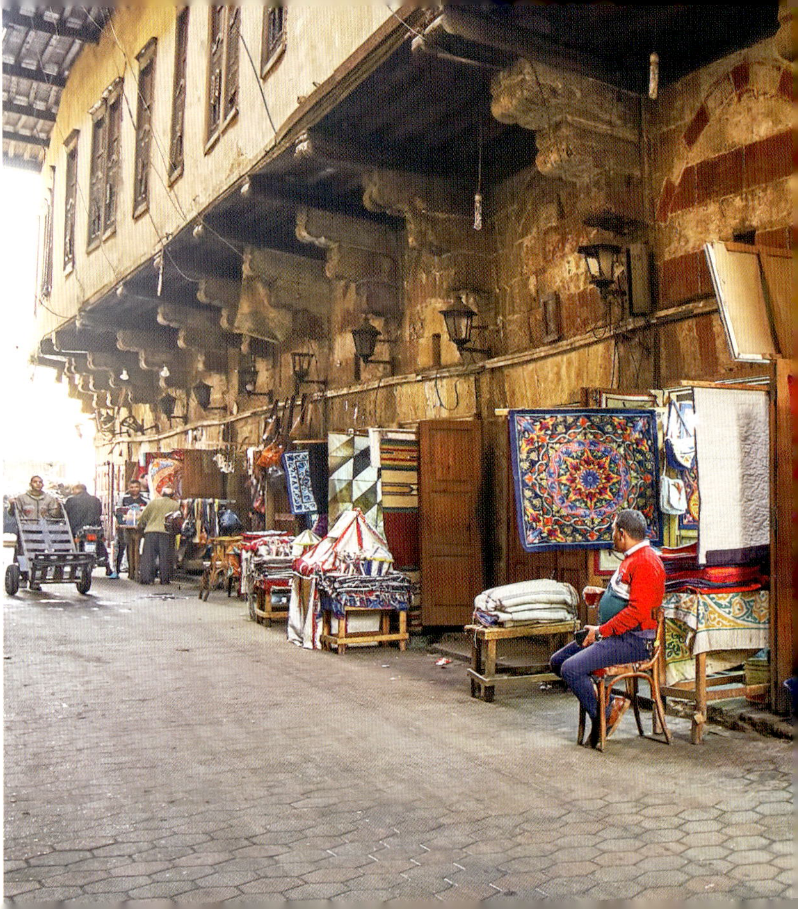

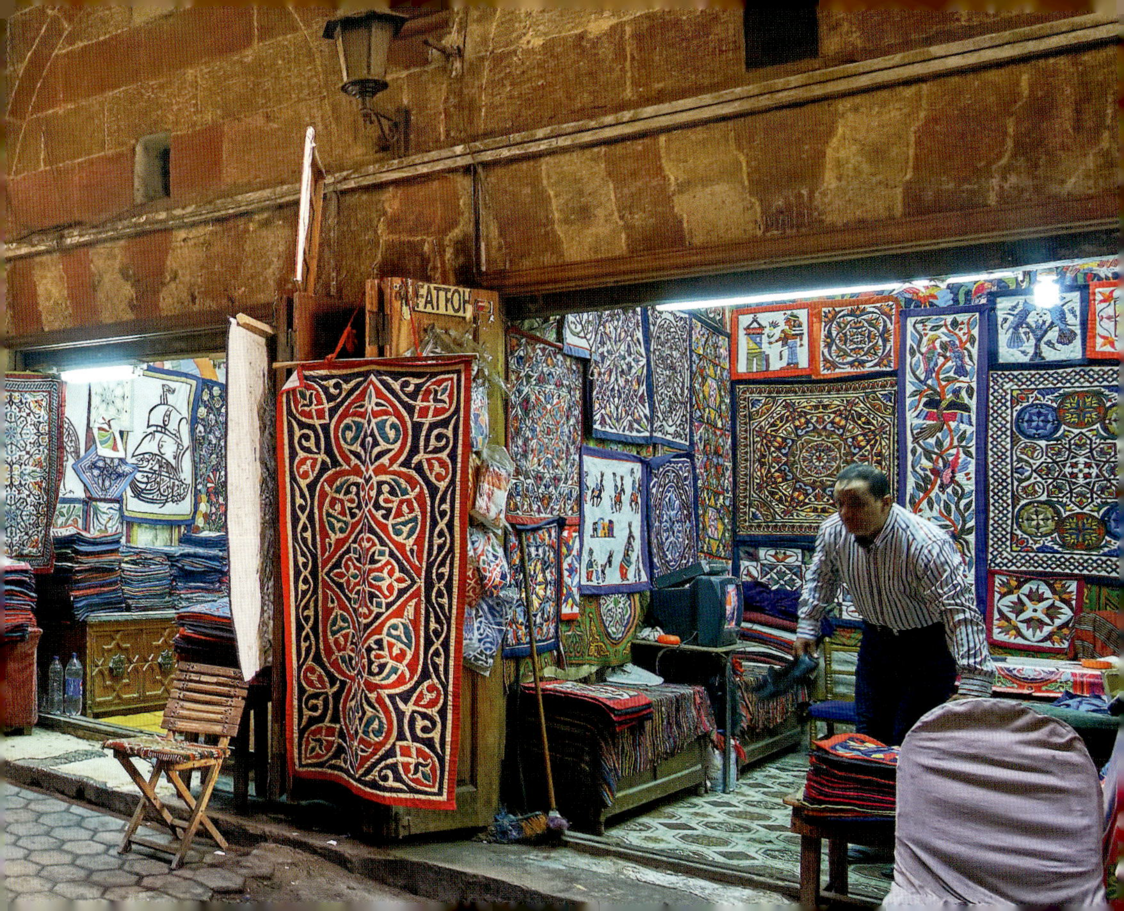
FATTOH

The Nile by Night

The city of Cairo comes alive after sunset and the Nile is its centre. The lights from its many boats, floating restaurants and hotels provide the backdrop to the noisy vibrant street life of Egypt. In the heat of summer, Cairenes of all ages come to the city to walk by the Nile and enjoy the cooling breeze in the evening.

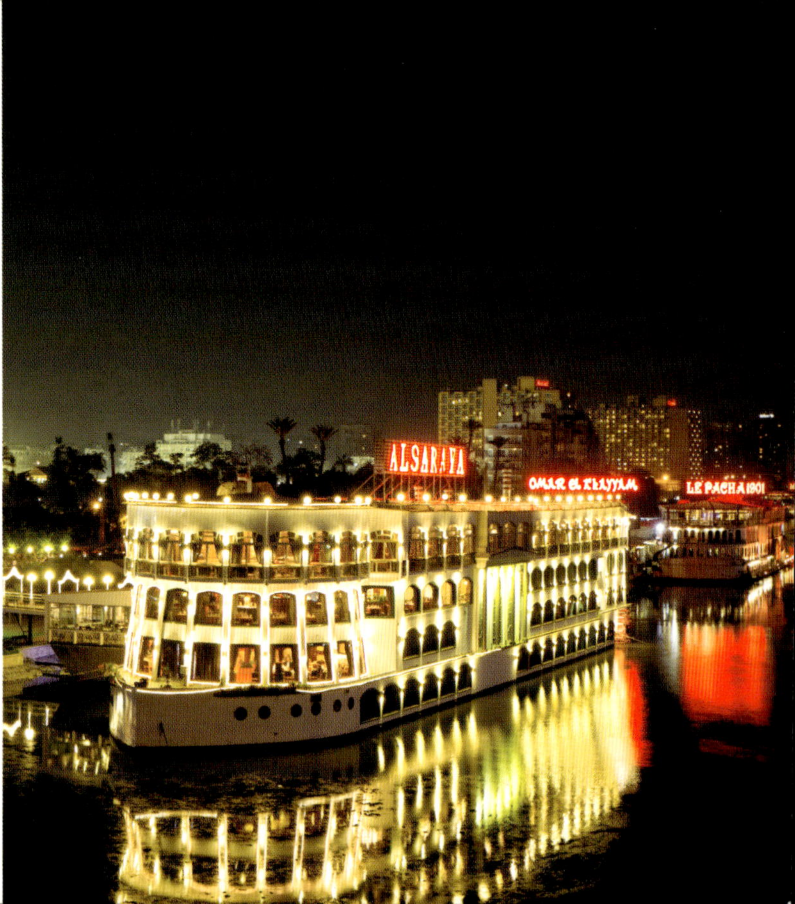

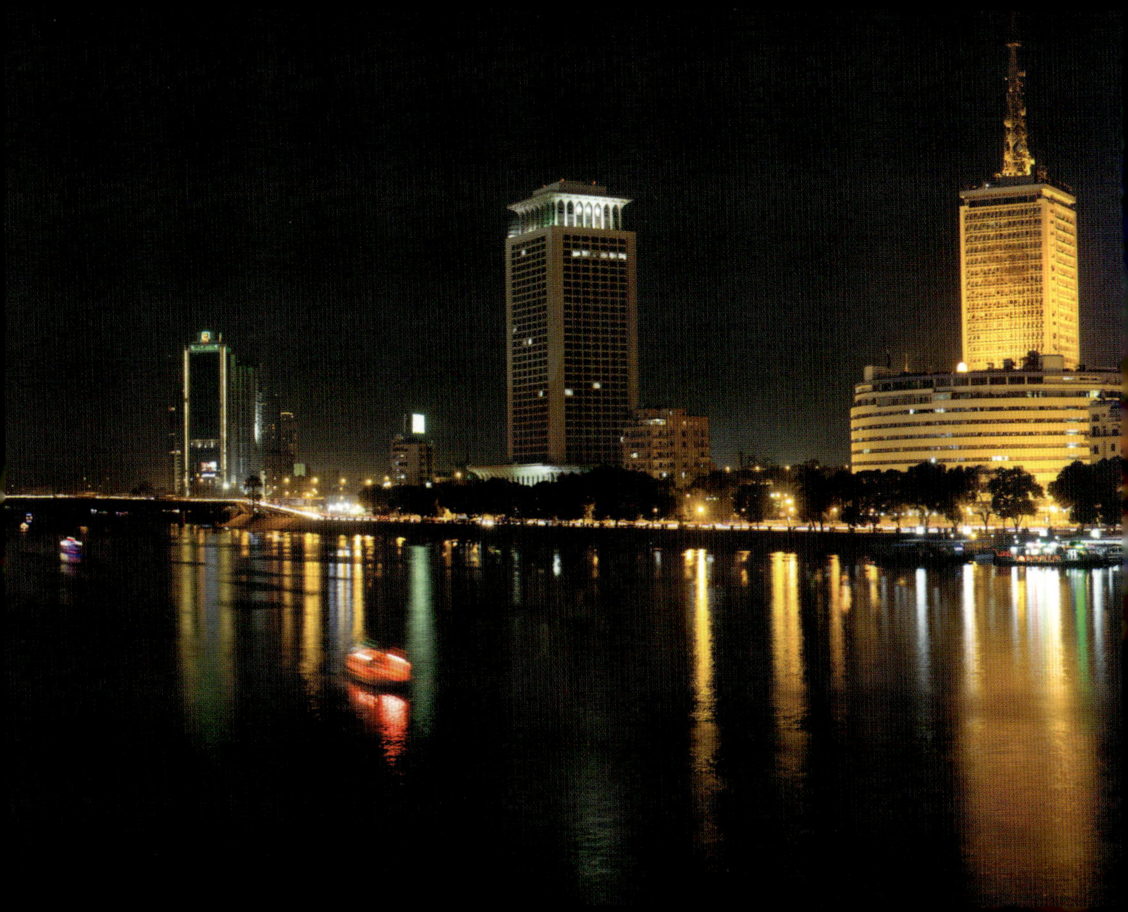

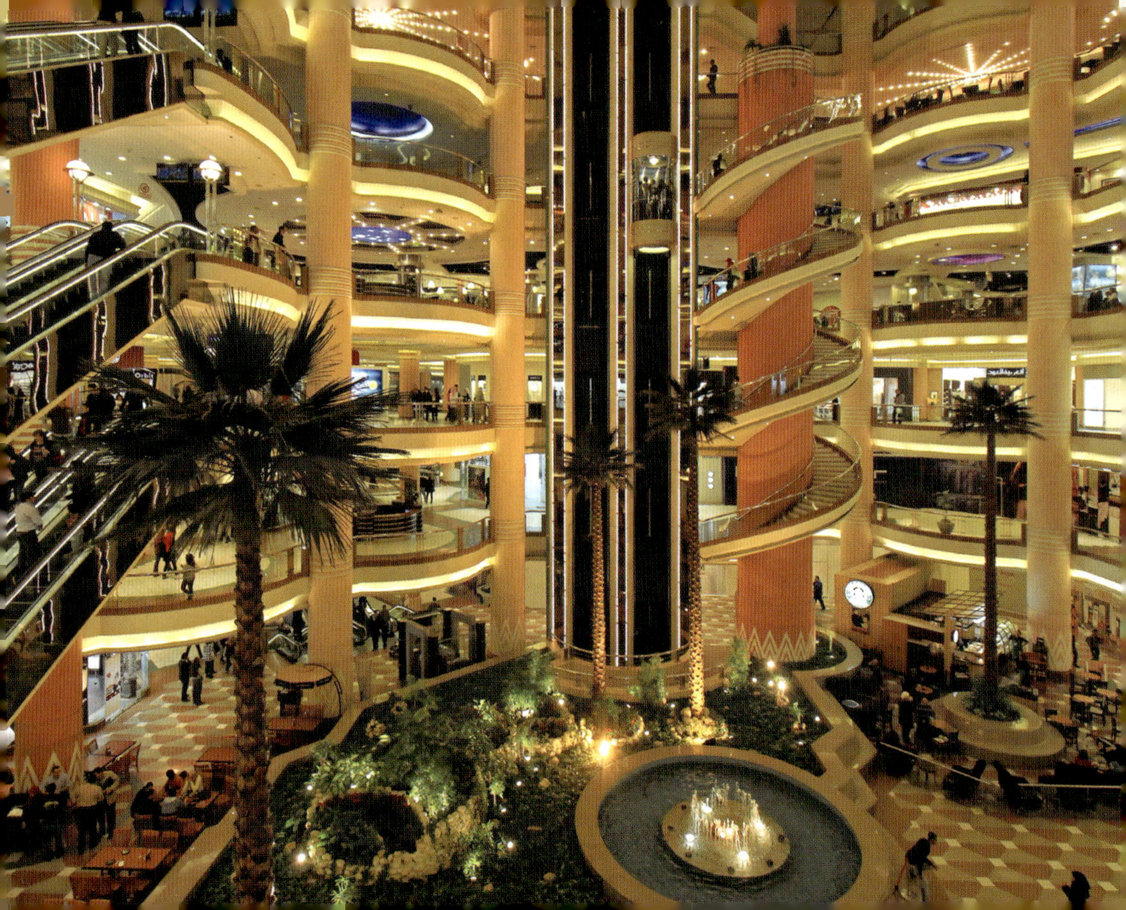

RIGHT:

Modern Egypt, Cairo

In recent years, there has been a rapid expansion in the number of modern shopping malls in and around Cairo. Egyptians love to shop and they also love eating out and spending time with their families. The arrival of these modern shopping centres, filled with international brands, cinemas and food courts, has been a great success.

OPPOSITE:

The Nile Corniche, Cairo

As in many cities across the Middle East, skyscrapers have begun to change their skyline. Cairo is no different, and with a view across the Nile as part of the offering, it's no surprise that developments along the river are proving popular.

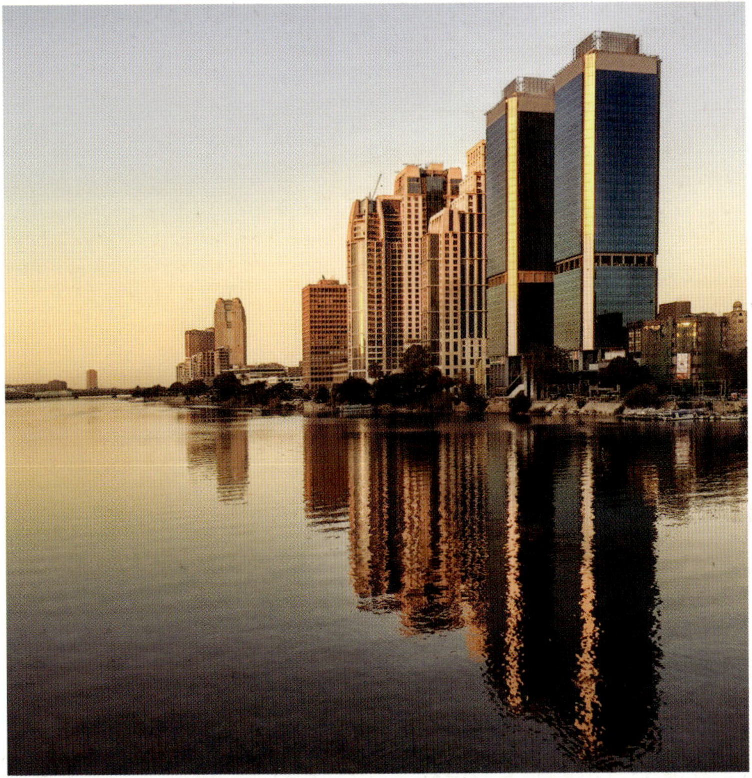

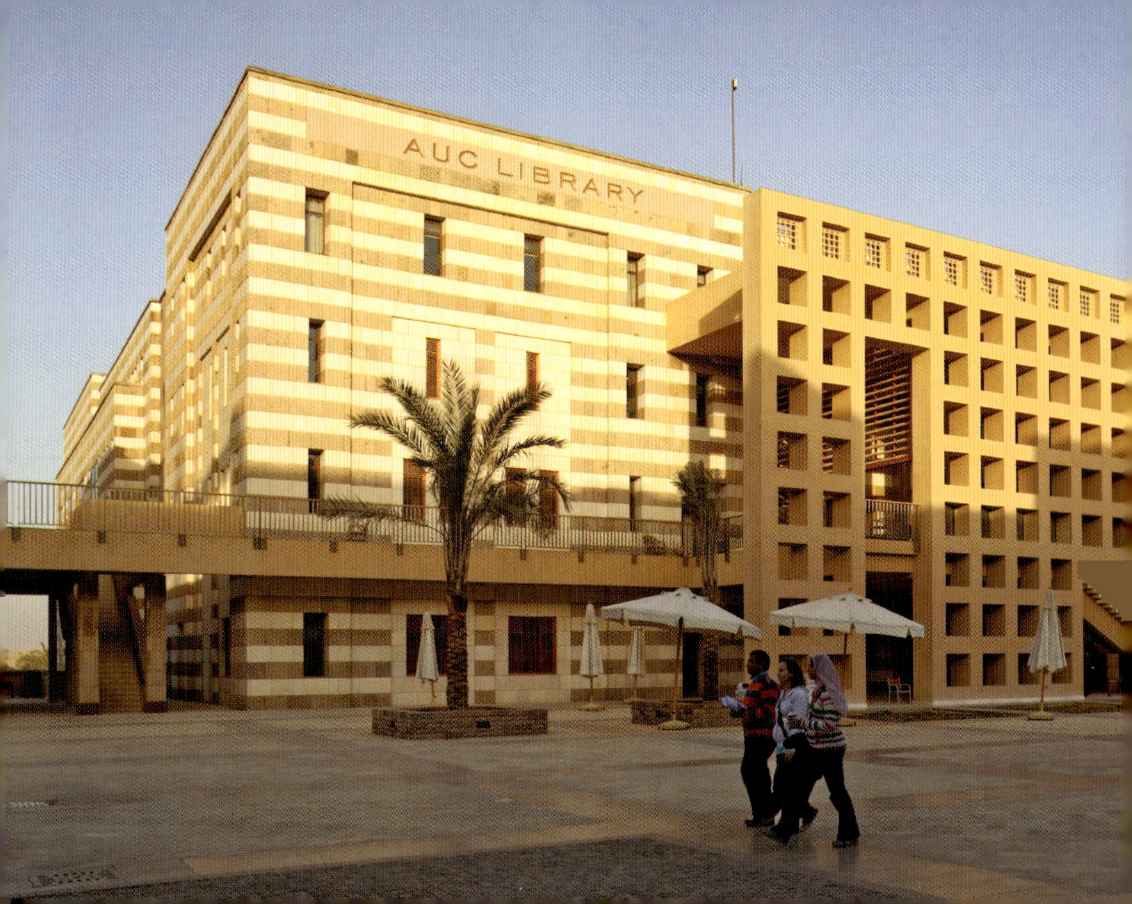
AUC LIBRARY

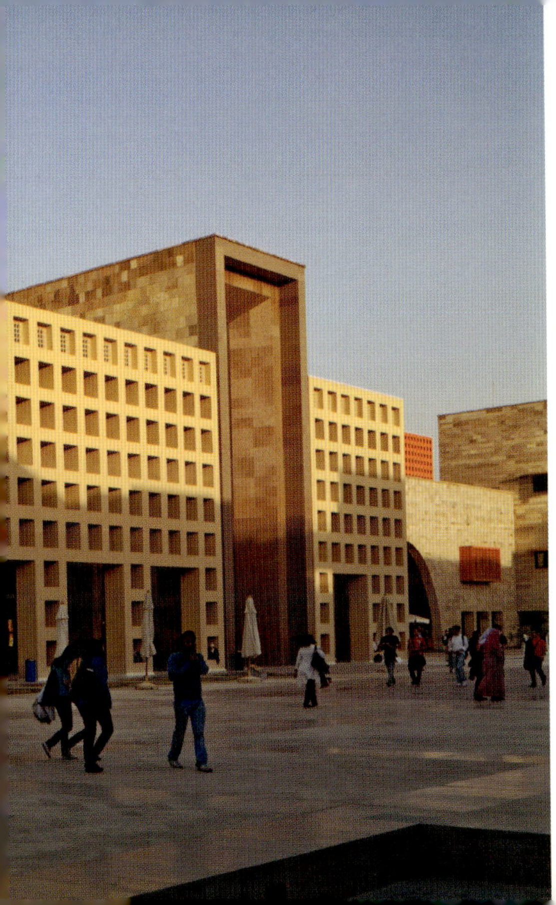

LEFT:

AUC Campus, New Cairo

The American University in Cairo (AUC) has provided an international education to Egyptians and students from around the world for 100 years. Recently, AUC moved to a purpose-built state of the art campus in New Cairo with facilities for more than 5000 students to enjoy.

BELOW:

AUC Campus, New Cairo

AUC is a premier English-language institution of higher learning in liberal arts and professional education. It is well known for building a culture of leadership, lifelong learning, continuing education and service among its graduates.

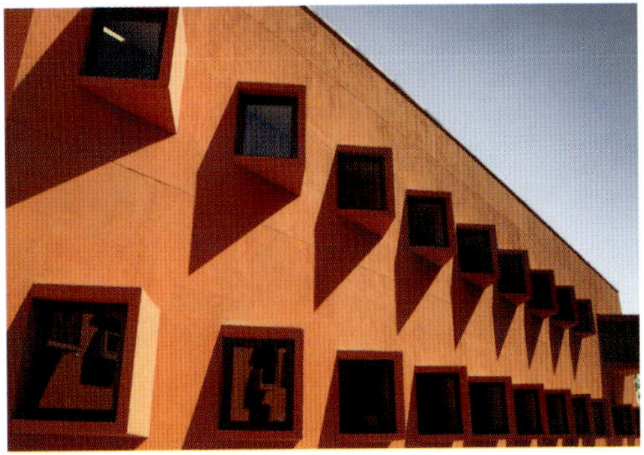

BELOW:

Street Festival, Cairo

In Sufism, there is a form of meditation which is performed in ceremonies by spinning around in circles whilst focusing on music and God. Practiced by whirling Dervishes in Turkey, this style of meditation has evolved into a form of performance dance, and in Egypt is called tanoura.

OPPOSITE:

Street Festival, Cairo

Tanoura is regularly performed at Sufi ceremonies, during street festivals and as a concert dance in Egypt. This picture captures a sense of the speed, colour and energy which tanoura dancers create as they turn these brightly coloured, weighted costumes.

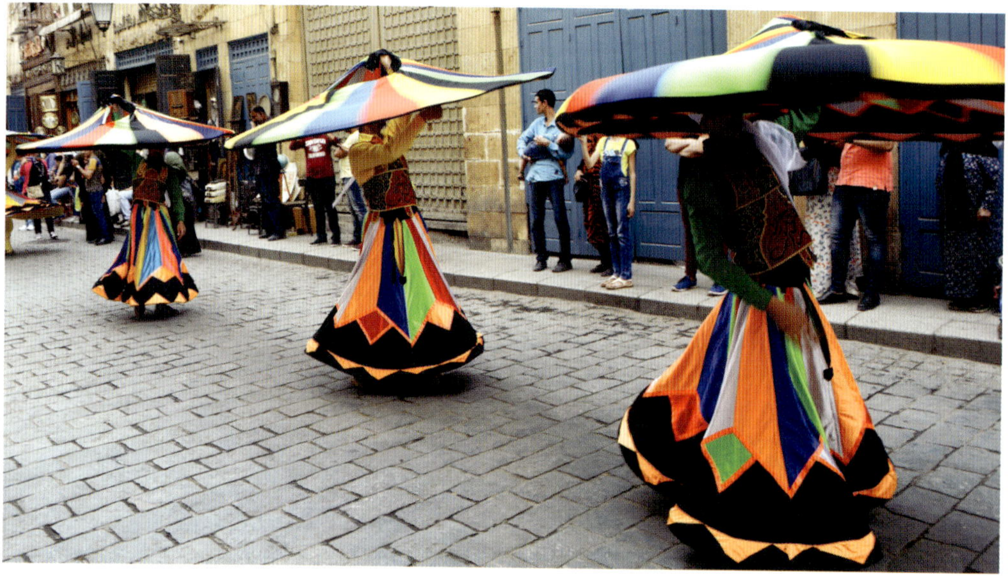

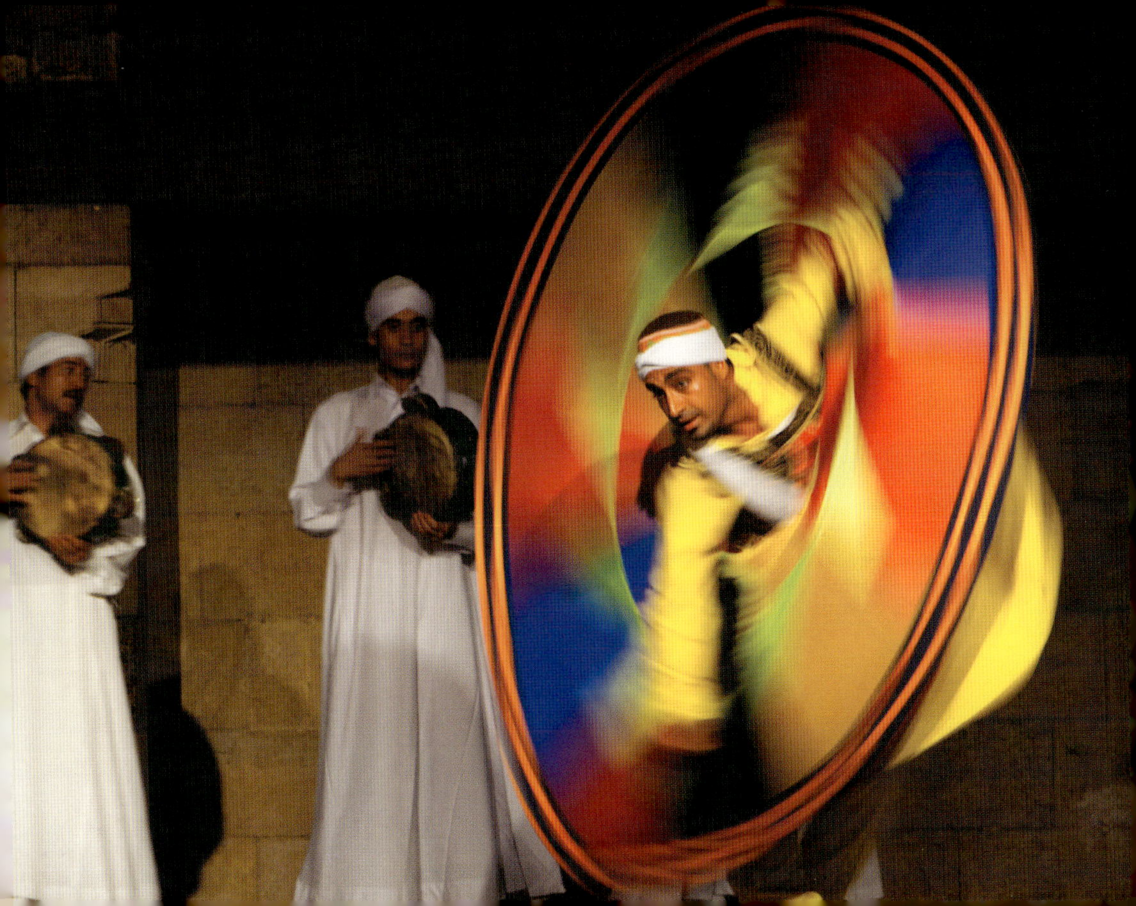

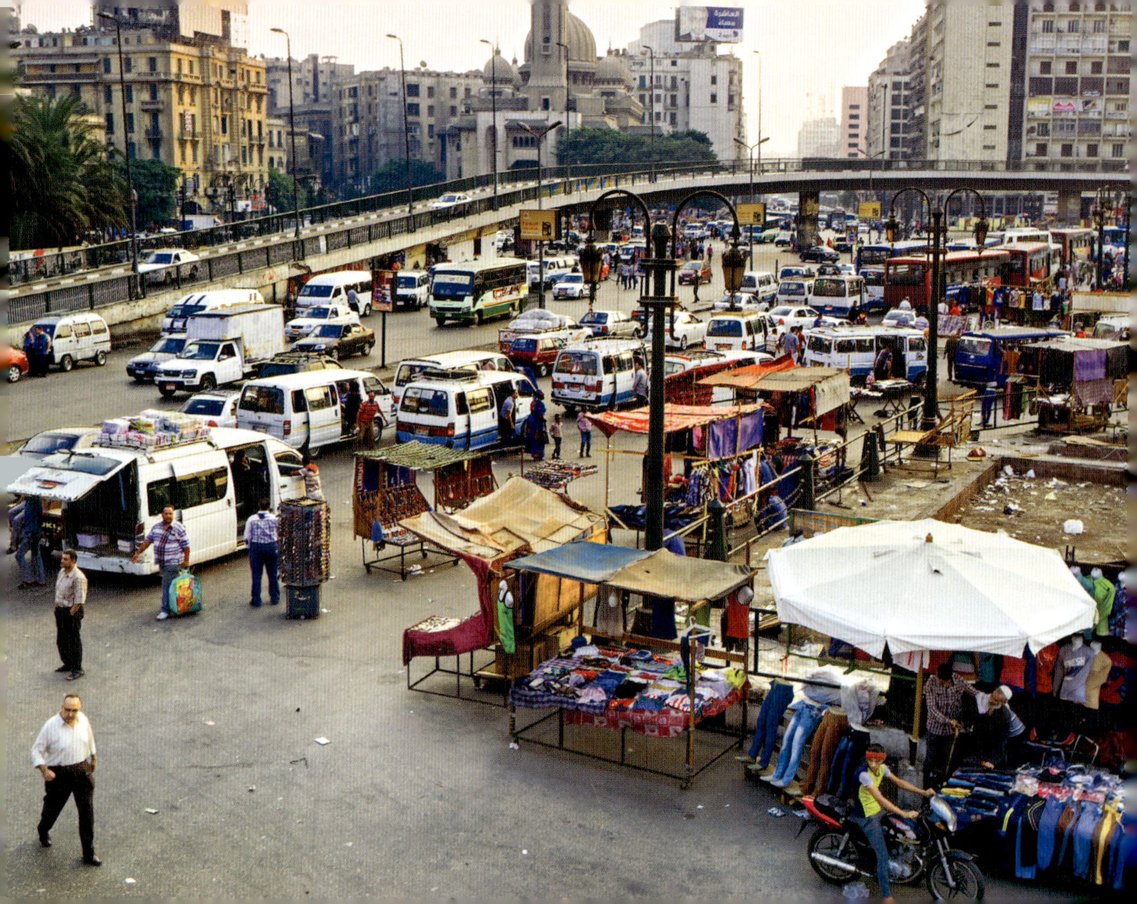

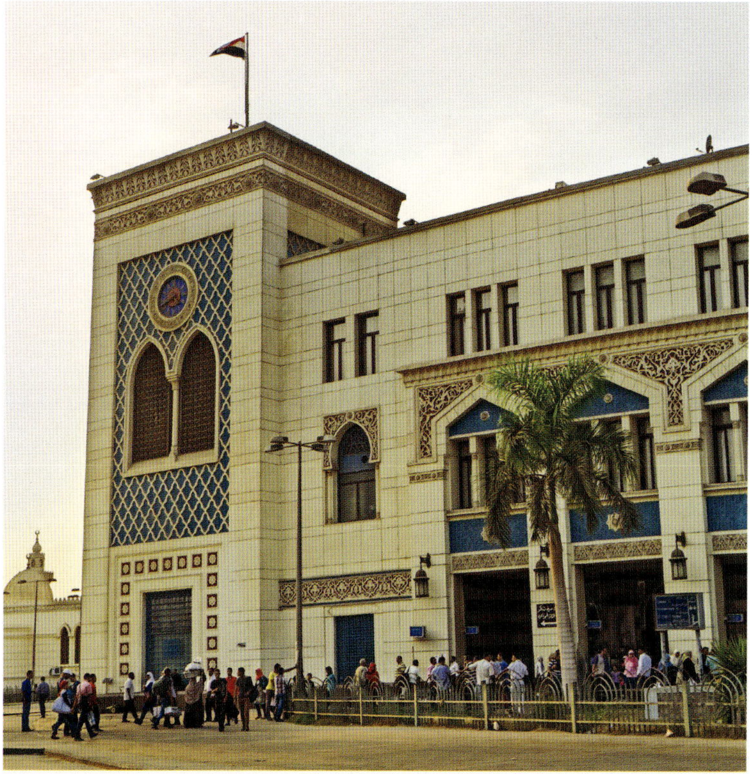

LEFT:

Ramses Train Station, Cairo

This semi-Islamic style building is at the centre of Egypt's national rail network. The building dates to the late 19th century and houses the Egyptian Railway Museum. The station is also worth visiting for its rather spectacular ceiling.

OPPOSITE:

Cairo Traffic

Ramses Square is one of Cairo's busiest intersections. The many roads which connect there join the city centre to a number of the city's residential areas. It is busy 24 hours a day with traffic and more recently, an informal market selling clothes, books and food.

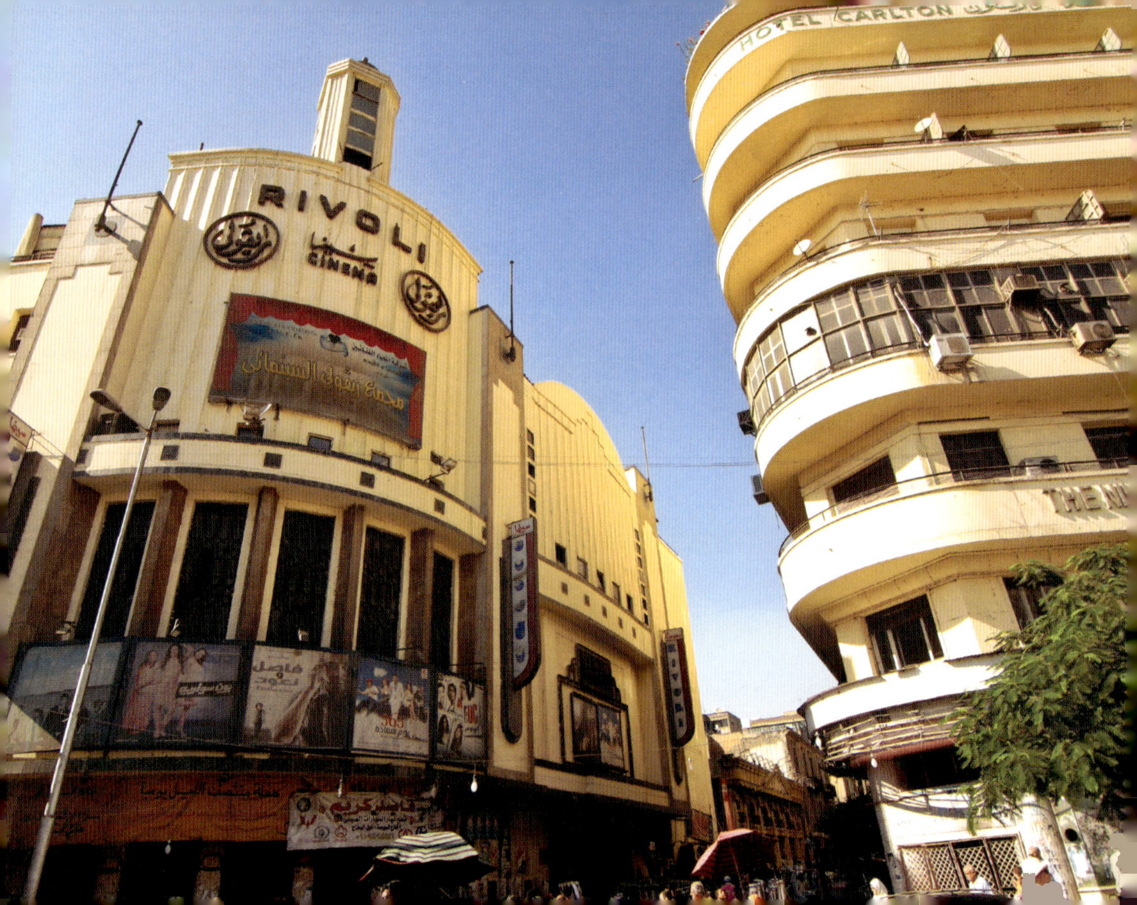

RIVOLI
CINEMA
HOTEL CARLTON

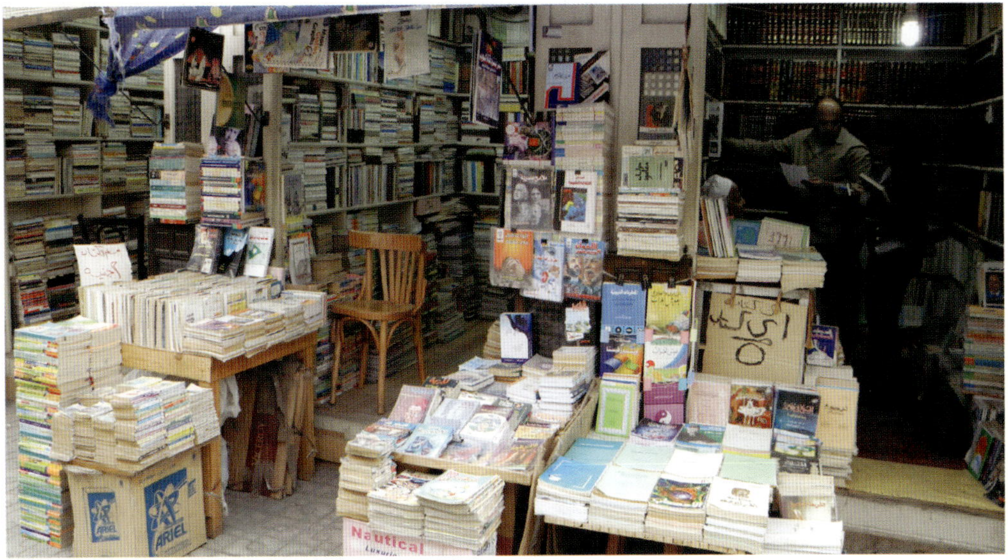

OPPOSITE:

Rivoli Cinema, Cairo

Here we see a movie house from Egypt's golden age of cinema. The Egyptian film industry mirrored the development of cinema in Europe and USA and became the centre of Arabic film-making for the whole Middle East. Known as the Eastern Hollywood, Cairo has produced major movies in every decade.

ABOVE:

Azbakeya Book Market, Cairo

By the gardens of Opera Square in Downtown Cairo is a famous market that is devoted to selling second-hand books and magazines in Arabic, English and other languages. Within each small unit, books of all ages are crammed together in no obvious order.

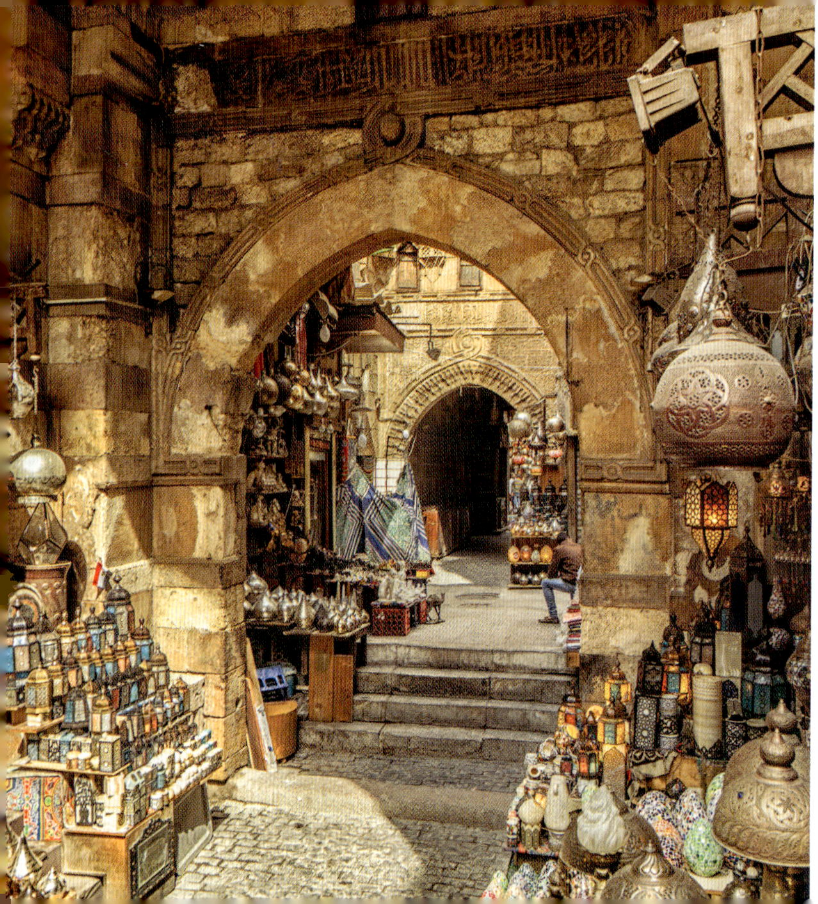

LEFT:

Khan al-Khalili Bazaar, Cairo

This area in Islamic Cairo is Egypt's most famous souk (market). Its many streets are divided into areas devoted to specific goods where sellers compete for your business.

OPPOSITE TOP LEFT:

Khan al-Khalili Bazaar

The Arabic word for slipper is 'shipship' and the leather market offers ample opportunities to buy a pair to take home.

OPPOSITE TOP RIGHT:

Khan al-Khalili Bazaar

These small lanterns can be used with electricity or candles and are to be found in any home. Known as 'fanous', they are especially popular during festivals and Ramadan.

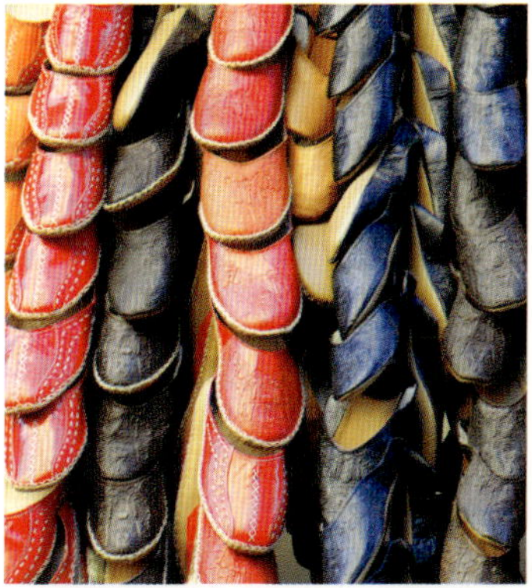

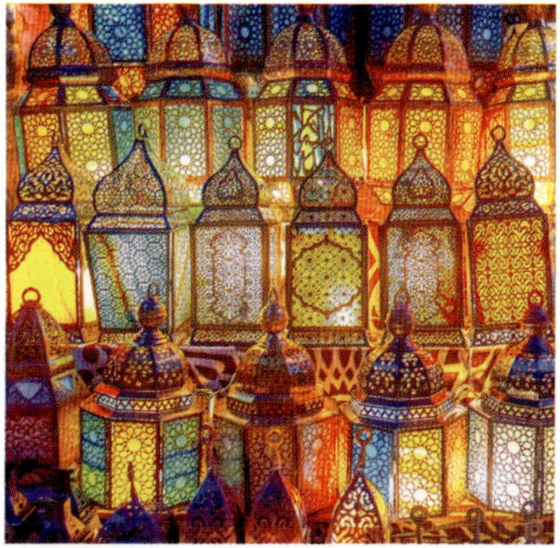

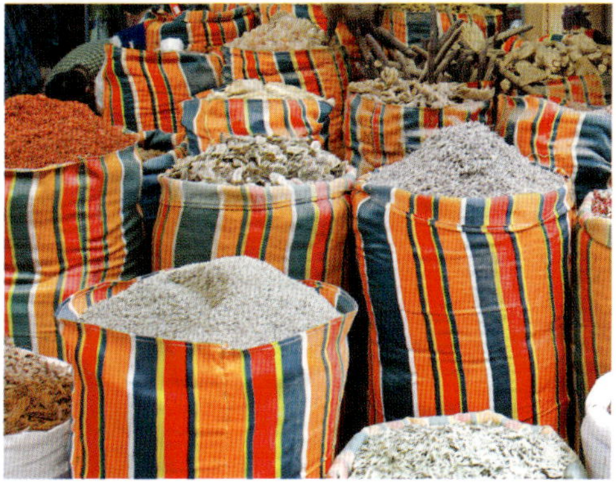

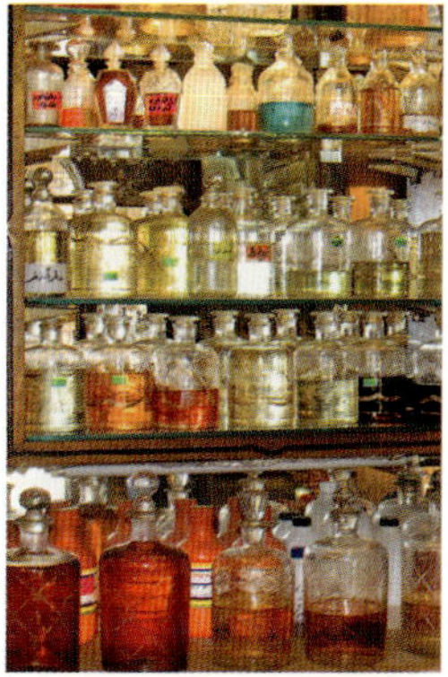

BOTTOM LEFT:

Khan al-Khalili Bazaar

The spice market is one of the most popular streets of all. Egypt has been at the centre of the trade routes for Africa and the Middle East for centuries.

BOTTOM RIGHT:

Khan al-Khalili Bazaar

The perfume bazaar reflects Egypt's longstanding tradition of creating fragrances. In Ancient Egypt, they were associated with the gods and it was believed that perfumes had a positive effect on your health and well-being.

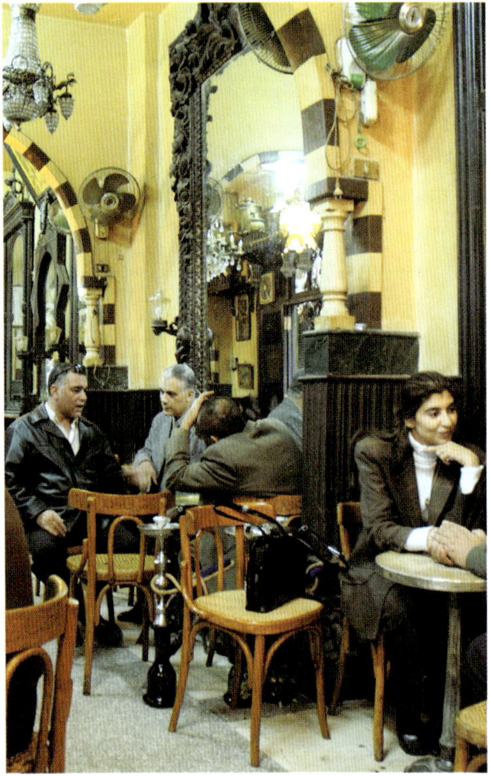

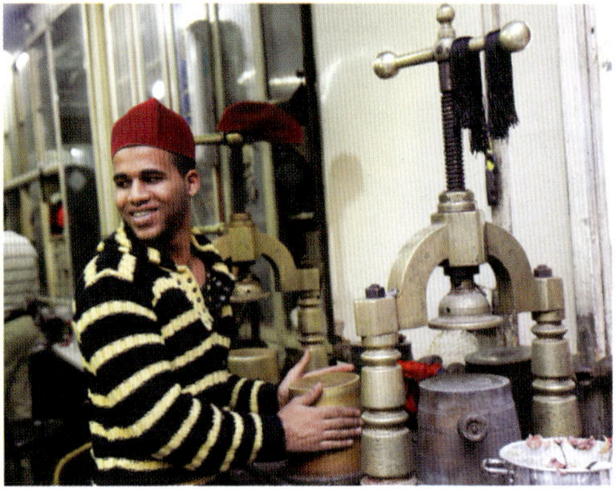

LEFT:

Khan al-Khalili Bazaar

Ensure you take time for coffee or tea while you shop. The backstreets of the bazaar are full of coffee shops, some of which have existed for centuries.

ABOVE:

Khan al-Khalili Bazaar

Often referred to as a fez, the Egyptian headwear called a tarboush was essential headwear in the 1950s and 1960s. Today the last tarboush makers ply their trade in the Khan al-Khalili.

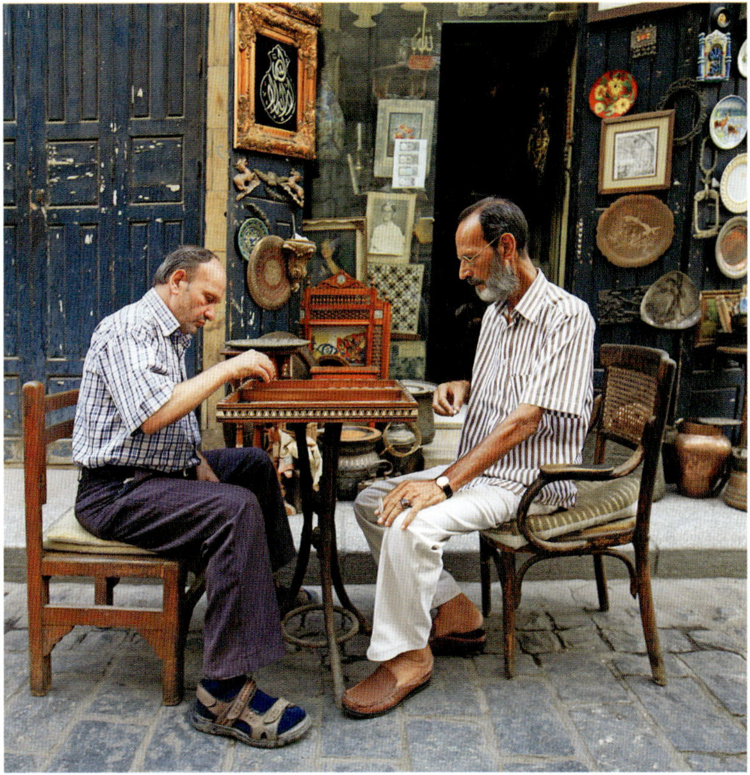

LEFT:

Khan al-Khalili Bazaar

All across Egypt, in pavement coffee shops and cafes, one may observe a game of Tawla or 'backgammon' underway. This game alongside chess has provided Egyptians with entertainment and quiet, steely competition for centuries. You may be invited to join in but be aware, local players are good at these games.

Picture Credits

Alamy: 6 (Barry Iverson), 28/29 (Barry Iverson), 33 (Buddy Mays), 46 top (agis), 47 (Arterra Picture Library), 56 (eFesenko), 59 (B.O'Kane), 72 (B.O'Kane), 94/95 (ONEWORLD PICTURE), 116/117 (B.O'Kane), 118 (Tor Eigeland), 120 (Rolf Richardson), 121 top (B.O'Kane), 123 (theodore liasi), 129 (DE ROCKER), 132 (wildviews/Charles Tomalin), 154 (Cavan), 155 (Arco Images GmbH), 163 (Cultura Creative), 165 (Martin Strmiska), 174 (Reinhard Dirscherl), 194 (Denis Cherkashin), 212 & 213 (B.O'Kane), 218 (theodore liasi), 219 (MuslimPhotos.Net/ Athar Akram), 221 top left (Michael Ventura), 221 bottom right (Peter Horree), 222 left (Mauricio Abreu)

Dreamstime: 8 (Stig Alenas), 10/11 & 12 (all Sculpies), 13 (Donyanedomam), 20 (Vladimir Melnik), 24/25 (Siempreverde22), 26 (Christophe Amerijckx), 27 (Thomas Wyness), 30 & 31 top (Hecke01), 31 bottom (Sergey Mayorov), 35 (Jaroslav Moravcik), 40 & 41 (Sculpies), 50/51 (Anton Macheev), 54 (Evgeniy Fesenko), 66 & 67 (Evgeniy Fesenko), 75 (Edwardgerges), 76 (Rasoul Ali), 77 (Edwardgerges), 82/83 (Khaled Eladawy), 85 (Evgeniy Fesenko), 90/91 (Baloncici), 98/99 (Evgeniy Fesenko), 101 (Evgeniy Fesenko), 106 (Evgeniy Fesenko), 110 (Baloncici), 119 (Jason Row), 128 (Adwo), 133 (Olya Solodenko), 134/135 (Igor Groshev), 146 (Nikita Buida), 152/153 (Petr Kasal), 160/161 (Ian Woolcock), 162 (Myroslavbozhko), 164 (Evgeniy Fesenko), 168 (Mrahmo), 170/171 (Emad Omar), 173 (Freeprod), 175 (Siempreverde22), 177 (Siempreverde22), 181 (Hecke01), 185 (Cristian Tzecu), 191 (Kylie Nicholson), 202/203 (Leonid Andronov), 208/209 (Frederic Cerez), 210 (Baloncici), 216 & 217 (Evgeniy Fesenko), 221 top right (Evgeniy Fesenko), 221 bottom left (Baloncici), 222 right (Edwardgerges)

Getty: 16 (Mohamed El-Shahed)

Getty/DeAgostini: 17 (A. Dagli Orti), 36 (W.Buss), 45 (C.Sappa), 46 bottom (G.Dagli Orti), 73 (A. Vergani)

Rex by Shutterstock: 102 (Khaled El Figi), 103 (Sipa)

Shutterstock: 7 (Matias Planas), 14 (eFesenko), 15 (MicheleB), 18/19 (paul Prescott), 21 (Cortyn), 22 (Dmitry Pleshakov), 23 (akimov Konstantin), 32 (Nick Brundle), 34 (Calin Stan), 37 (eFesenko), 38 (Anton_Ivanov), 39 (Graficam Ahmed Saeed), 42/43 (Prin Adulyatham), 44 (Matias Planas), 48 (Olab214), 49 (Cyril PAPOT), 52 (Kayihan Bolukbasi), 55 (eFesenko), 57 (hakuna-jina), 58 (Eric Valenne geostory), 60/61 (javarman), 62 (INTERTOURIST), 63 (Syahtuah Mohamed), 64 (Whitehaven), 65 (Waj), 68 (krechet), 69 (suronin), 70/71 (Octasy), 74 (rasoulali), 78 (Leonid Andronov), 79 (Nancy Ezzat), 80 (Yaser Alamoudi), 81 (Khaled ElAdawy), 84 (Victor Jiang), 86/87 (Orhan Cam), 88 (Kazzazm), 89 (Khaled Magdy Mahmoud), 92 (Orhan Cam), 93 (Kazzazm), 96 (Mohamed Monem), 97 (masud2k4cse), 100 (Dr Ajay Kumar Singh), 104/105 (eFesenko), 107 (Merlin74), 108/109 (Sun_Shine), 111 (Lisa S), 112 (Eric Valenne geostory), 114/115 (Gilles Gaonach), 121 bottom (NAPA), 122 (Patryk Kosmider), 124 (paul Prescott), 125 (meunierd), 126/127 (George Nazmi Bebawi), 130 (suronin), 136/137 (Repina Valeriya), 138/139 (Anton_Ivanov), 140 (Birute Vijeikiene), 141 (joachim affeldt), 142/143 (Igor Grochev), 144 (Iryna Yanchukovich),147 (Kazzazm), 148/149 (Vova Shevchuk), 150 (Ioknamilan), 151 (LedyX), 156/157 (John_Walker), 158 (Mohamed Hakem), 159 (Taya Bright), 166 (Mr_ Karesuando), 169 (Nader El Assy), 172 (Amr mahmoud Soliman), 176 (Anton_Ivanov), 178/179 (Ieshiy985), 180 (Anton_Ivanov), 182/183 (Olha Solodenko), 184 (Sun_Shine), 186/187 (Cherkashin Denis), 188 (Kazzazm), 189 (Enrico Montanari), 190 (dibrova), 192/193 (Michail_ Vorobyev), 195 (Jiann), 196 (Leonid Andronov), 198 (MikeDotta), 199 (eFesenko), 200 (Mahmoud Haikal), 201 (Kazzazm), 204/205 - 206/207 (eFesenko), 211 (Abdoabdalla), 214 (Nae84), 215 (Pius Lee), 220 (Merydolla), 223 (Eric Valenne geostory)